The Campus History Series

The University of Tennessee at Martin

On the Front Cover: Dr. Paul Meek, University of Tennessee Martin Branch (UTMB) chancellor, and Andy Holt, president of the University of Tennessee (UT) System, lead a group of faculty out of the Hall-Moody Administration Building on their way to commencement around 1960. (Courtesy of the University of Tennessee at Martin Archives.)

Cover Background: Students and ROTC cadets walk outside the ROTC Building around 1950. Looking east, this view of campus includes the Sociology Building (left), the dining hall (later repurposed as the Communications Building, center), and the Hall-Moody Building in the background. (Courtesy of the University of Tennessee at Martin Archives.)

The Campus History Series

The University of Tennessee at Martin

Samuel Richardson, Nathan Morgan, and Karen Elmore

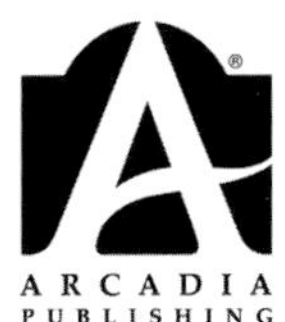

ISBN 978-1-4671-6296-8

Published by Arcadia Publishing
Charleston, South Carolina

Printed in the United States of America

Library of Congress Control Number: 2025941274

For all general information, please contact Arcadia Publishing:
Telephone 843-853-2070
Fax 843-853-0044
E-mail sales@arcadiapublishing.com

Visit us on the Internet at www.arcadiapublishing.com

Contents

Acknowledgments

This pictorial history of the University of Tennessee at Martin (UTM or UT Martin) would not have been possible without the support and contributions of many individuals, to whom we extend our deepest gratitude. First, we sincerely thank Dr. Jacquelyn Johnson, associate vice chancellor for alumni relations and chief engagement officer, for her tireless efforts in ensuring the contract was approved and signed promptly, allowing us to meet our production deadline. We are also grateful to Bud Grimes, vice chancellor of communication and marketing, for his invaluable guidance and insights throughout the process. Special thanks go to all those involved with the university's newspaper, the *Pacer/Vollette*; the *Spirit* yearbook staff over the years, and the former university relations team and photographers whose work helped preserve the history of UTM. Their dedication to documenting the university's legacy made this project possible. We also appreciate the contributions of Bob Carroll and Neil Graves, whose previously compiled histories were instrumental in the development of this book. Finally, we would like to acknowledge Dr. Yancy Freeman, UTM chancellor, for his unwavering support of the 125th Anniversary Committee and its mission. All images appear courtesy of the University of Tennessee at Martin Archives and University Relations.

Introduction

Nestled in the quiet town of Martin in rural northwest Tennessee, the University of Tennessee at Martin sits between the Tennessee and Mississippi Rivers, just 10 miles from the Kentucky border. While modest in size, Martin has long been a hub for higher education. By the early 20th century, it was home to two colleges: McFerrin College, founded by the Methodist Church in 1890, and the Hall-Moody Institute, established in 1900 by the Beulah Baptist Association.

Hall-Moody was built on land donated by Ada Gardner Brooks and took shape under the leadership of Dr. L.N. Penick, pastor of Martin's First Baptist Church. Named in honor of Baptist leaders Elder J.N. Hall and Dr. J.B. Moody, the school offered a 13-year educational track that extended from primary grades to college-level coursework. Hall-Moody opened with five faculty members and held its first classes on September 2, 1901. The campus's original building, noted for its distinctive tower, served many functions until it was destroyed by fire in 1970. Over the years, Hall-Moody expanded its academic scope and physical campus, adding dormitories, a science building, and a gymnasium to support its student body.

Despite growth, the school struggled financially. In 1927, the Tennessee Baptist Convention consolidated Hall-Moody with Union University in Jackson. Local leaders, fearing the loss of educational opportunities in northwest Tennessee, quickly rallied to bring a new institution to Martin. Attorney and Hall-Moody trustee George C. Rowlett, newly appointed to the University of Tennessee Board of Trustees, helped secure legislative support and local funding commitments, which included tax bonds from the city and county.

On March 29, 1927, Gov. Austin Peay signed legislation creating the University of Tennessee Junior College (UTJC), which opened that fall on the former Hall-Moody campus. UTJC focused on agriculture, home economics, and industrial arts. Under founding executive officer Calvin Porter Claxton, the college began with 120 students and 14 faculty members. Early years brought foundational developments—including new academic buildings, a steam plant, and a greenhouse—to support its educational mission.

In 1934, Paul Meek became chief executive, guiding UTJC through the Great Depression and World War II. During the war, enrollment dipped, but a Navy flight training program provided critical financial support. Postwar, enrollment surged with returning veterans supported by the GI Bill. The college responded with rapid expansion, building dormitories and student housing from surplus military materials.

In 1951, the state authorized the college to offer four-year degrees in agriculture and home economics, transforming UTJC into the University of Tennessee Martin Branch (UTMB). This marked the beginning of a new era of growth. Throughout the 1950s and 1960s, enrollment increased steadily, and the campus expanded with the construction of key facilities such as a new administration building, science buildings, and a library. In 1961, UTMB enrolled its first African American student, reflecting national progress in civil rights.

The institution officially became the University of Tennessee at Martin in 1967, symbolizing its evolving role within the UT System. The decade saw the introduction of student organizations, Greek life, and greater diversity in academic offerings. By 1970, enrollment exceeded 4,600, and the university continued to construct buildings to meet student needs, including the Fine Arts Building and Gooch Hall for nursing and education.

The 1970s and 1980s brought challenges and innovation. As enrollment fluctuated, the university responded with targeted recruitment strategies, new academic initiatives like the Honors Seminar and University Scholars Program, and improved support services for nontraditional students. Infrastructure developments included a residential swimming pool and the West Tennessee Agriculture Pavilion, later named the Ned McWherter Agricultural Complex in honor of Gov. Ned Ray McWherter.

During the 1980s and 1990s, UTM embraced modernization and regional engagement. The university launched its first capital campaign, met ahead of schedule, and began offering additional graduate and professional programs. The campus footprint expanded through the construction of new facilities and the modernization of existing academic buildings. UTM achieved national recognition for campus safety and landscaping, and it transitioned to NCAA Division I athletics, rebranding from the Pacers to the Skyhawks in 1995.

The 2000s marked a period of strategic expansion. The university focused on enhancing campus life with new residence halls and student-focused facilities, creating a more vibrant and supportive environment. UTM extended its reach through off-campus centers in Jackson, Ripley, Parsons, Selmer, and Somerville, making education more accessible across West Tennessee. Programs in engineering, education, business, and agriculture flourished. A centennial celebration in 2000 reflected on the university's legacy and growth.

In the decade that followed, UTM reached record enrollment, peaking at more than 8,400 students. The university continued expanding its impact through academic and cultural initiatives, including the All-Steinway School campaign. Outreach efforts such as the WestStar Leadership Program—founded in 1989 to support regional development—grew in prominence. Capital improvements topped $100 million, and new programs in health sciences, STEM (science, technology, engineering, and mathematics), and the arts helped meet the needs of a changing student population.

By the 2020s, UTM had become a recognized leader in regional public higher education. It navigated the COVID-19 pandemic while maintaining academic continuity, student support, and enrollment stability. The university completed its most ambitious fundraising campaign—RISE—raising over $178 million. Investments in facilities, including the Latimer-Smith Engineering and Science Building and a future College of Business and Global Affairs, positioned UTM for continued growth.

Today, UTM stands as a comprehensive, future-focused university grounded in its community roots. From its beginnings as Hall-Moody to its present-day role as a regional and statewide leader, the university remains committed to expanding access to education, fostering student success, and driving economic and civic development across Tennessee and beyond.

One

Hall-Moody Institute

1900–1927

At the turn of the 20th century, Martin was home to two colleges. The Methodists founded McFerrin College in 1890, and in 1900, the Beulah Baptist Association, along with local Baptist churches, established the Hall-Moody Institute. The institution was built on land donated by Ada Gardner Brooks, a member of Martin's First Baptist Church. Hall-Moody, which later became the University of Tennessee at Martin, initially operated from a modest two-story brick building with just five faculty members.

Dr. L.N. Penick, pastor of Martin's First Baptist Church, was the driving force behind Hall-Moody's creation. Concerned about the lack of educational opportunities in northwest Tennessee, he rallied support from local churches and the Beulah Baptist Association. Named after Baptist ministers Elder J.N. Hall and Dr. J.B. Moody, the school was founded to provide both general education and religious instruction. Offering a 13-year program from primary education through the equivalent of a first-year college curriculum, Hall-Moody focused on denominational training, which its founders believed public schools could not provide.

On October 2, 1900, construction began on the administration and classroom building, which featured a distinctive tower dubbed the "witch's hat." After storm damage in 1912, the tower was removed, and four columns were added. The building remained in use until it burned down in 1970. Hall-Moody officially opened on September 2, 1901, with Pres. O.E. Baker and four teachers. Over the next five years, three others served as president until Dr. H.E. Waters took over in 1905. During his tenure, student enrollment grew from 200 to 500, meeting the school's original goal.

Financial struggles plagued Hall-Moody, and in 1927, it became clear that the school could not sustain itself. The Tennessee Baptist State Convention decided to consolidate Hall-Moody with Union University in Jackson, focusing resources on a single institution. Hall-Moody held its final commencement on May 19, 1927, closing after 27 years.

Though Hall-Moody failed, it was on this foundation that laid the beginnings of what would become the University of Tennessee at Martin.

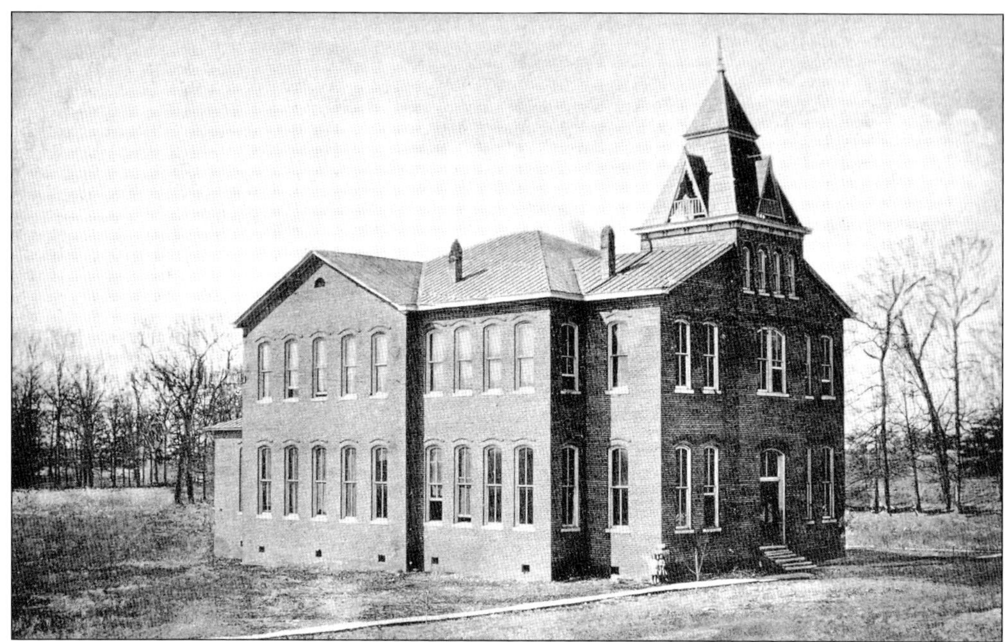

Located on the west side of town, Hall-Moody started in a modest two-story building with only five instructors. This building served as administrative offices, classrooms, and eventually, the library from 1900 to 1927. With the railroad running north and south through the middle of town, it was said that the Methodists lived on the east side of the railroad and the Baptists on the west. This perhaps determined the placement of the two colleges. McFerrin College was placed on the east side of Martin.

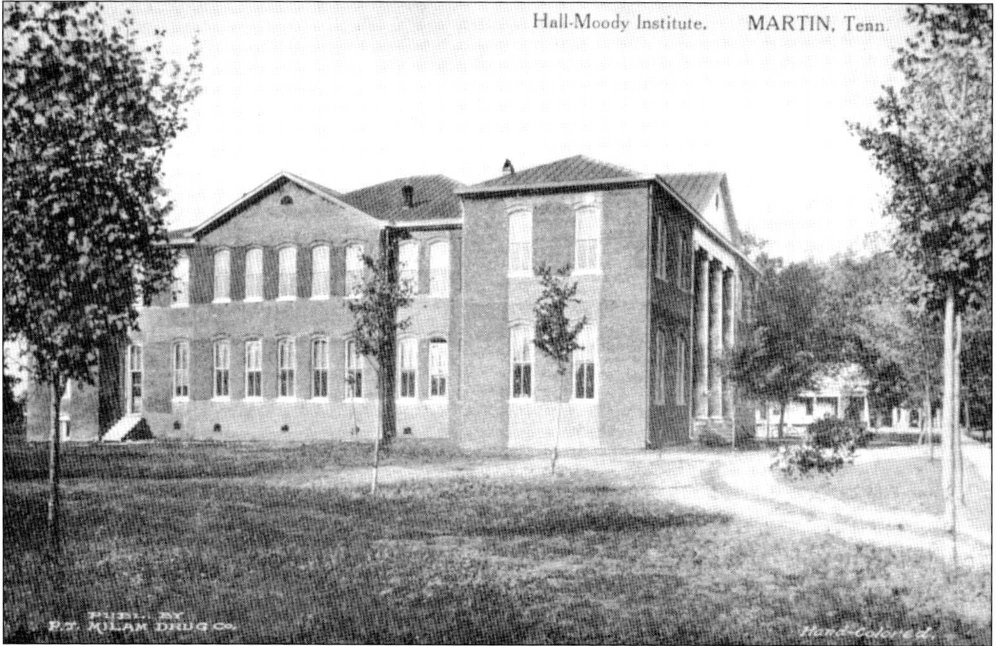

Due to wind damage in 1912, the tower on the administration building was removed, and two front wings with classrooms were added, along with four columns. This building would remain the center of activity on campus until 1959, when the new administration building was completed.

J. N. HALL

The founders chose to name the school in honor of two influential Baptist ministers: Elder J.N. Hall of Fulton, Kentucky, who was also the editor of the *American Baptist Flag*, and Dr. J.B. Moody, who led the school's theological department from 1905 to 1915. The *Last Leaf*, the final yearbook published by Hall-Moody, noted, "Although there have been some slight changes to better reflect the school's mission, the original name, Hall-Moody, has always remained dear to the hearts and minds of both its founders and those who followed in their footsteps."

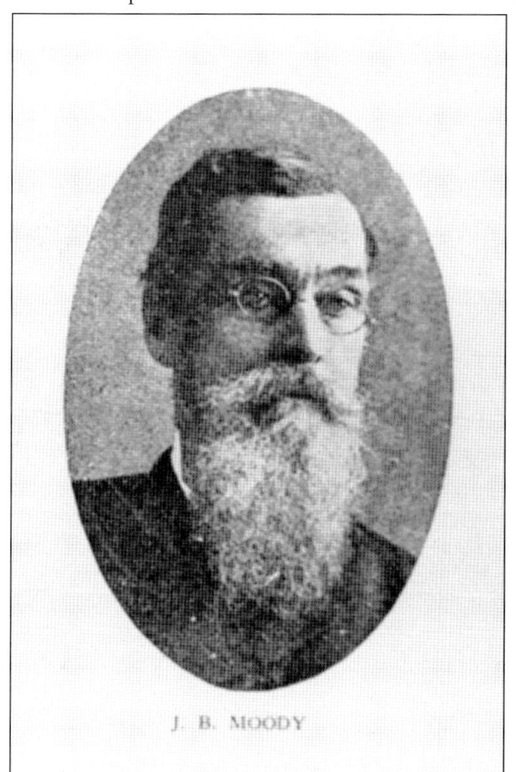

J. B. MOODY

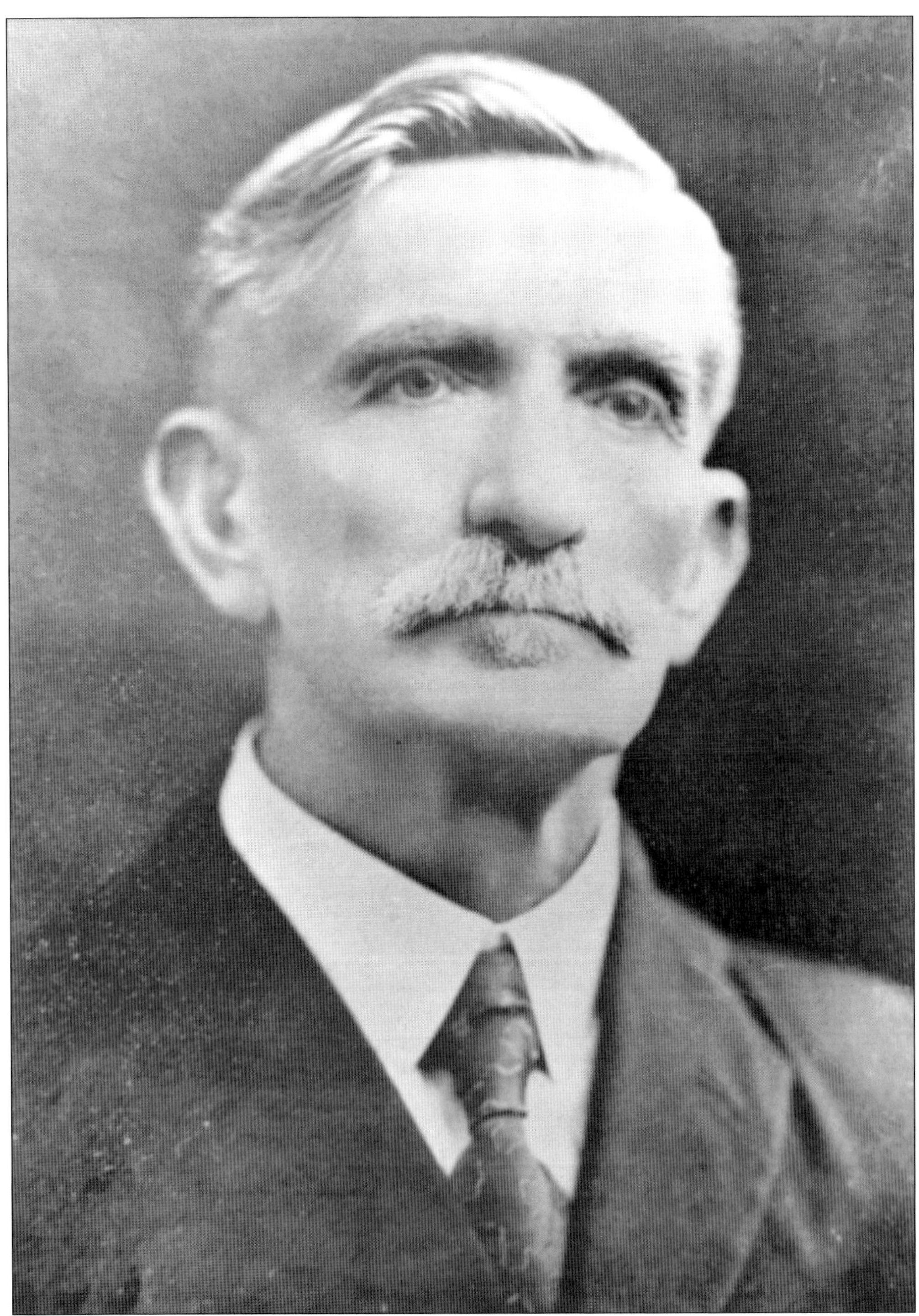

I.N. Penick served as pastor of First Baptist Church in Martin and was one of the driving forces in the founding of Hall-Moody. Believing there was a lack of educational opportunities in northwest Tennessee, he led the effort to establish a school for religious and denominational training, along with general courses in education.

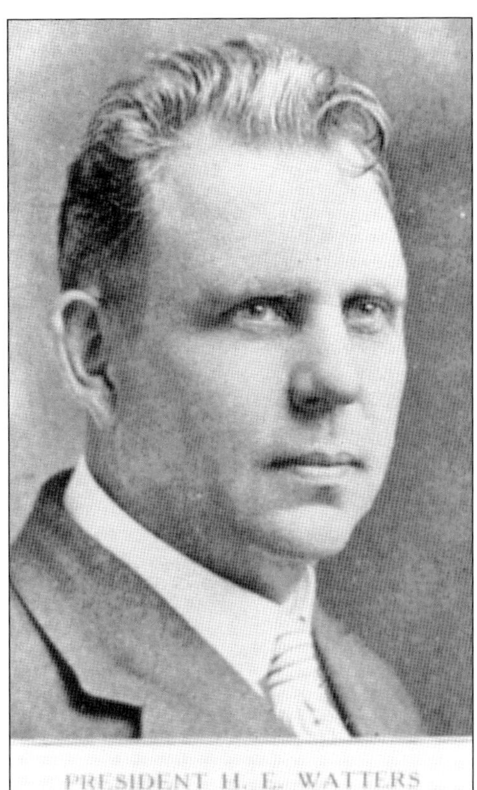

H.E. Watters joined Hall-Moody in 1904 as vice president and business manager. The following year, at just 29 years old, he became president. During his 11-year tenure, he assembled a strong faculty and oversaw a period of steady growth for the institution. Watters remained president until 1915. In this group photograph labeled "Teachers" from 1910, Watters is pictured in the third row, wearing a dark suit, on the side of the Hall-Moody Building.

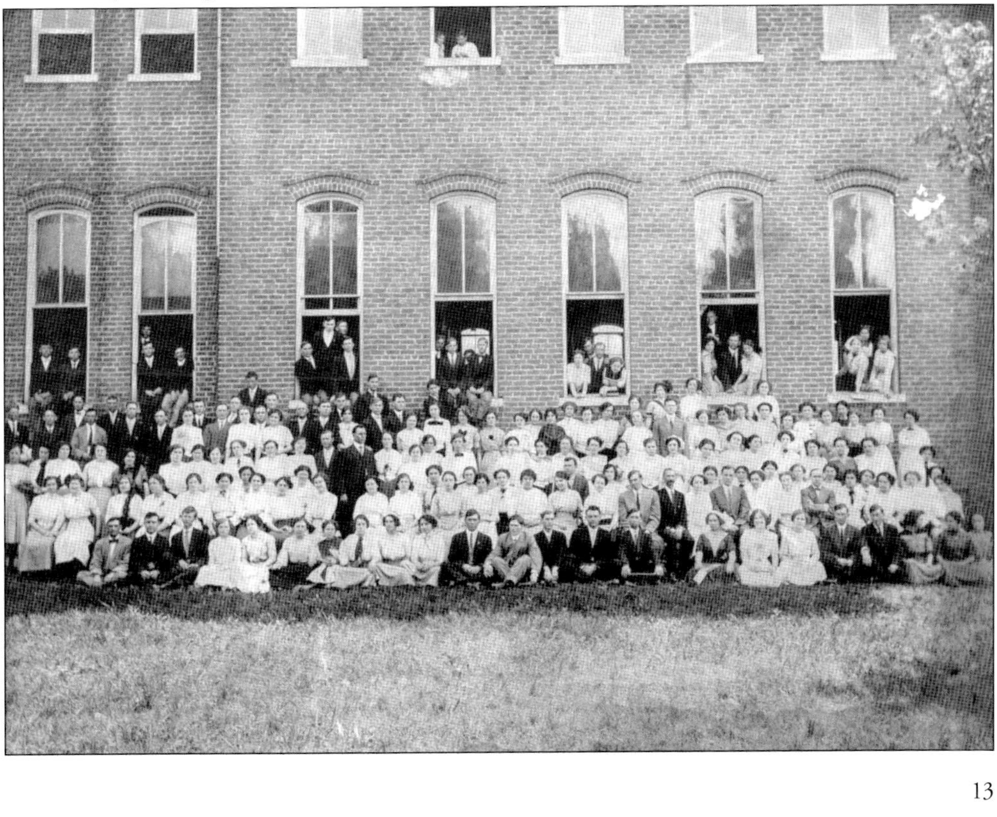

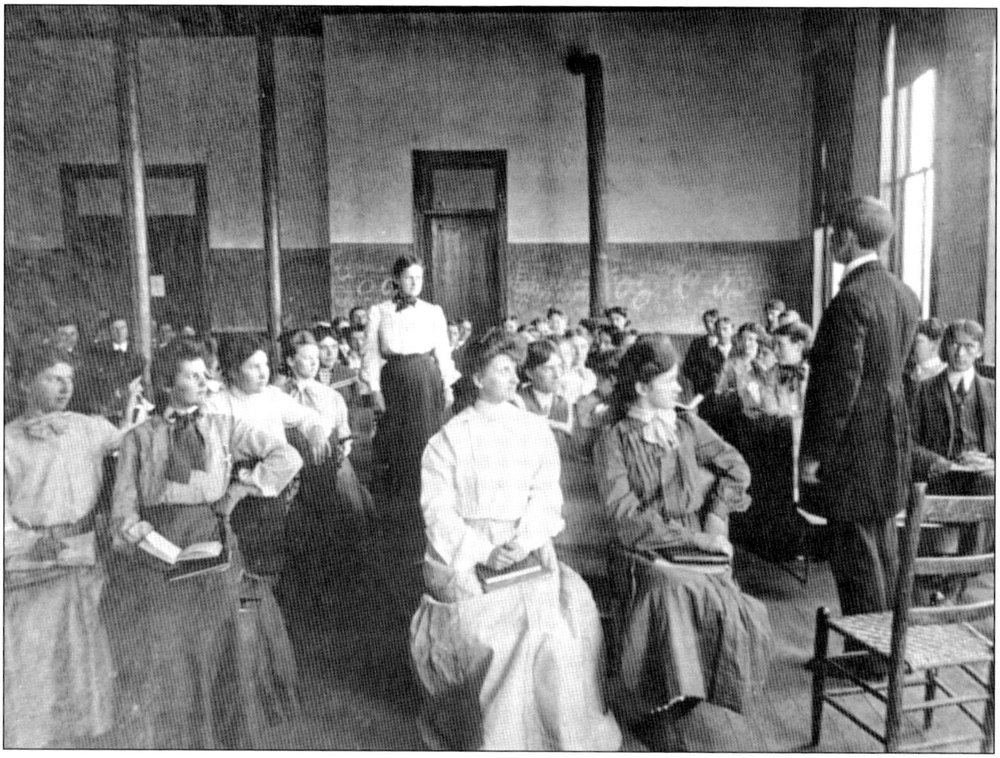

In 1904, Hall-Moody offered an English grammar class as part of a comprehensive 13-year academic program. The curriculum began at the primary level (grades one through six) and extended through what was termed the "Extended Level," equivalent to college-level coursework beyond the 11th grade. At the time, clear distinctions between high school and college curricula had not yet been established, allowing institutions that offered instruction beyond the 11th grade to be designated as colleges.

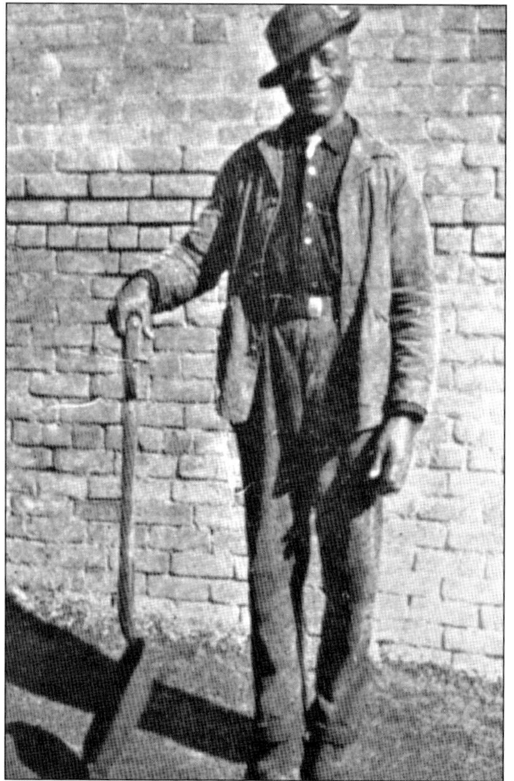

Bob Wilkins was a highly regarded and cherished custodian who dedicated his service to both Hall-Moody and UTJC. Beginning his work at Hall-Moody in 1907, he remained a steadfast presence for over 40 years. He was recognized as one of the institution's most devoted employees, with his contributions leaving a lasting impression on all who were part of the school, as reflected in the sentiment that his "work is written in the memory of every person who has been connected with the institution."

The junior class of 1909 at Hall-Moody reflected the school's steady growth since its founding, with enrollment reaching 560 students during the 1908–1909 academic year. A significant portion of the older students were preachers and teachers pursuing further education and professional development.

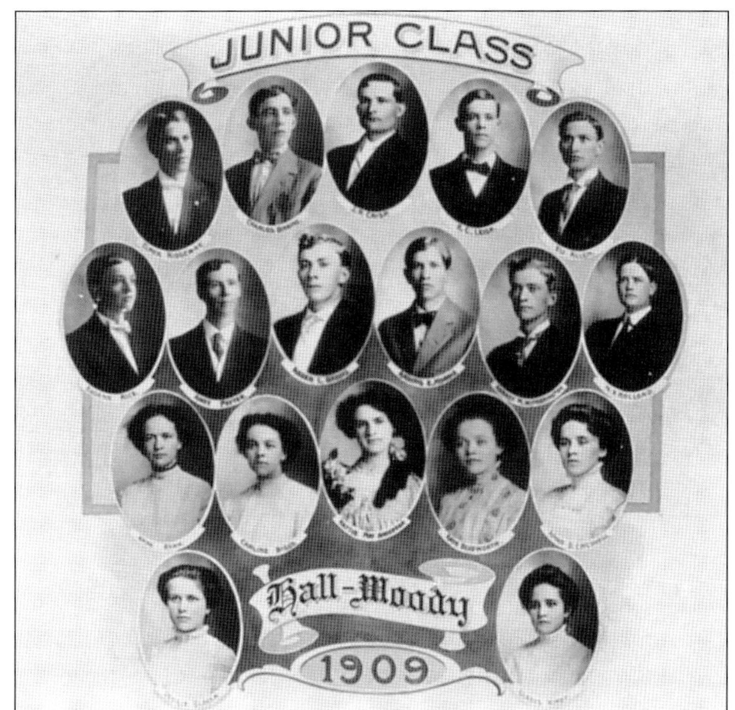

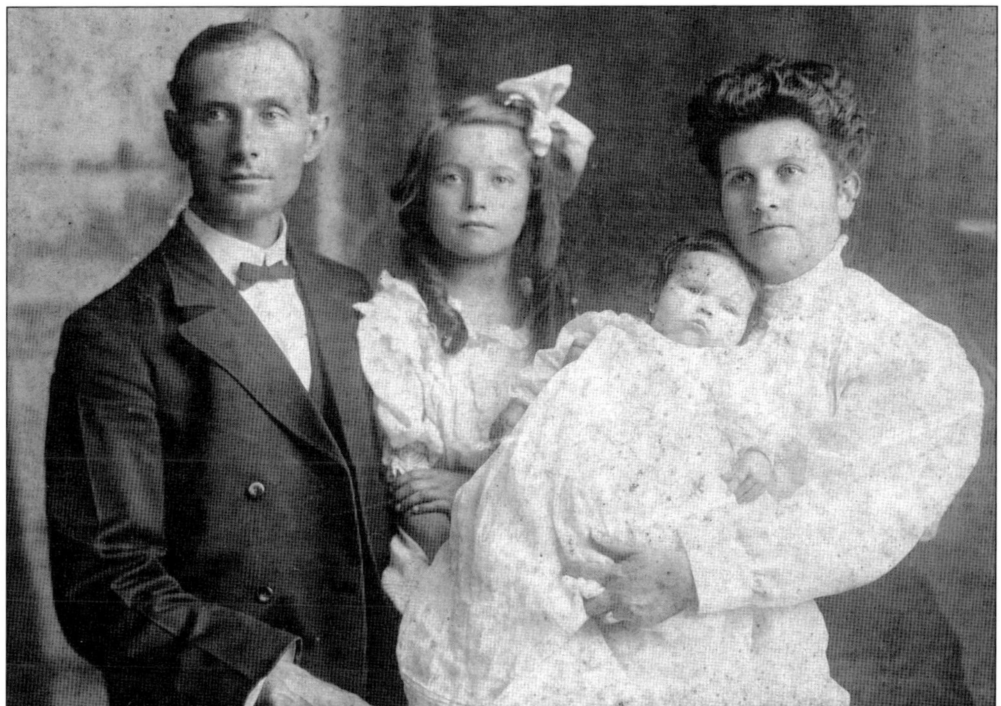

In 1900, M.W. Robinson and his family were active members of the community. Robinson served as vice president of Hall-Moody for six years during President Watters's administration. He later held the position of assistant superintendent of public instruction for Tennessee from 1911 to 1912 and, in 1913, was appointed as the state supervisor of high school industrial education.

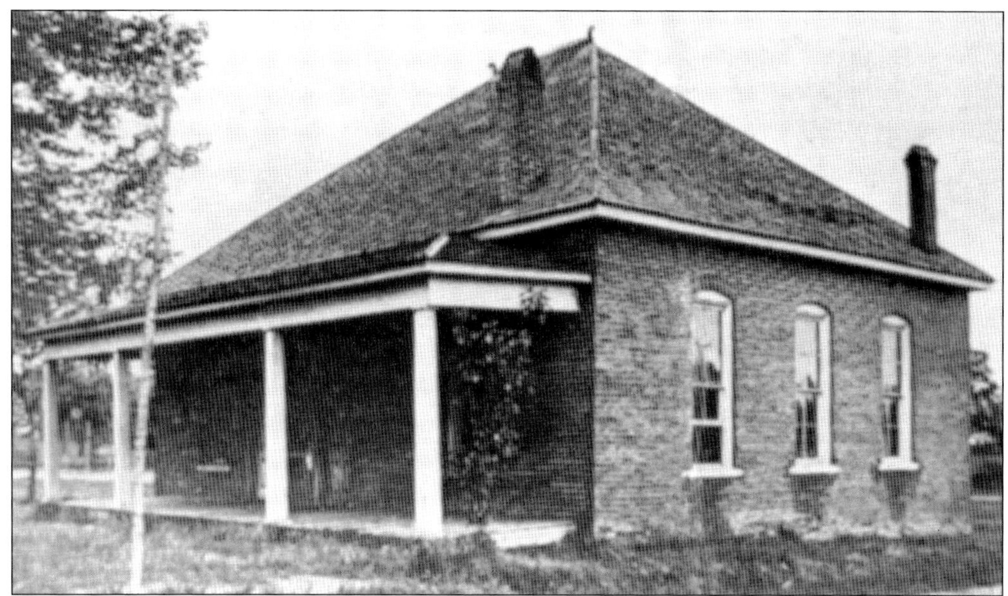

The old Science Building was one of the original structures from the Hall-Moody Institute era. Originally constructed in 1907 as a separate laboratory facility, the building measured 32 by 40.5 feet and housed a single classroom/laboratory. It served as the junior college's first science building until the Science Building (later to become the Sociology Building) was completed. After 1929, it was briefly used as a Soils Laboratory before being repurposed as the bookstore and post office from 1931 to 1950. The building was eventually demolished to make way for Browning Hall, a men's dormitory that is now the Business Administration Building.

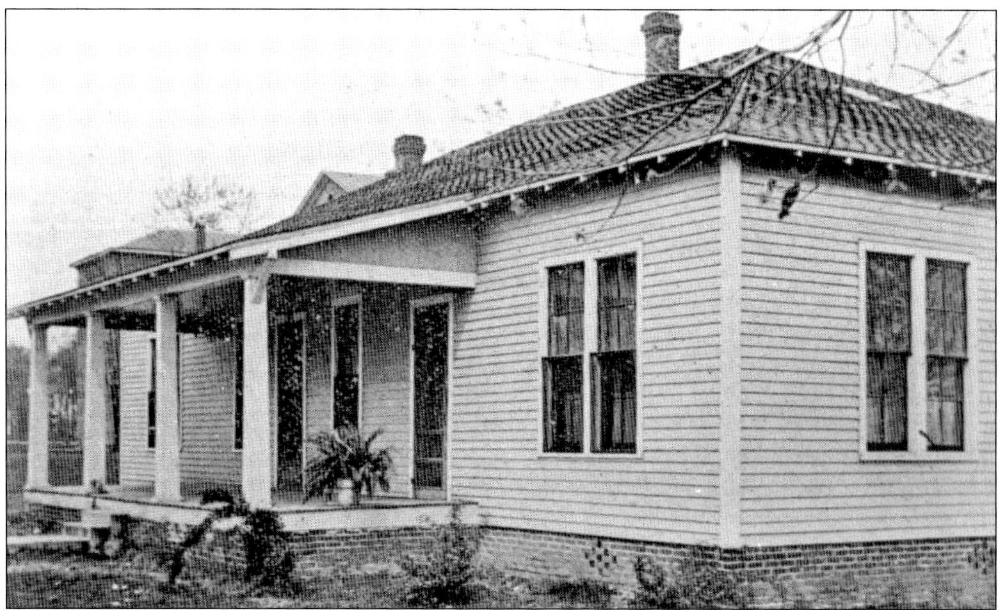

The old dining hall could accommodate up to 125 students when it was fully operational. It contained a dining hall, pantry, storeroom, and kitchen. The building was constructed between 1913 and 1926 and was one of the original structures purchased by the University of Tennessee. It was replaced by a new dining hall in 1935.

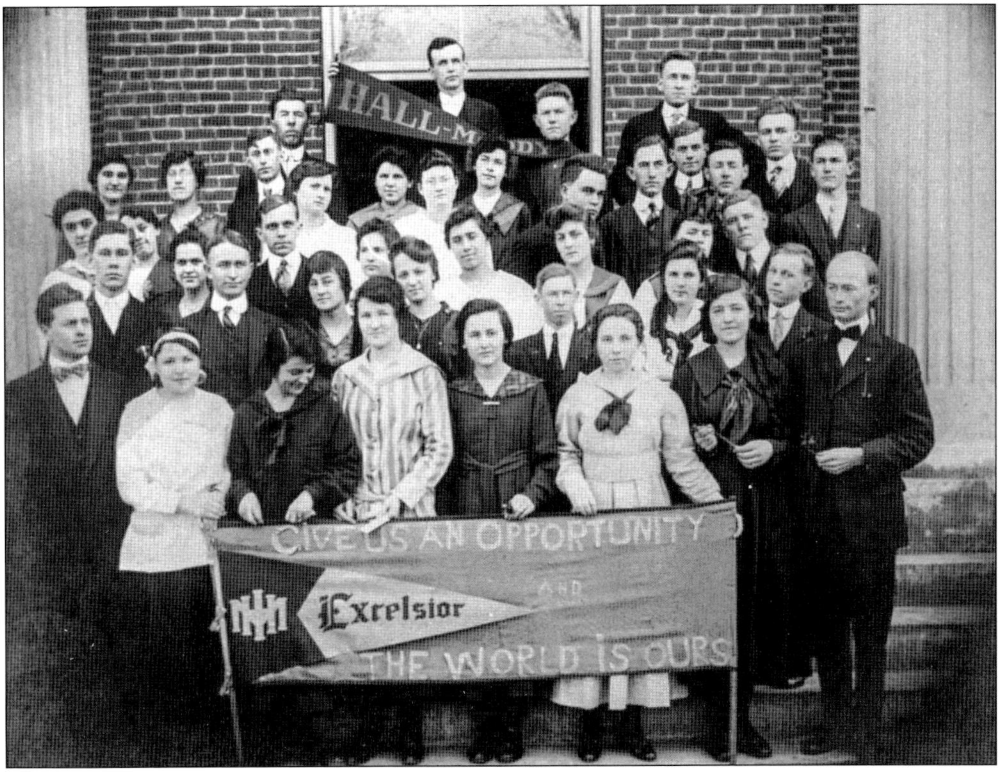

From its earliest years, Hall-Moody placed importance on student participation in public programs by maintaining student organizations that offered training in this area. This was primarily accomplished through literary societies. Prior to 1916, each class formed its own society, which met on Monday afternoons to present programs featuring debates, readings, and musical performances. In 1916, a new administration introduced changes to the literary society system. Rather than having multiple class-based societies, the school consolidated them into two main organizations: the Excelsior Literary Society (pictured) and the Cliosophic Literary Society. These two societies developed a spirited rivalry as they competed for members and engaged in various activities.

Like their predecessors, the Excelsior and Cliosophic societies offered students opportunities to participate in debates, music, readings, and oratory competitions. In the absence of interscholastic athletics at the time, they also organized athletic contests between the two groups. Literary societies such as the Excelsior remained a vital part of campus life, offering both intellectual and recreational outlets for Hall-Moody students.

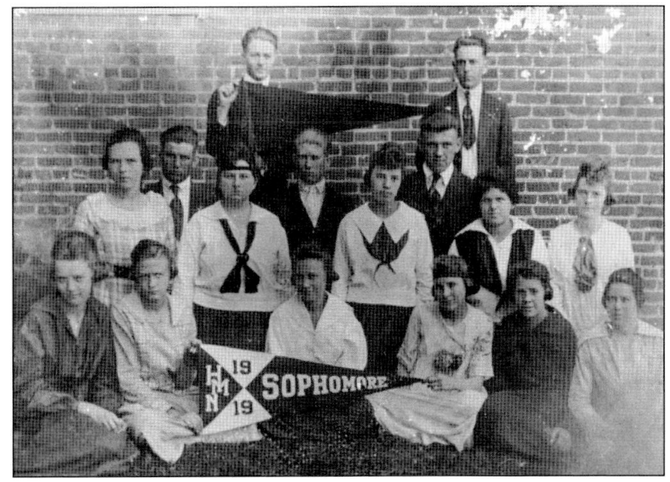

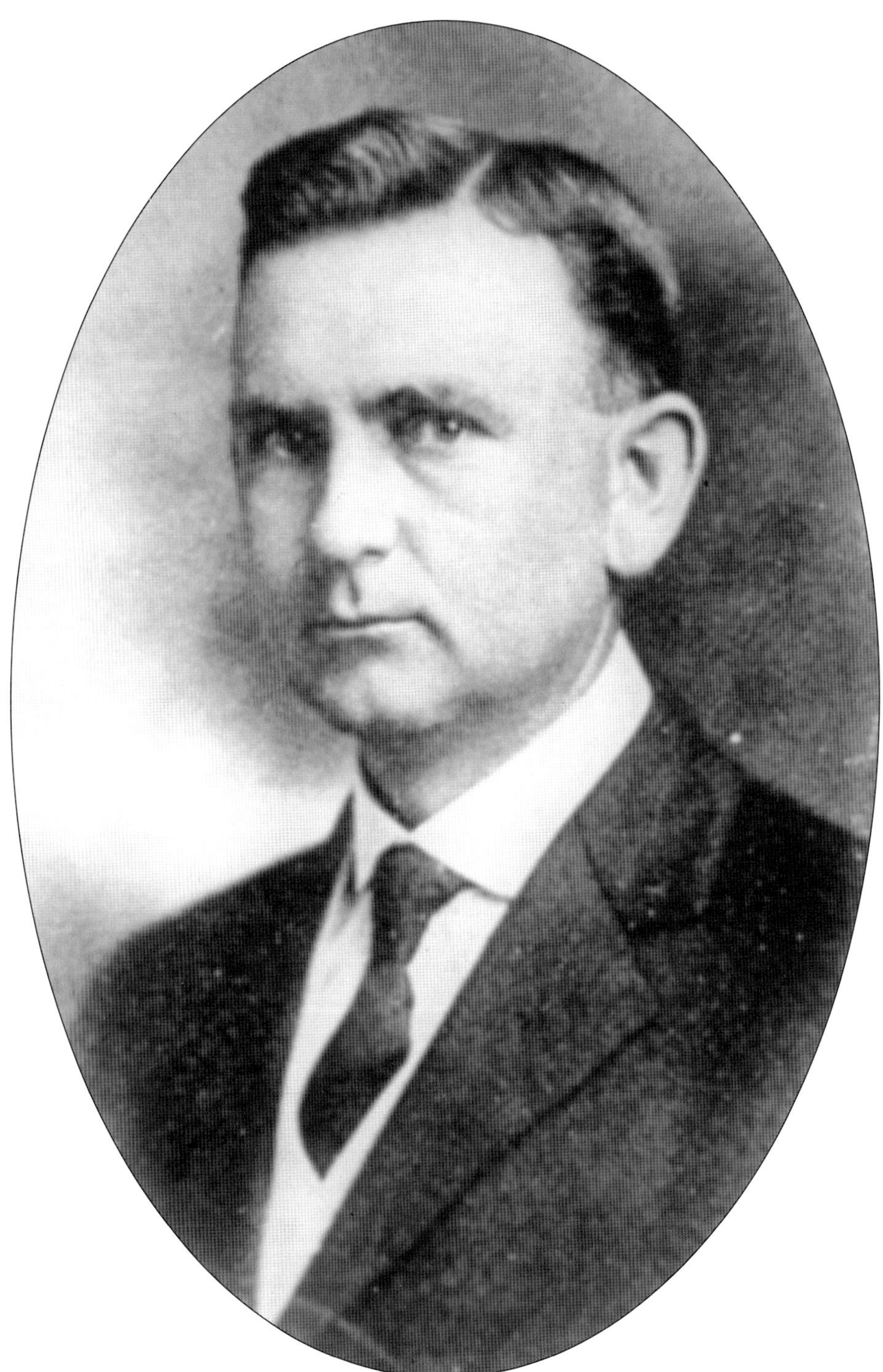

James T. Warren was president of Hall-Moody from 1917 to 1926. During Warren's tenure, the elementary and high school curriculum was further standardized to meet the requirements established by Tennessee's Department of Education. A clear distinction was made between the high school and college curriculum, allowing the college to confer an associate of arts degree on the junior college graduates.

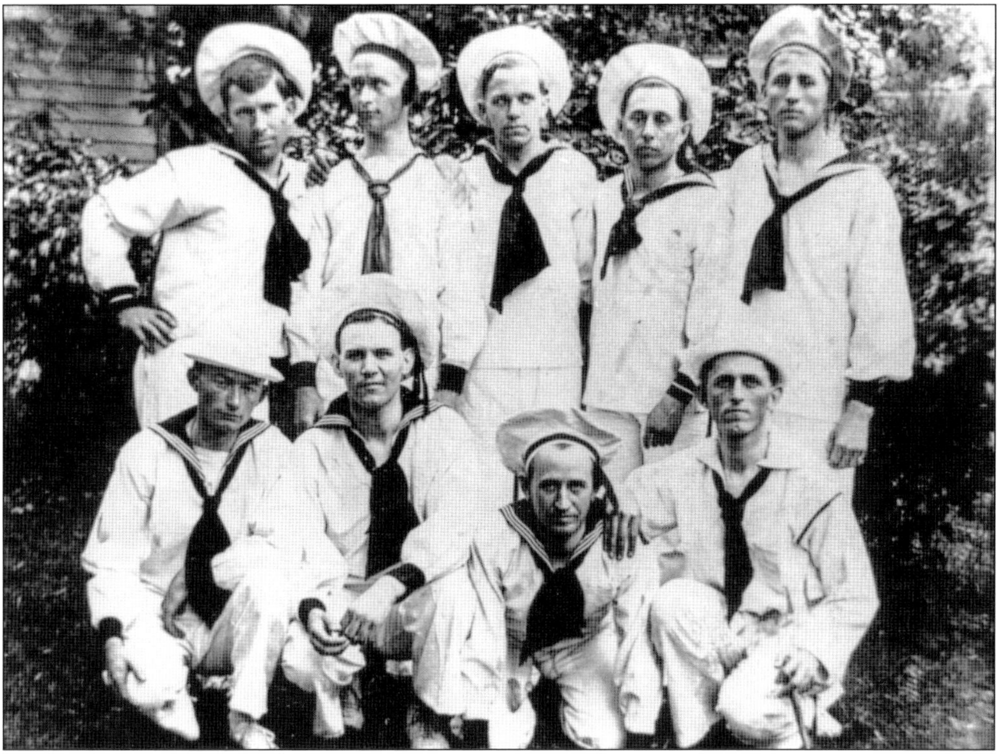

Bolstered by Prof. Musa Hall, music was emphasized by fine arts and was a vital part of life at Hall-Moody. Musical groups were an important outlet for many of the college's students. It became routine for the school to present recitals, concerts, music during chapel, and operettas. Students above in 1914–1915 are dressed for a musical performance, and the cast of the 1924 performance of *In India* is seen below.

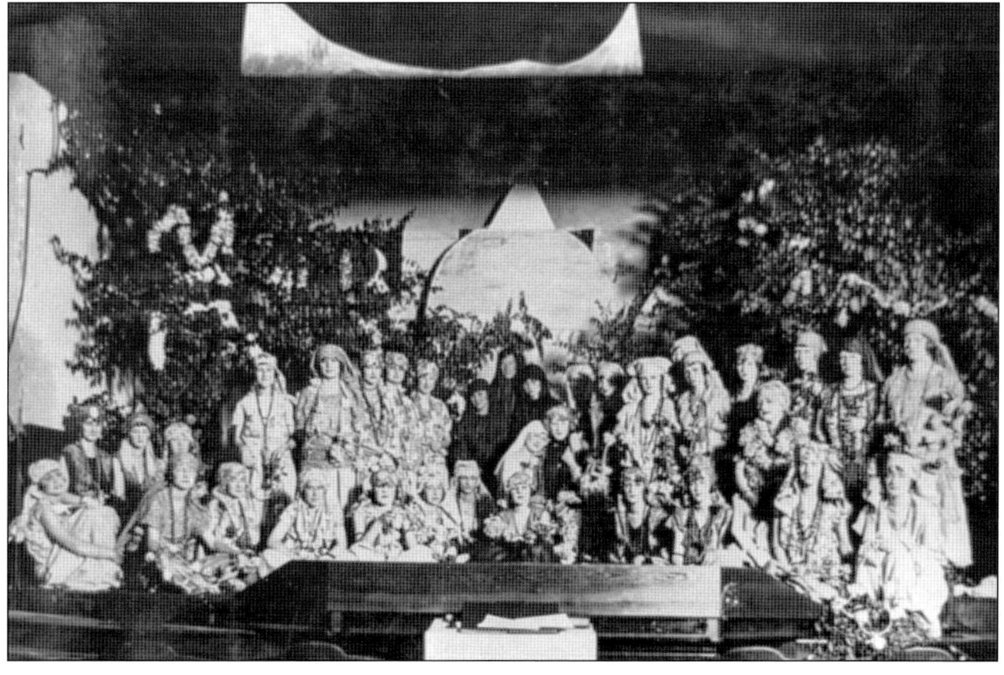

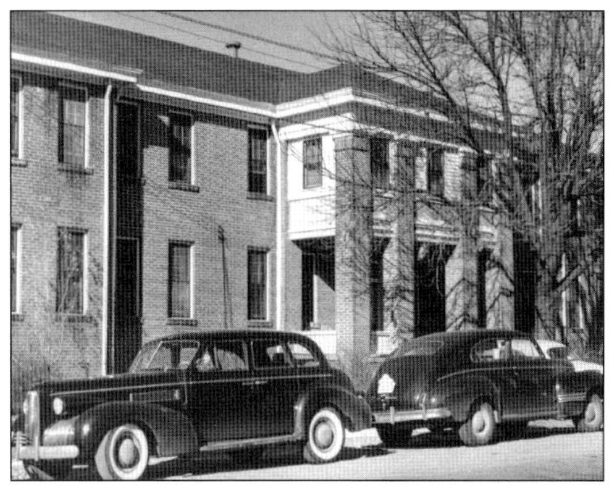

To accommodate growing enrollment, the Hall-Moody began constructing a dormitory in 1919. Originally named the Ellis Home for Young Women, the building honored Baptist elder G.L. Ellis. It was located directly east of the old Administration Building and connected to it by a covered breezeway. After the Hall-Moody campus was acquired for use as a state junior college, the dormitory was renamed Reed Hall. It continued to serve as a women's residence hall until 1975, when it was demolished to make way for more modern facilities. It is pictured here in the 1950s.

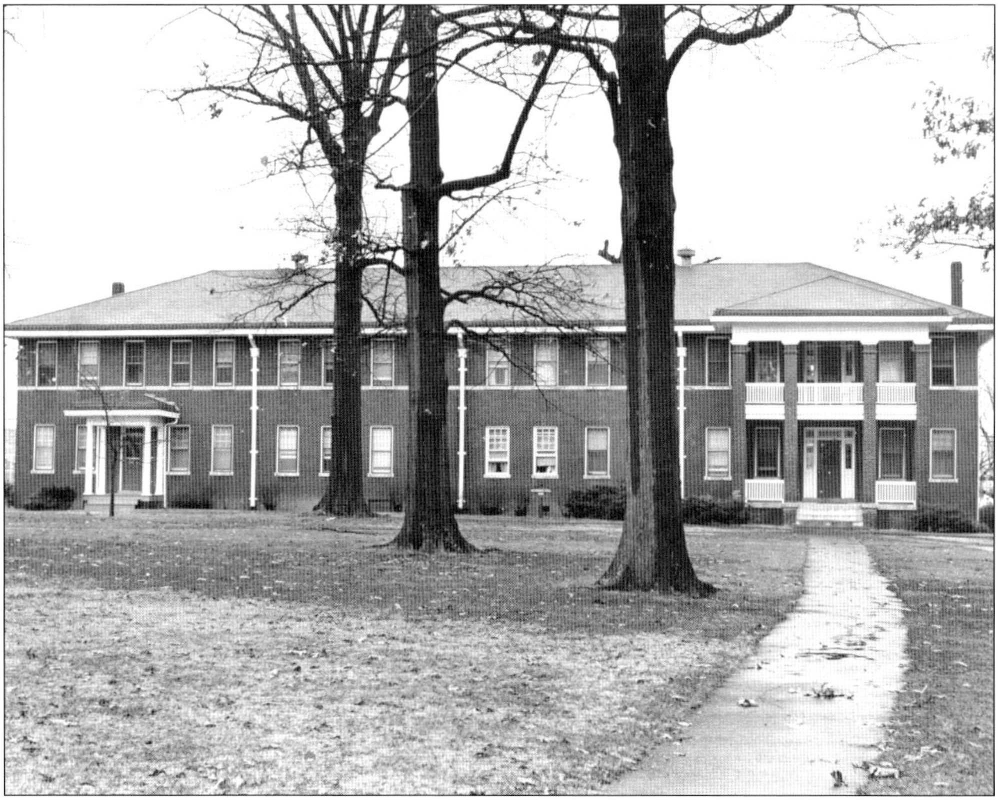

In response to increasing enrollment, Hall-Moody began building a new men's dormitory in 1921. Completed later that year, the dormitory was named the Lovelace Home for Young Men in honor of W.N. Lovelace, who had donated the land on which it was built. When the University of Tennessee acquired the Hall-Moody property, the building was renamed Freeman Hall and served as a men's dormitory from 1921 until 1973. Some sources from the 1930s curiously referred to it as Blackman Hall. After 1969, newer dormitories located on the south side of campus began housing students. Freeman Hall was ultimately demolished in the summer of 1973 to make way for the construction of Gooch Hall. During World War II, the building was left mostly vacant as many male students left the junior college for military service. In 1943, following the expansion of the UTJC flight training program by the Civil Aeronautics Administration, Freeman Hall was temporarily renamed the Atlanta Barracks and housed Navy pilot trainees.

In 1926, following the resignation of James T. Warren—who left to become vice president of Tennessee College—William Hall Preston assumed the presidency of Hall-Moody. At the time, the institution was facing financial difficulties. Less than a year into Preston's tenure, the Baptist State Convention opted to merge Hall-Moody with Union University in Jackson, Tennessee, making Preston the final president in the school's history.

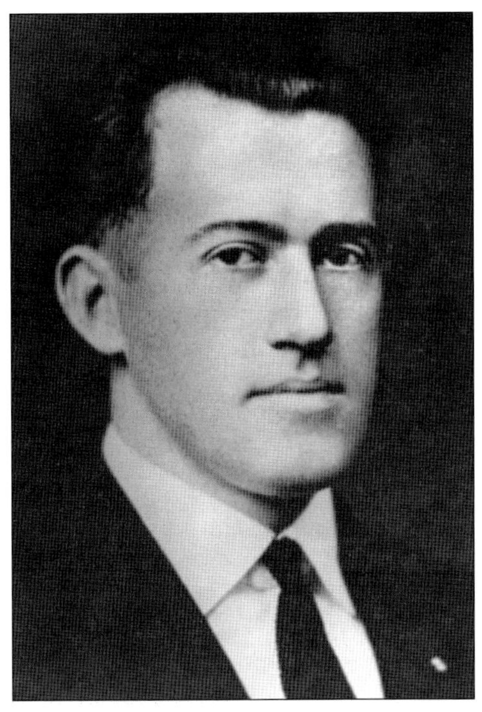

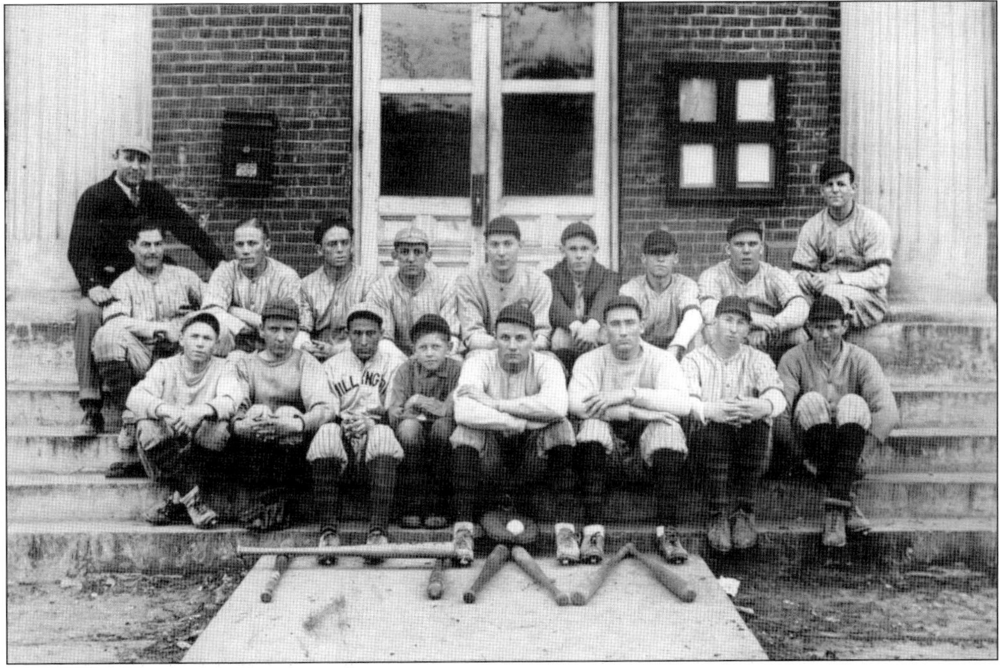

The 1925–1926 Hall-Moody baseball team marked the beginning of the coaching career of H. Kirk Grantham (pictured left) at the school. Previously a successful high school coach in Newbern, Tennessee, Grantham joined Hall-Moody in 1925 as both head coach and director of athletics. That same year, Hall-Moody began competing against strictly collegiate opponents. Due to the limited number of nearby junior colleges, the schedule primarily featured senior colleges. The 1926 team finished the season with a 10-8 record, and much of the athletic program's early success was credited to Grantham's leadership.

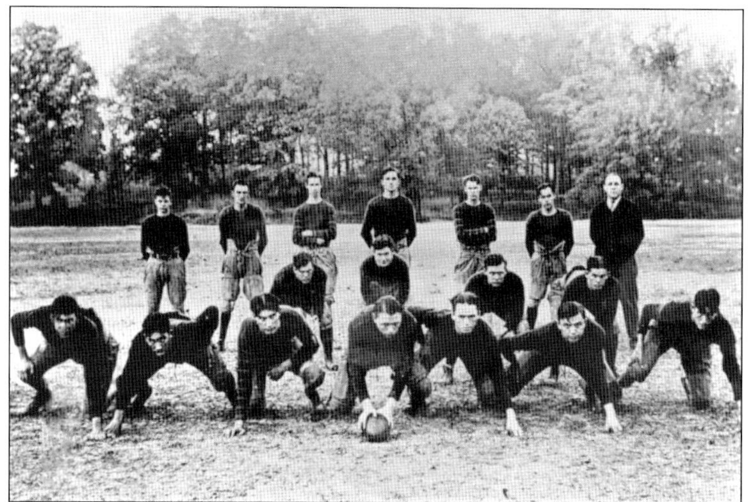

The 1926–1927 Hall-Moody football team, led by Coach Grantham, marked the final season of intercollegiate football for the institution. The team finished the 1926 campaign with a record of 3-5-1. Hall-Moody's athletic teams were known as "the Sky Pilots"—a nickname derived from a frontier-era term for preachers.

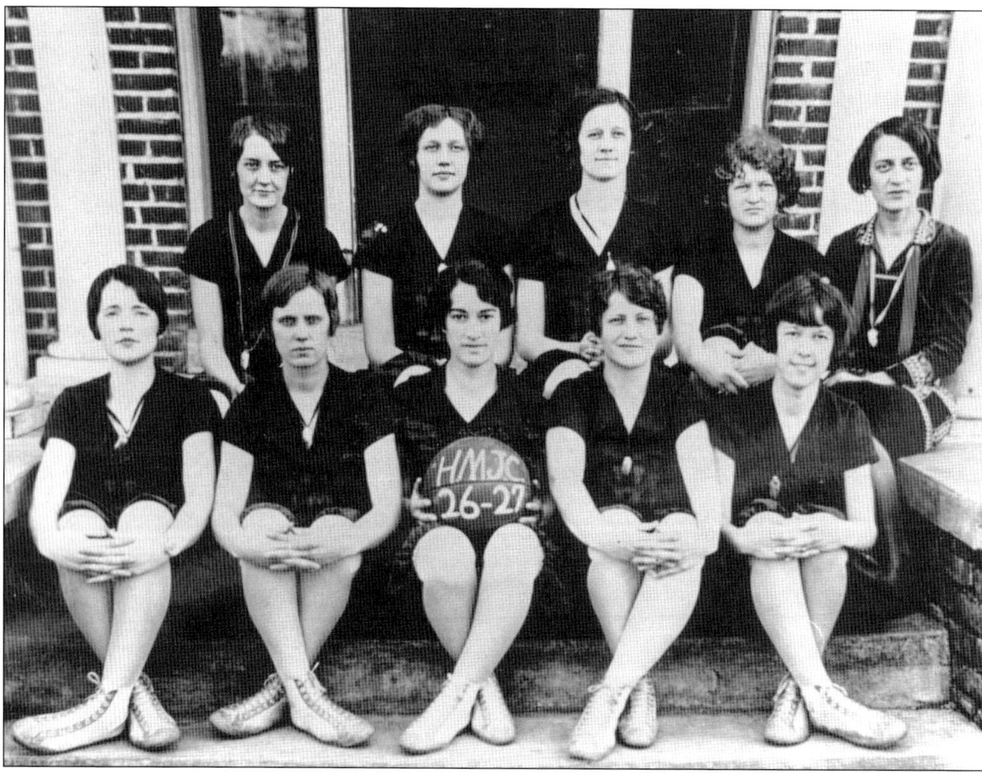

The members of the 1926–1927 women's basketball team are, from left to right, (first row) Ruth Rucker, Lillian Tucker, Grace Avery, Virginia Falghum, and Elizabeth Callicut; (second row) Virginia Poyner, Winnie Kennedy, Grace Hansbro, Lucille Woods, and coach Martha Williford. Under the leadership of Coach Williford, the Hall-Moody women's basketball team concluded the season with a 2-4 record. During that year, they competed twice each against Lambuth, Union University, and Bethel. In the program's early years, the women's team played a mixed schedule comprising both high school and college teams. However, in Hall-Moody's final two seasons, the schedule was exclusively against collegiate opponents, with their record demonstrating a commendable level of performance against college competition.

Hall-Moody Junior College

Martin, Tennessee

"The College of High Ideals"

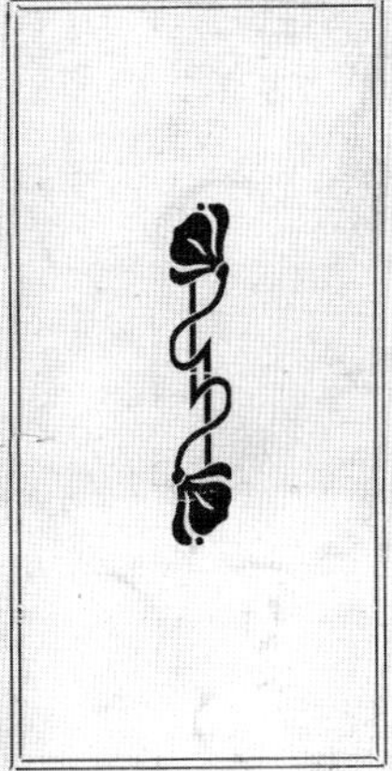

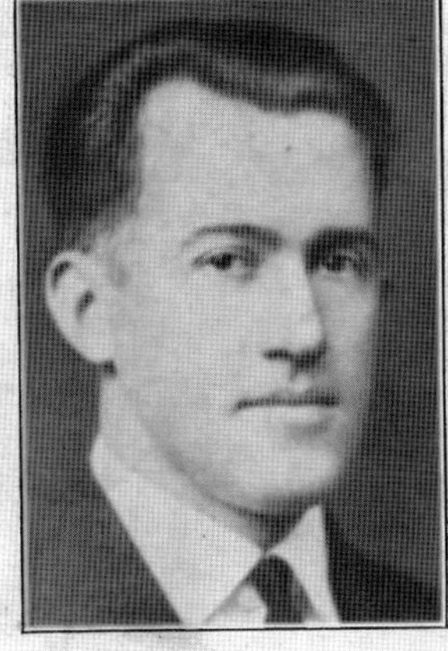

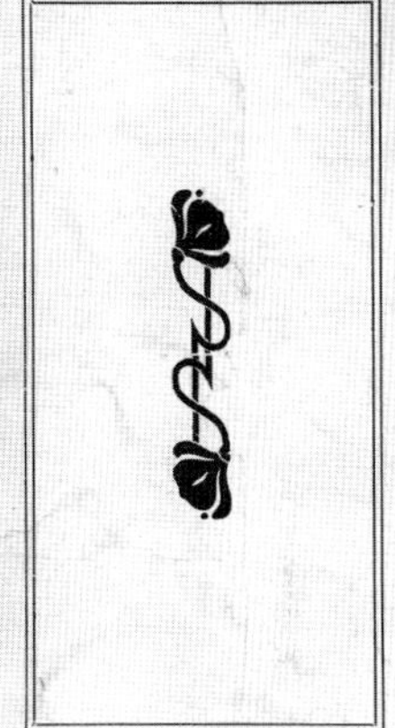

WILLIAM HALL PRESTON
President of Hall-Moody Junior College

Ten Big "Whys" For Attending Hall-Moody Junior College

1. HIGH STANDARDS—
   It is a Standard Junior College With Christian Ideals. Its graduates enter the Junior Class of Senior Colleges and Universities with full credit for work done in Hall-Moody.
2. CO-EDUCATIONAL—
   It is a Baptist Co-Educational School offering wholesome, helpful school and social life during the high school years and the first two years of College.
3. RELIGIOUS LEADERSHIP—
   It offers opportunities to develop the qualities of leadership in Religious Work. The B.Y.P.U., the Sunday School, the Y.W.A., the Missionary and the Evangelistic Clubs, along with the regular work in the local churches afford places for real service.
4. DEBATE AND ORATORY—
   It provides opportunities for developing the qualities of leadership in debating and oratory. Each year Hall-Moody has at least two inter-collegiate debates. Oratorical contests are held at commencement time to determine the winners of medals offered by friends of the College.
5. DRAMATICS—
   It gives the students an opportunity to take dramatics and expression along with the regular literary work. At least two plays are given during the school year.
6. GLEE CLUB AND ORCHESTRA TOURS—
   It provides for developing the voices in the College. Hall-Moody has a Glee Club and tours of this section of the State are being planned for 1926-1927 for the Orchestra and Glee Clubs.
7. ATHLETICS—
   From Fall until Spring (especially) every effort is made to have each student develop himself or herself physically—Football, Basketball (for girls and boys), Baseball and other clean sports are fostered. A new Gymnasium makes these sports more attractive.
8. TEACHERS CERTIFICATES—
   Graduates of Hall-Moody Junior College, who have taken the requirements in education, are given professional high school certificates good in any except first class high schools. They are also entitled to a permanent professional elementary certificate.
9. EXPENSES LOW—IDEALS HIGH—
   The expenses at Hall-Moody are as reasonable or more so, than any other school of like standing in the South. Board and room $5.50 per week. Tuition about $96.00 per school year of nine months. Other expenses between $50.00 and $100.00. Situated in a small city with high moral standards, pure water, and healthful climate.
10. LOAN FUND AND SCHOLARSHIPS—
    A loan fund is available for worthy students who may need financial assistance to remain in school. A few scholarships are also offered. Come to "The College of High Ideals"!
    Fall Quarter opening September 6th, 1926.

A brochure from the 1925–1926 academic year for Hall-Moody Junior College proudly featured the institution's motto, "The College with High Ideals." Even in the early 20th century, colleges utilized promotional materials to attract prospective students. This brochure highlights "Ten Compelling Reasons to Attend Hall-Moody Junior College."

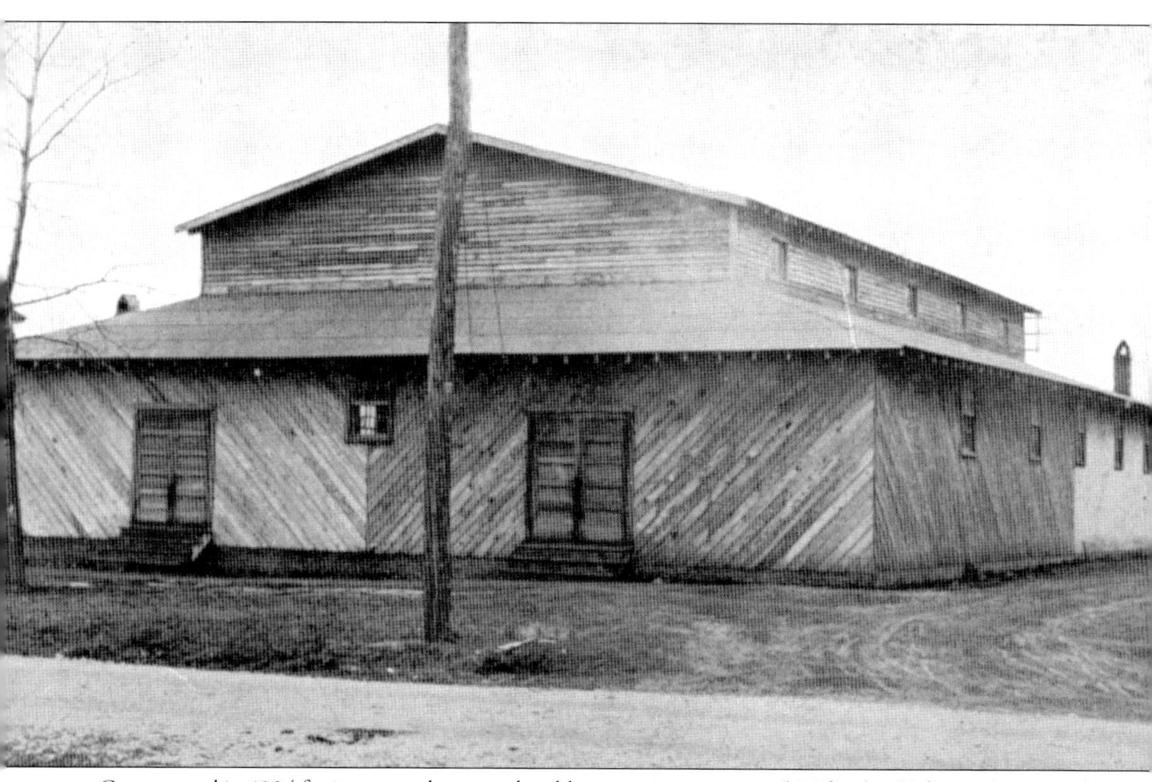

Constructed in 1924 for intermural sports, the old gymnasium measured 91 feet by 64 feet and consisted of a regulation basketball court. It was a wooden structure that was constructed to allow the outside to be faced with brick, but it was incomplete when the campus was purchased for the University of Tennessee in 1927. The building was demolished in 1931 after the completion of the new Physical Education Building.

Two

The University of Tennessee Junior College 1927–1951

With the closure of Hall-Moody, one of Tennessee's most esteemed small colleges, leaders and citizens of northwest Tennessee feared its impact on education and employment in the region. Even before its doors shut, local leaders sought another institution to establish a college in Martin. George C. Rowlett, a Martin lawyer and trustee of Hall-Moody Junior College, had recently been appointed to the University of Tennessee Board of Trustees. Using his influence, community leaders petitioned the state to take over the Hall-Moody campus and create a junior college under UT's umbrella.

Though UT president Harcourt A. Morgan was initially reluctant, the City of Martin and Weakley County underscored their commitment by each approving a \$100,000 tax bond to acquire the Hall-Moody campus and 80 acres from nearby Woodley Farm. On February 10, 1927, state senator Sam R. Bratton introduced Senate Bill 301 to establish the University of Tennessee Junior College (UTJC) in Martin. Gov. Austin Peay signed the bill into law on March 29, officially creating the college. The act mandated the establishment of a junior college for agriculture, industrial arts, and home economics. UTJC opened on September 12, 1927, with existing Hall-Moody buildings and a modest campus infrastructure.

Calvin Porter Claxton served as UTJC's first executive officer until 1934, overseeing nearly all campus operations except faculty hiring, which was controlled by UT Knoxville. The college began with 120 students and 14 faculty members, including H. Kirk Grantham, the only holdover from Hall-Moody. Under Claxton, the campus expanded significantly, adding new facilities, including a home economics building, a science hall, a gymnasium, and an industrial arts center.

In 1934, Paul Meek became UTJC's chief executive officer, inheriting a school struggling through the Great Depression. His leadership revived the institution, and by 1946, *Look* magazine ranked UTJC among the nation's top 15 junior colleges. World War II threatened enrollment, but Meek secured a Navy pilot training center that kept UTJC operational. Postwar, aided by the GI Bill, enrollment surged, necessitating further expansion. The university repurposed wartime materials from Fort Tyson Army Base to construct additional student housing and facilities, ensuring UTJC's continued growth.

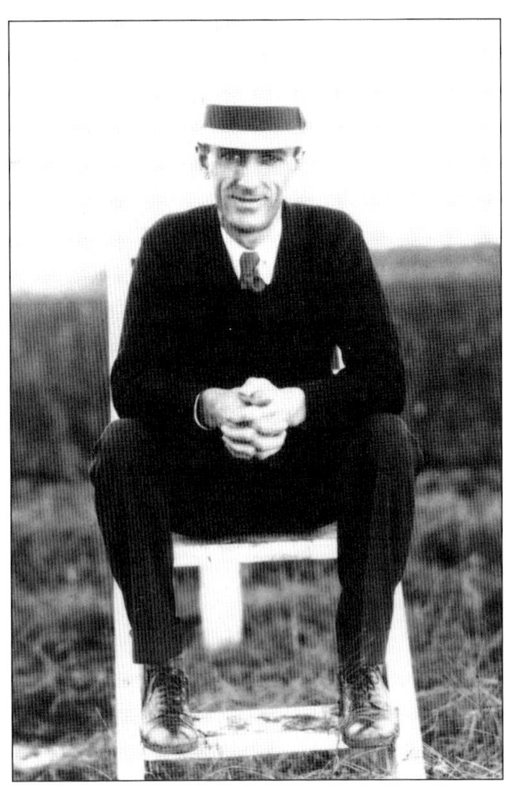

Calvin Porter Claxton was the first executive officer of the University of Tennessee Junior College. He was responsible for establishing the new institution. Claxton was respected as a caring and generous administrator and an excellent teacher. He served UTJC until 1934, when he was recalled to the Knoxville campus.

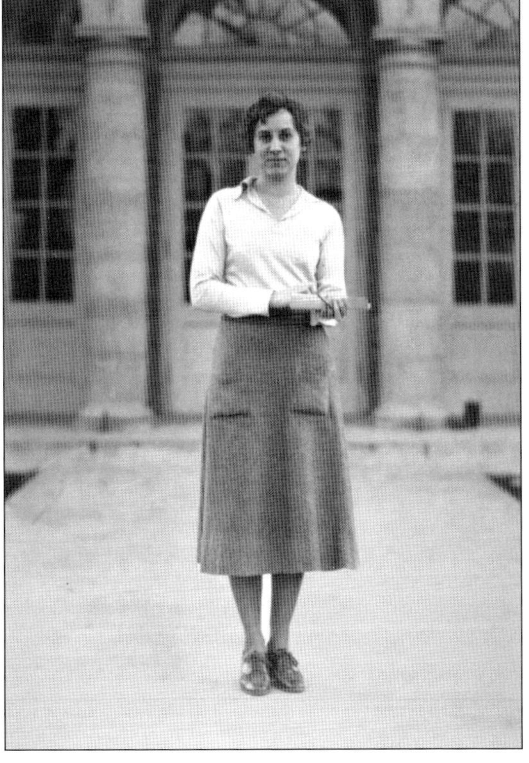

At the start of Claxton's tenure at UTJC, enrollment rose to 180 but dropped to 92 by 1933, for which he was blamed. Additionally, concerns were raised about his relationship with physical education teacher Evelyn Mabry (right). Although both were single, some considered their relationship inappropriate. As a result of these complaints, UT recalled Claxton to Knoxville. Their relationship, however, proved serious—Claxton married Mabry in March 1934.

Coming from Newbern, Tennessee, Hall-Moody hired H. Kirk Grantham in 1925 as head coach and director of athletics. He was the only Hall-Moody faculty member to be retained at UTJC. Along with being the head of the Department of Physical Education and director of athletics, Grantham coached football, baseball, and men's basketball. He served in these positions until 1937, when he left UTJC and entered private business.

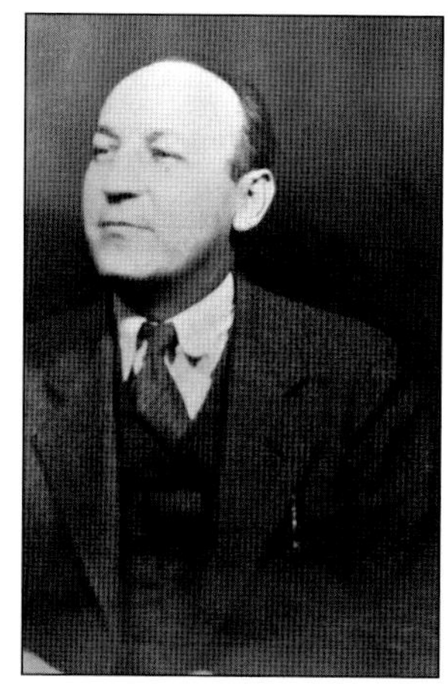

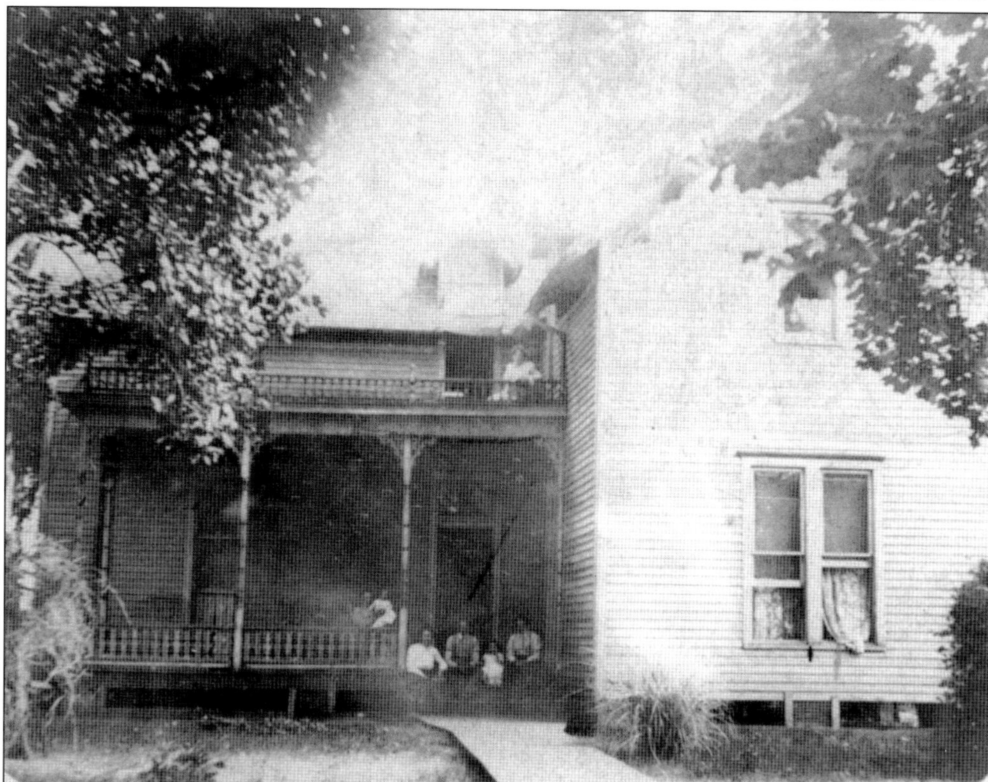

The University of Tennessee at Martin now occupies much of what was once Woodley Farm, originally owned by James Evans Freeman in the mid-1880s. His wife, Elizabeth Rast Freeman, named the property for its abundance of hickory, oak, poplar, and elm trees, some of which still stand today. The Freemans built a 13-room house on the land—now the site of the Paul Meek Library—and surrounded it with various outbuildings, including barns, storage sheds, and tenant housing. In its prime, the farm served as both a productive agricultural site and a social hub, even hosting the Martin Lawn Tennis Club. After Elizabeth's death in 1915, the farm declined rapidly and was eventually sold in 1928 by Otis Freeman to the University of Tennessee for $18,000. The land became a central part of the UTM campus, and although many changes have occurred, traces of the original farm, like segments of Union City Road, remain visible today.

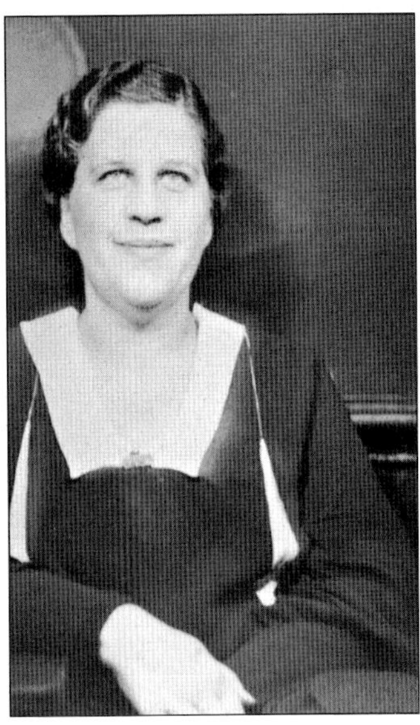

Myrtle Phillips served as the registrar of UTJC from 1929 to 1964. In the absence of an alumni director, she also took on alumni relations, writing and distributing *Campus Chatter*, a publication sent to former students. Her husband, J. Paul Phillips, led the education department and taught psychology and other subjects at UTJC from 1927 until his passing in 1953.

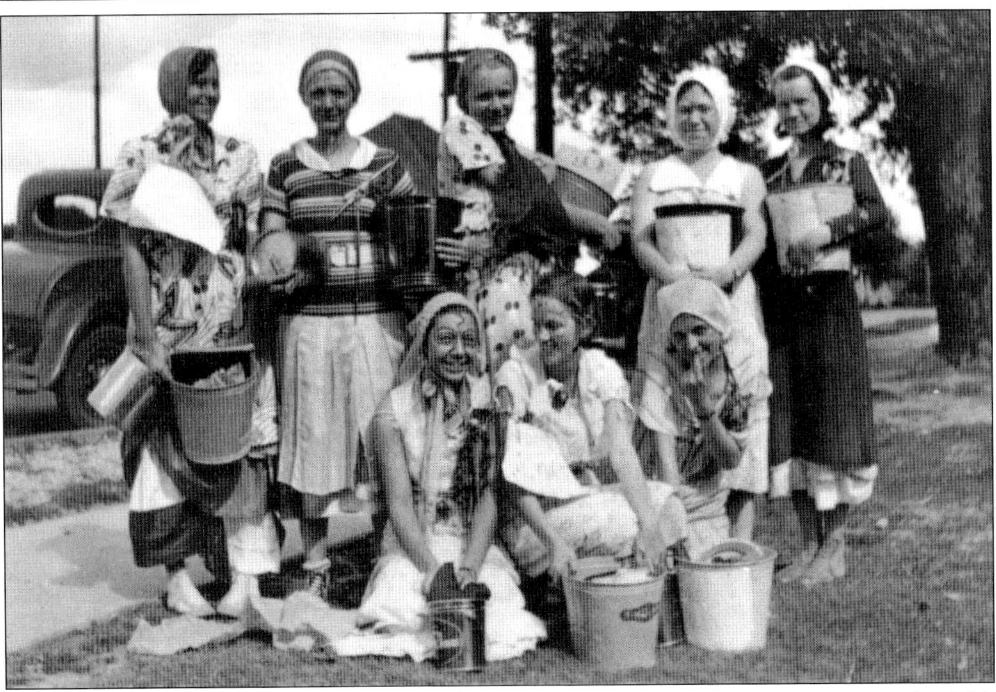

In 1932, students were formally inducted into the Home Economics Club. Founded in 1927, the club's membership was restricted to students enrolled in home economics courses. Initially, the club comprised only 30 members, but it grew alongside the department. The organization aimed to promote fellowship among students, strengthen the relationship between home and academic life, encourage community leadership, and assist members in developing personal skills and social confidence. At that time, about 85 percent of the female student body at UTJC was enrolled in the home economics department. The curriculum was designed with dual objectives: to prepare students for roles as homemakers and to equip them for professional and commercial careers within the field. While primarily attended by women, the program was inclusive; in 1937, seven men were enrolled, and by the following year, this number had risen to 67.

Erected in 1929, the Home Economics Building was constructed to serve as offices and classrooms for the home economics department. In 1987, the building was renamed the Holland McCombs Center and Archives and housed the McCombs archives and the university museum. Since 1995, when the museum and archives were moved to the newly renovated Paul Meek Library, the McCombs Center has been used to house the University Scholars Program. It is the oldest building on campus.

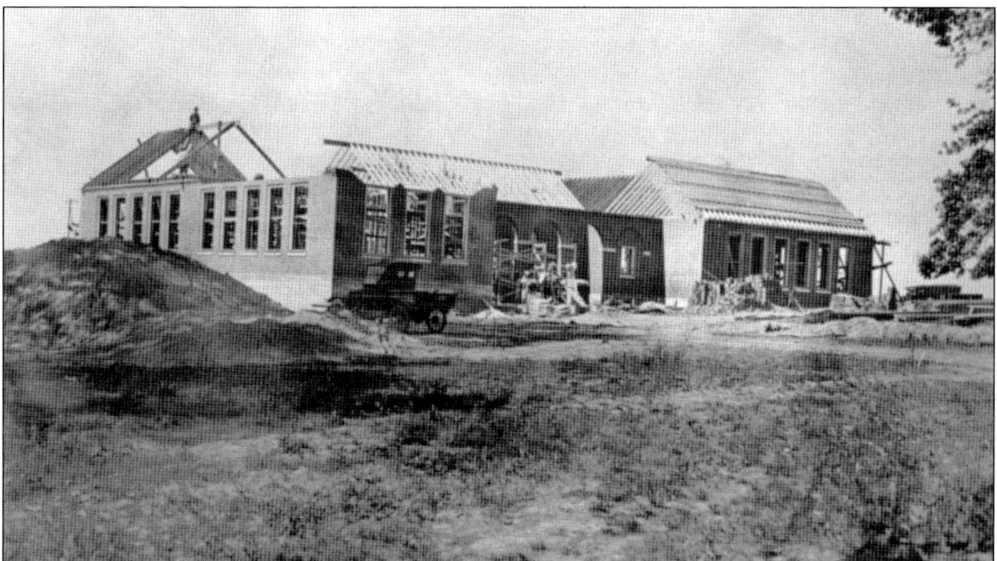

Shortly after construction began on the Home Economics Building, work commenced on a site for a new Science Building. Foundations were laid, and the structure—now known as the Sociology Building—was erected facing the Home Economics Building across the quadrangle. Originally, between 1929 and 1961, it housed offices and classrooms for the physical and industrial sciences department. Following the completion of the Engineering and Physical Sciences Building in 1961, the structure was repurposed for overflow classrooms, the faculty club, and as the main facility for the All-Students Association. Later, it became home to the social sciences department, which included drama programs and the Vanguard Theater. Since 1971, the building has served as the headquarters of the sociology department.

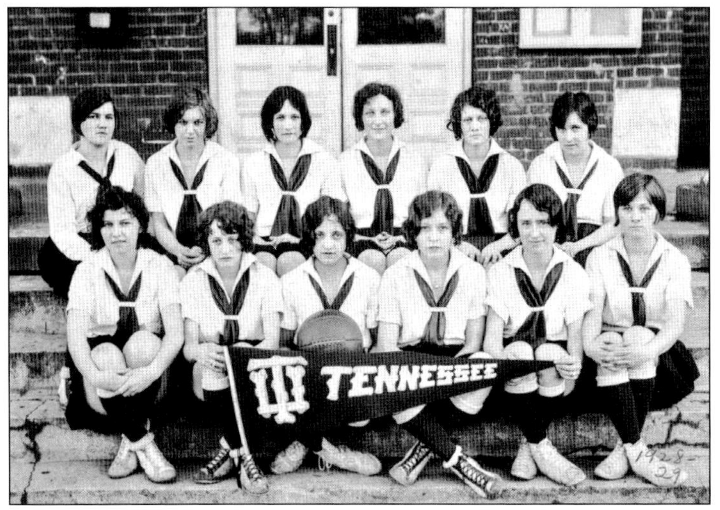

The 1928–1929 women's basketball team of UTJC performed admirably given the level of competition they faced. Many of their opponents were four-year institutions, primarily located in western Tennessee, western Kentucky, and southern Illinois. Notable competitors included Murray State, Bethel, Union, Southern Illinois, and West Tennessee State Teachers College (now the University of Memphis).

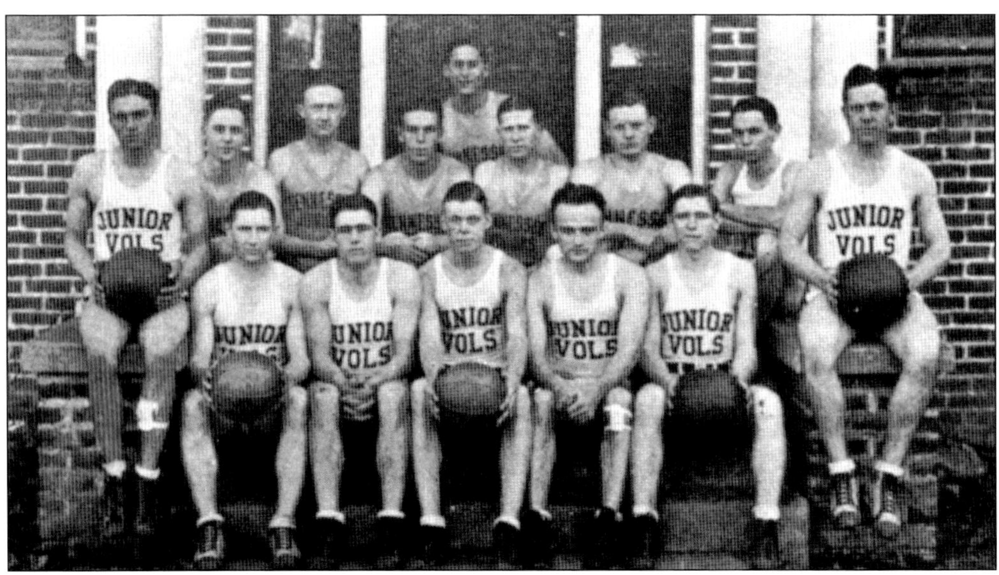

The 1930 University of Tennessee Junior College basketball team included the following members, from left to right, (first row) captain Clifton Pritchett, William Aycock, Conrad Lewis, William Stout, Bruce Tucker, Frank Adair, and William Minton; (second row) Frank Taylor, Maynard Reed, William Pybass, Brownlow Brundige, Mercer Boone, Otis Hastings, and Sam Moffat. Although the 1930 UTJC basketball team did not initially meet the expectations set for the season, their performance improved progressively over time. The successes attained were the result of the collaborative efforts of Coach Grantham and the dedicated squad under the leadership of captain Clifton Pritchett. Despite an inconsistent start marked by fluctuating outcomes and some challenges within conference play, the team's resolve and determination remained steadfast throughout the season. While luck may not have favored them on the court, the Junior Vols consistently exerted maximum effort in pursuit of victory. Ultimately, the team stood as a source of pride for the University of Tennessee, exemplifying resilience, commitment, and the enduring spirit of the Junior Volunteers.

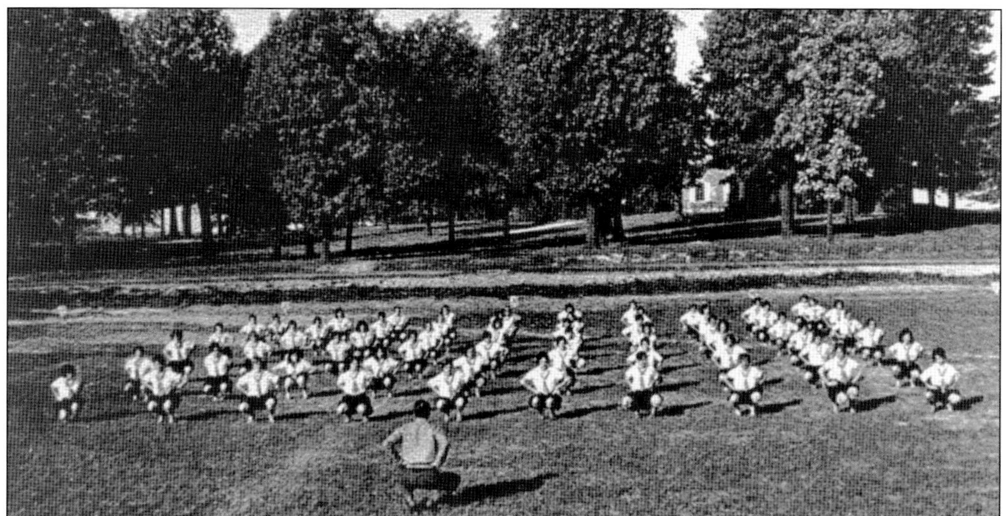

In 1930, formal calisthenics were introduced under the guidance of Coach Grantham. As the sole Hall-Moody instructor retained by UTJC, Grantham began leading the Department of Physical Education and established the department that year. He earned widespread respect from the community, students, faculty, and staff for his dedication both as a coach and an instructor.

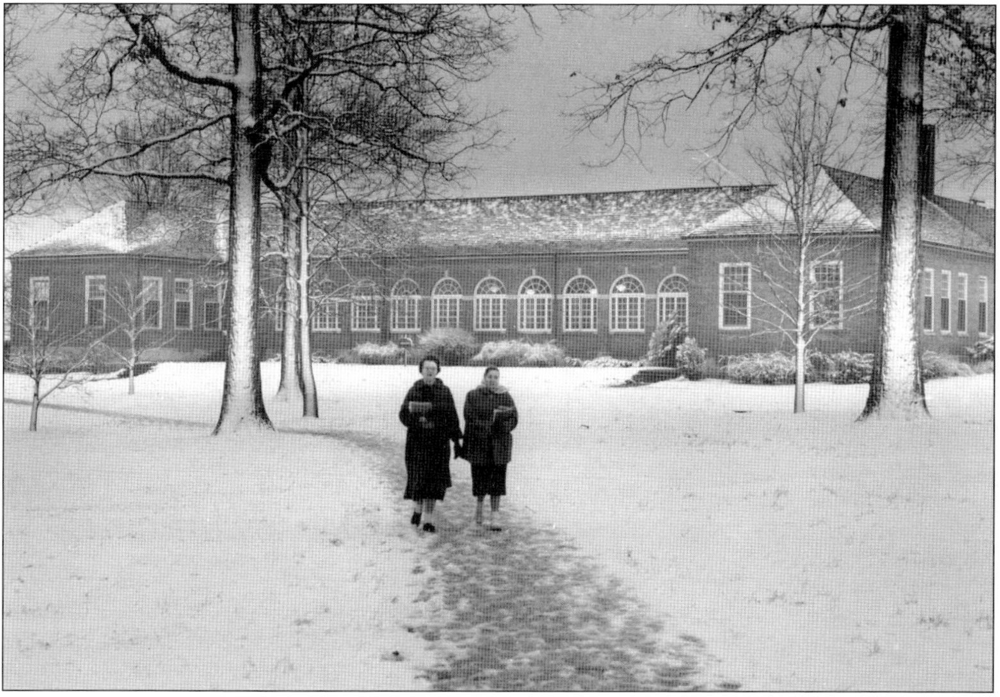

Two young students walk away from Crisp/Cooper Hall on a wintery day. Completed in 1930, the building originally housed offices and classrooms for the industrial arts program. In 1941, a fire gutted the structure, prompting UTJC to seek financial support from Gov. Prentice Cooper for reconstruction. With the secured funds, the structure was rebuilt and renamed Cooper Hall in 1969 to honor the governor. From 1942 to 1961, it served as offices and classrooms for the engineering department. Since the early 1970s, it has housed public safety, and in 1989, the campus computer center also relocated there. In 1996, the building was renamed Crisp Hall in honor of Harry L. Crisp Sr., a respected businessman.

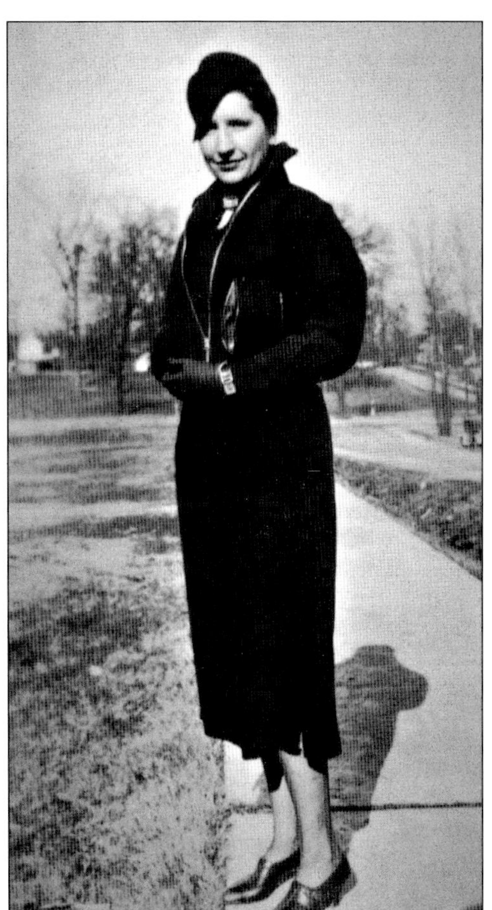

Florence Elliot Hillis, who was affectionately called "Miss Flossie," was a UTJC alumna who joined the UTJC faculty in 1933 to teach physical education. Among other subjects, she taught ballroom dancing. To her surprise, all the male students showed up for dancing instruction at the first session.

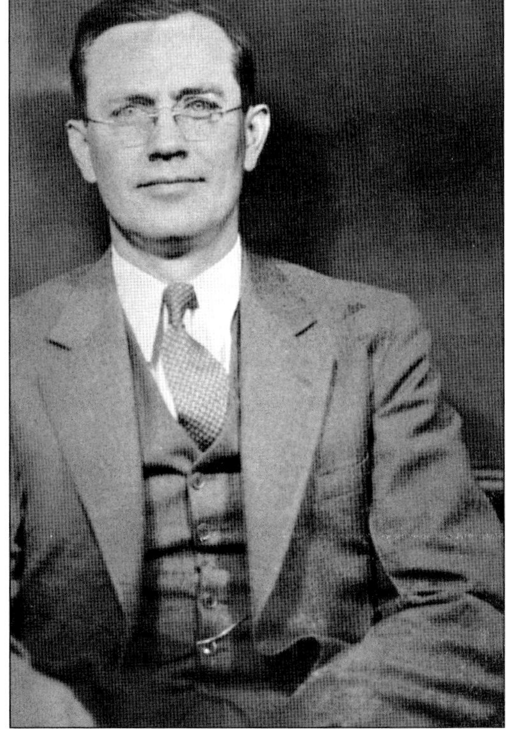

Born and raised in Weakley County, nobody did more for the success of the university than Paul Meek. He came to UTJC in 1934 to serve as chief executive after the departure of Calvin Porter Claxton. Along with being UTJC's executive officer, Meek served through the school's iterations as dean, UT vice president, or chancellor from 1934 until his retirement in 1967. He is still the university's longest-serving chancellor.

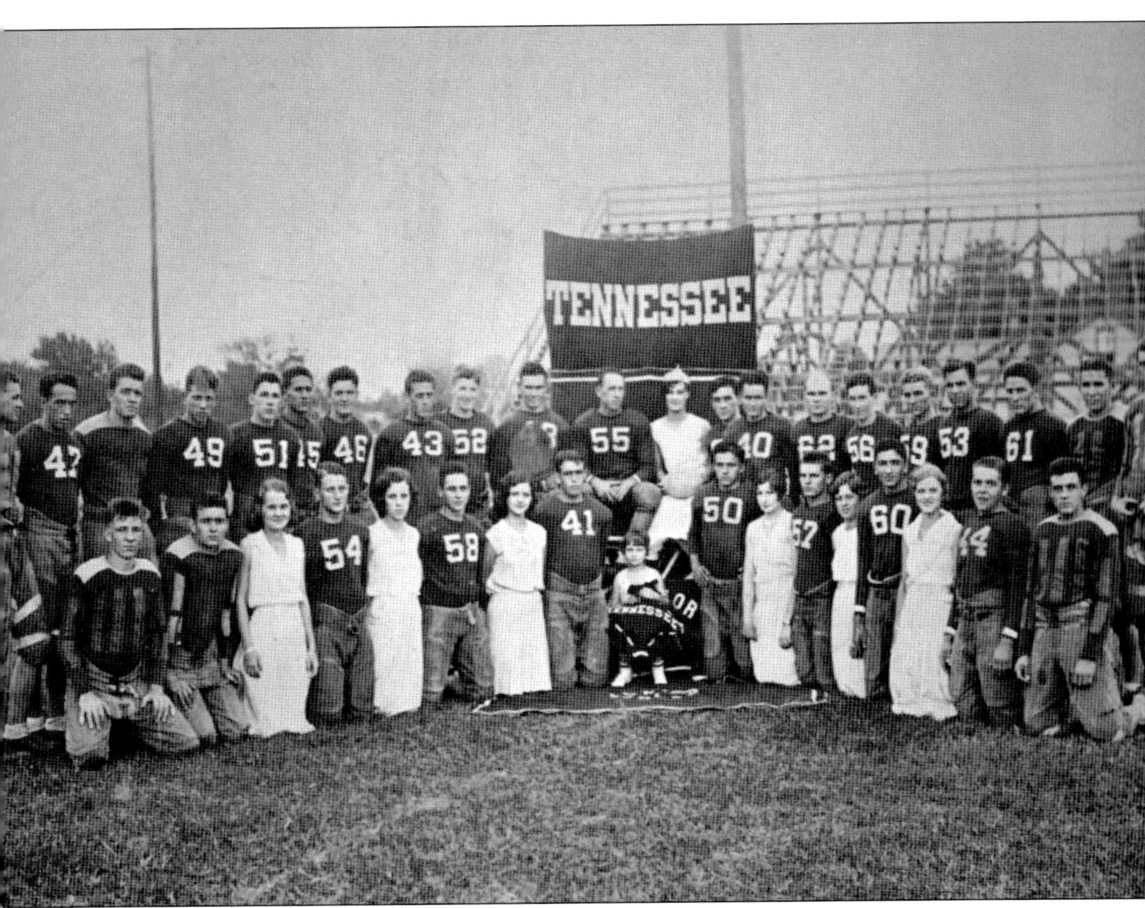

In 1930, a new chapter began for the UTJC Junior Vols football team as they commenced play in a newly constructed stadium equipped with lights. Night football was a novel experience for both players and spectators. The team enjoyed a successful season, securing eight victories and suffering only two defeats. Their sole major setback came in the final game, where they narrowly lost the Mississippi Valley Conference championship to West Tennessee Teachers College—now the University of Memphis—by a score of 14-13. In 1933, amid the economic challenges of the Great Depression, UTJC made the decision to discontinue all intercollegiate athletic programs. However, due to mounting public pressure and declining student enrollment, intercollegiate sports were reinstated in 1934.

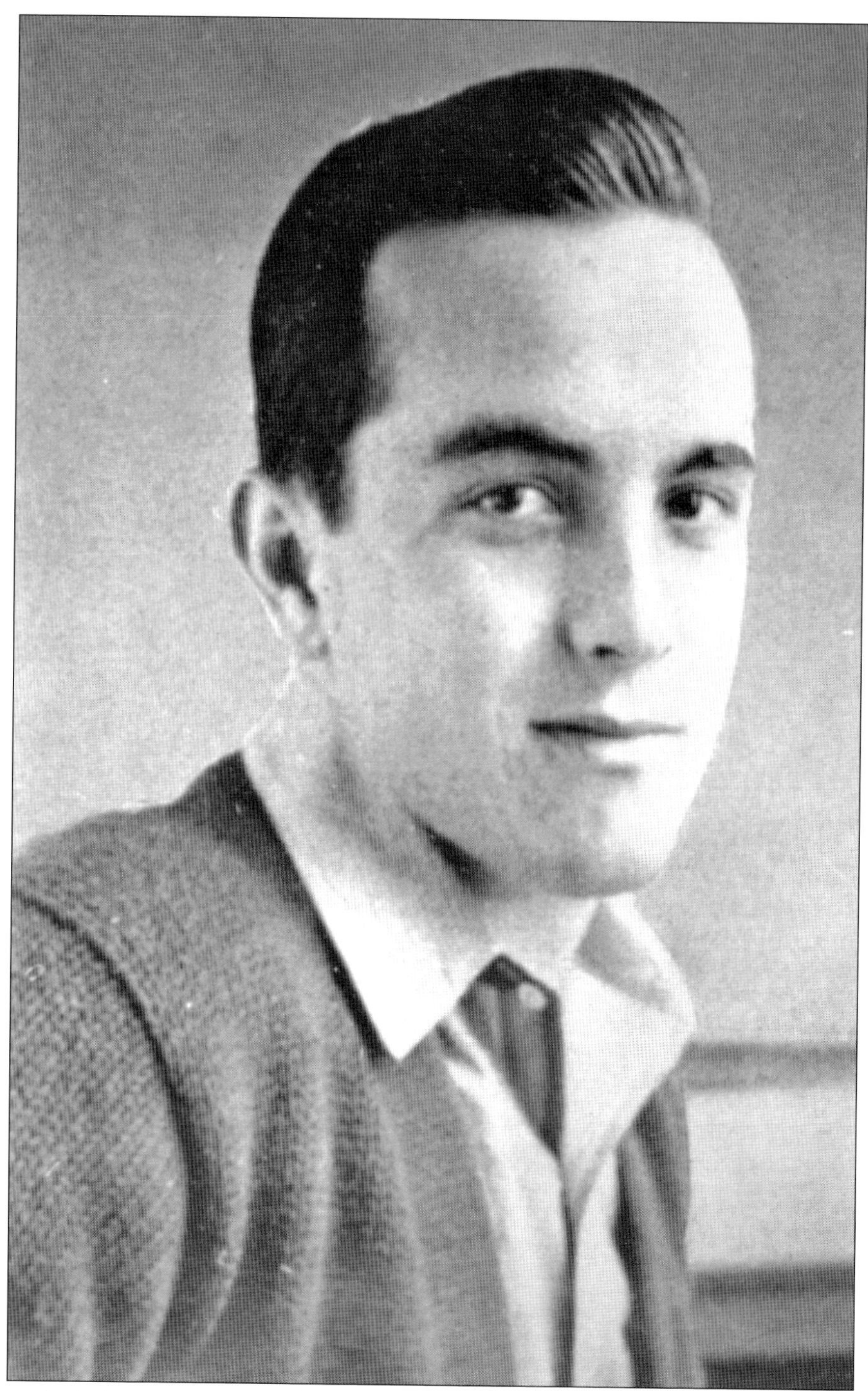

During a football game in 1935, sophomore tailback James Edward "Jimmy" Long from Union City sustained a fatal head injury. While playing against Northwest Mississippi Junior College in Senatobia, Long broke free for a 40-yard run but suffered a severe impact to his head when tackled, causing a ruptured blood vessel in his brain. He was quickly transported by ambulance to a hospital in Memphis, but despite medical efforts, he passed away the following day.

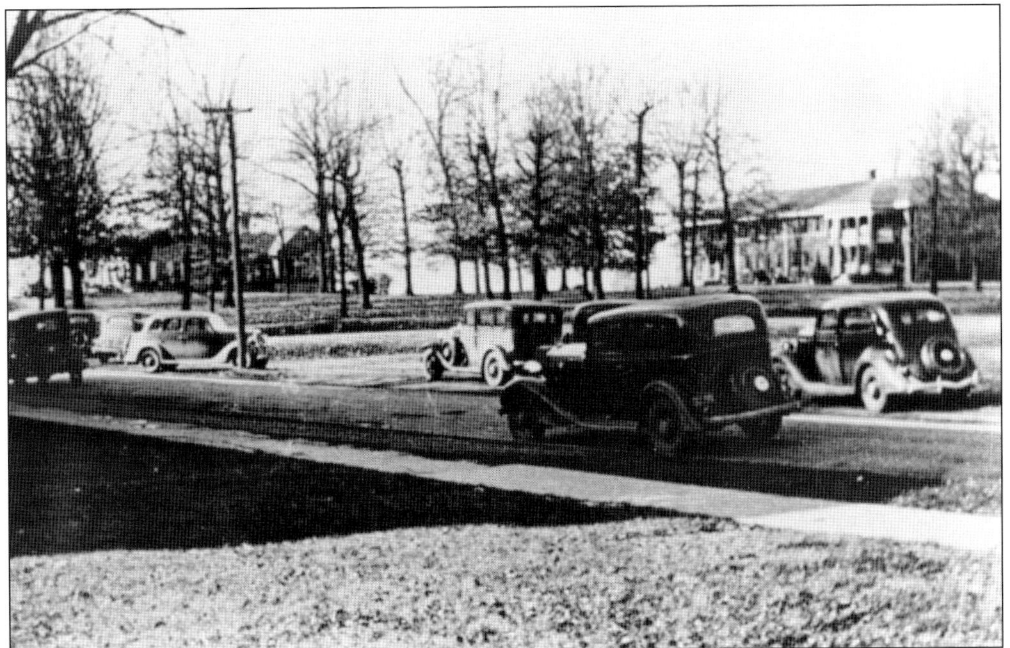

This is a panoramic view of UTJC during the 1930s, looking northwest across the quadrangle. The Home Economics Building is situated on the left, while Freeman Hall, the men's dormitory, stands to the right. This image captures the early architectural layout and atmosphere of the campus during that era.

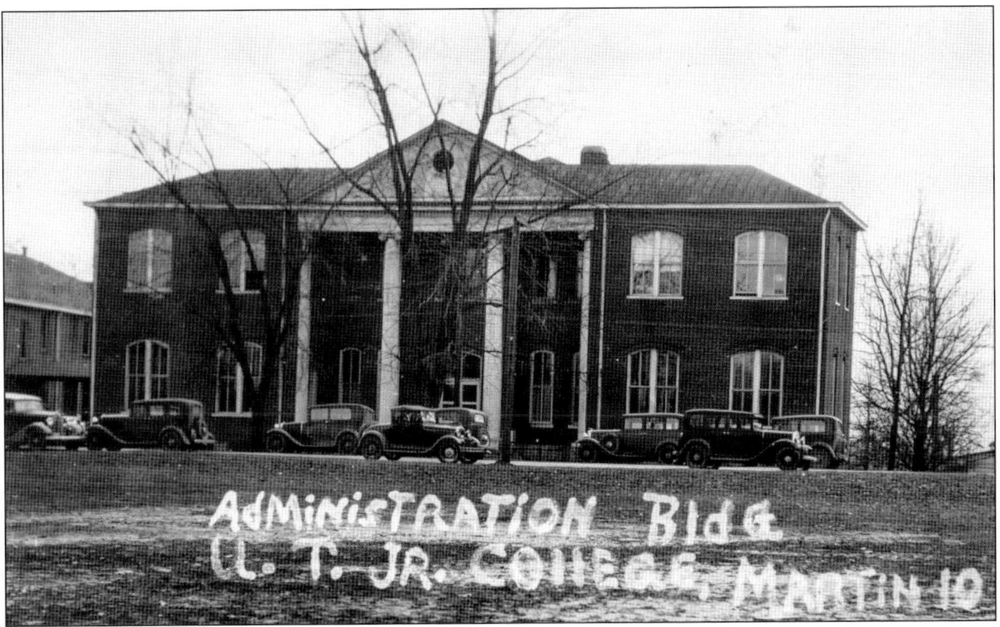

A general view of the Administration Building at UTJC in the 1930s, facing south, is shown here. The photograph captures the architectural style and scale of the building during this period, reflecting the institution's growth and commitment to higher education. This structure served as a central hub for administrative functions and played a vital role in supporting the college's academic mission throughout the decade.

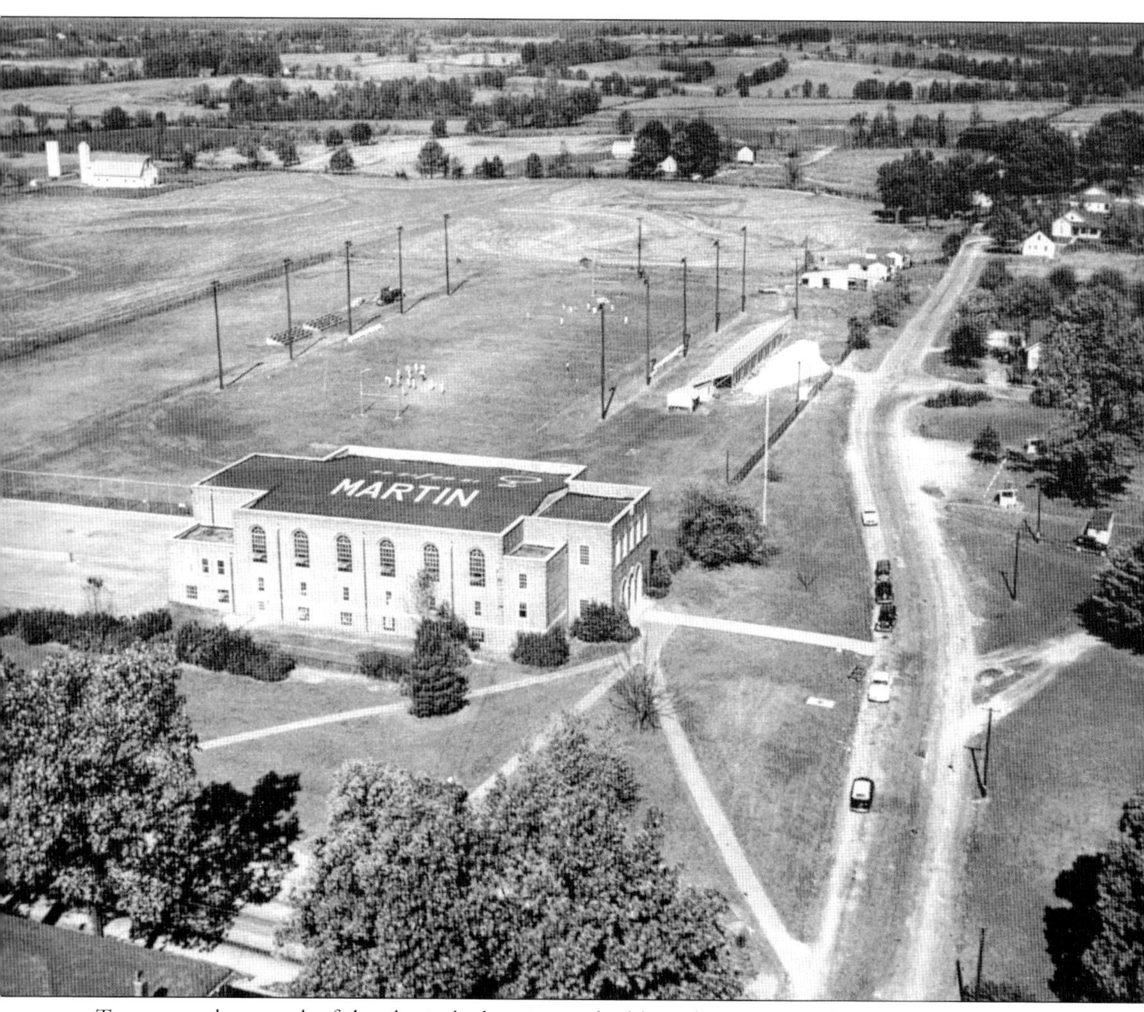

To support the growth of the physical education and athletic departments, the University of Tennessee began constructing the Physical Education Building in late 1929. When it opened in 1930, it was hailed as the most modern facility of its kind in the state. For 33 years, the gym served as the hub for UTJC's physical education department, housing offices, classrooms, and a gymnasium. It also hosted basketball games, student dances, annual Carnicus celebrations, and commencements. During World War II, the gym became a center for physical conditioning in 1943–1944, when a branch of the Navy's V-5 flight training program operated on campus and was temporarily renamed the Tennessee Barracks. Following the opening of the new Physical Education and Convocation Center in the summer of 1963, the building was repurposed as the Women's Physical Education Building. After those programs relocated to the new Elam Center, the facility transitioned into the offices and gymnasium for varsity-level athletic programs and now serves as the home of the university's football program. Remarkably, the original floor and the bleachers along the south wall remain intact.

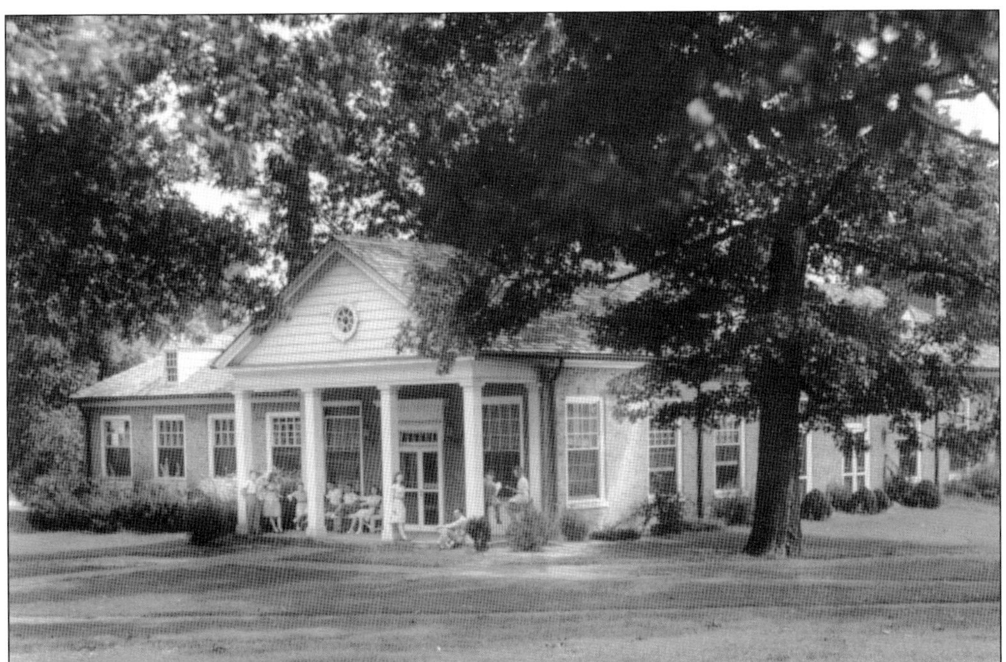

The dining hall and social building, as it was originally known, broke ground on October 15, 1934, with a "dirt-breaking" ceremony at the site. According to UTJC newspaper, the *Volette*, the first shovel of dirt was turned by a student named Jean Heidelberg, then president of the Home Economics Club. The building, which opened in January of the following year, replaced an earlier facility dating back to the Hall-Moody era. A quote from the October 22, 1934, issue of the *Volette* regarding the pending construction said it best, "It is intended thtat [sic] this building shall serve as the center of the social life of the college. While the Junior College is young, it has already developed a distinct spirit which has grown along with the architecture of its buildings." During World War II, it also provided meals for trainees in the War Training Service program. In 1947, the dining hall underwent renovations and functioned as a cafeteria until the completion of the new student center in 1965. Sometime before 1968, the space was repurposed into an instructional television studio for WLJT-TV. In 1979, it was officially renamed the Communications Building. This structure was demolished to make way for the Latimer-Smith Engineering and Science Building in 2019.

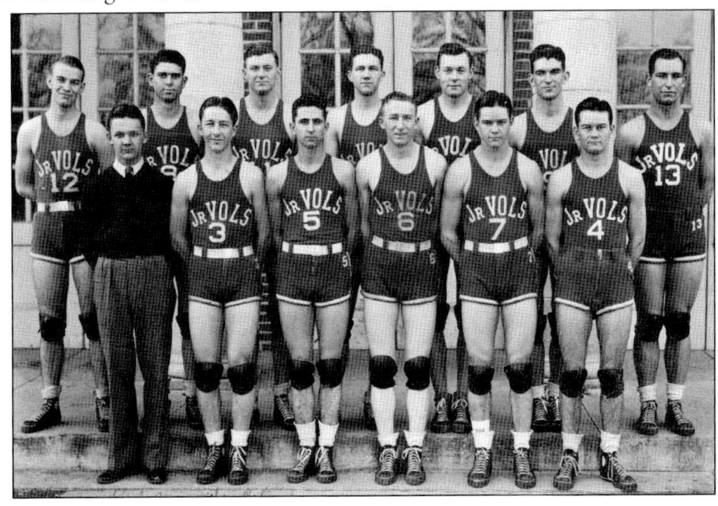

Under the leadership of Coach Grantham, the 1937 UTJC team had an outstanding season, securing victories in 19 of the 25 games they played. They concluded the season as runners-up in the Mississippi Valley Conference Tournament, falling to Freed-Hardeman in the championship game with a final score of 51-30.

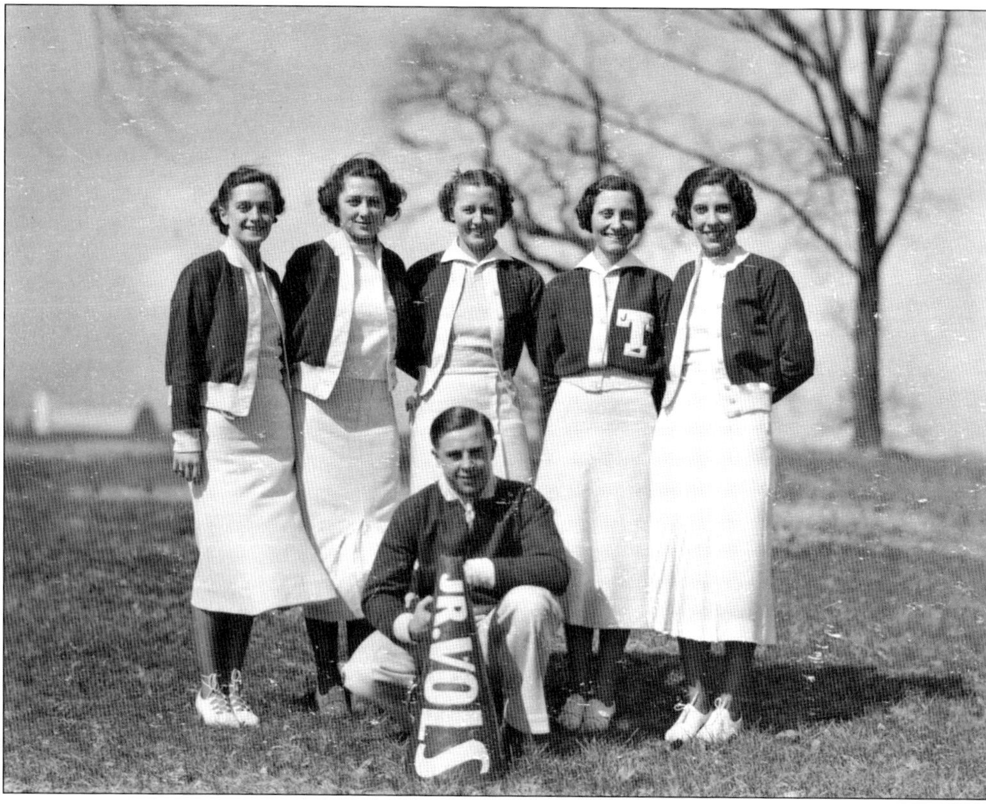

The 1937 cheerleaders are, from left to right, (first row) Joe Gower; (second row) Edith Edwards, Frances Hansbrough, Marth Frazier, Cora Rice, and Nell Warren. The cheerleaders, dressed in their orange and white uniforms, consistently brought energy and enthusiasm to the games. Regardless of the outcome, they could be seen cheering passionately, clapping, and at times, displaying intense emotion. They continually experimented with new routines and refined complex, spirited chants. Their presence infused both football and basketball games with vitality and excitement. Whether the team was leading or trailing, the cheerleaders and pep squad remained a steadfast source of motivation and encouragement, inspiring the players in their pursuit of victory.

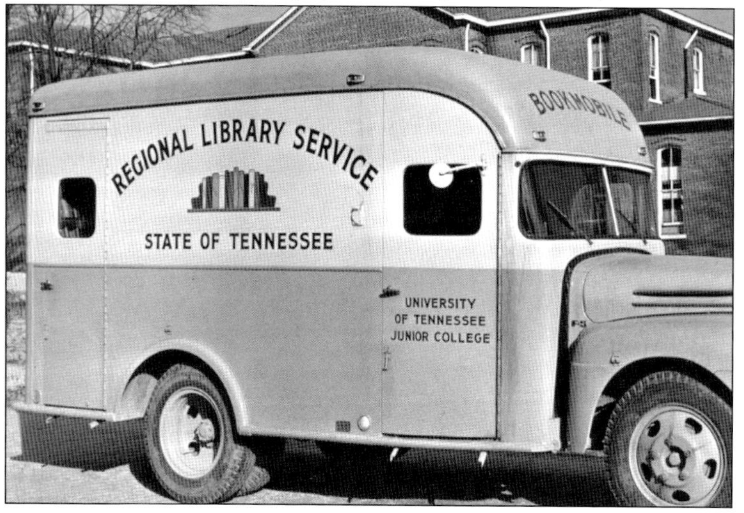

Along with offering books to the students at UTJC, the regional library extended the college's library services into the communities of West Tennessee. The regional library's "Book Mobile" could be seen every day traveling away from the college, providing fiction and nonfiction to community members.

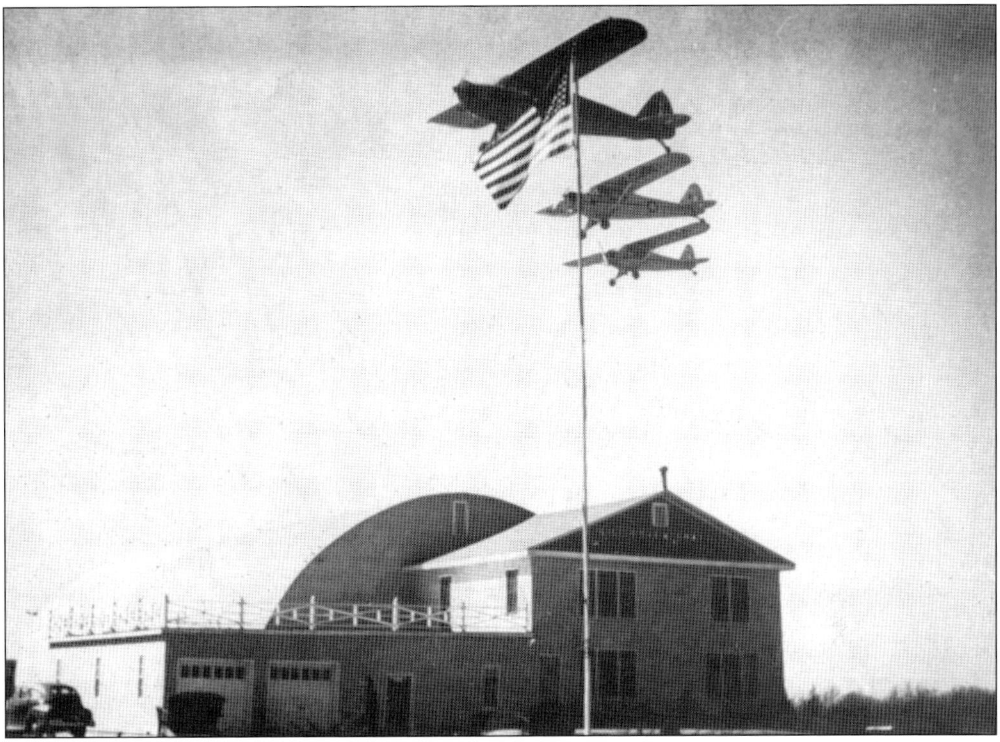

Gill-Dove Airfield operated from 1945 to 1946. Due to World War II, UTJC experienced a decline in enrollment, dropping to just 115 students, including only 24 male students. This decline sparked public concern about the school's future. Fortunately, Paul Meek, UTJC's chief executive officer, successfully persuaded the Civil Aeronautics Administration to establish a Civilian Pilot Training program on campus. In 1943, with the growing demand for military pilots, the program was expanded into one of several Navy pilot training centers. This initiative ultimately saved UTJC from insolvency and ensured its survival.

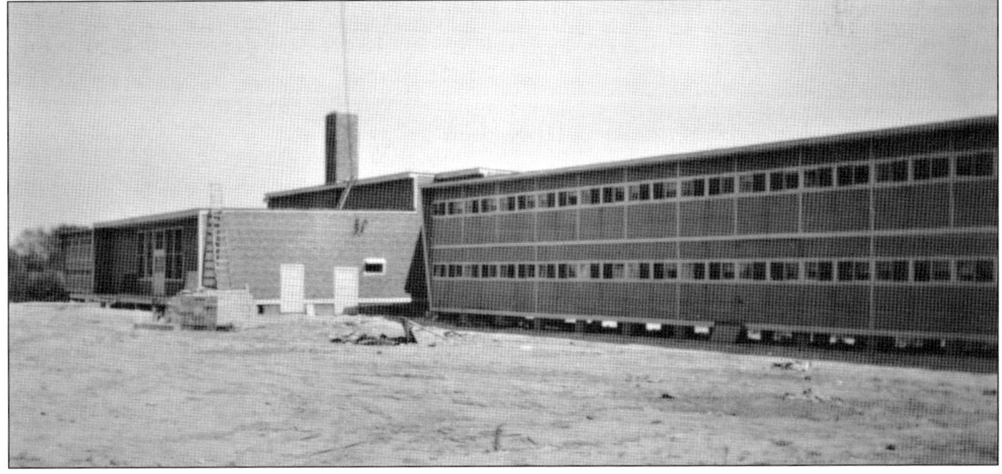

After World War II, with the support of the GI Bill, veterans enrolled in colleges and universities across the United States, including UTJC. By 1946, UTJC's enrollment had reached 649 students, 532 of whom were male. Providing housing for these students became a priority, and in 1947, the college constructed the "Wooden Box," a prefabricated dormitory for men.

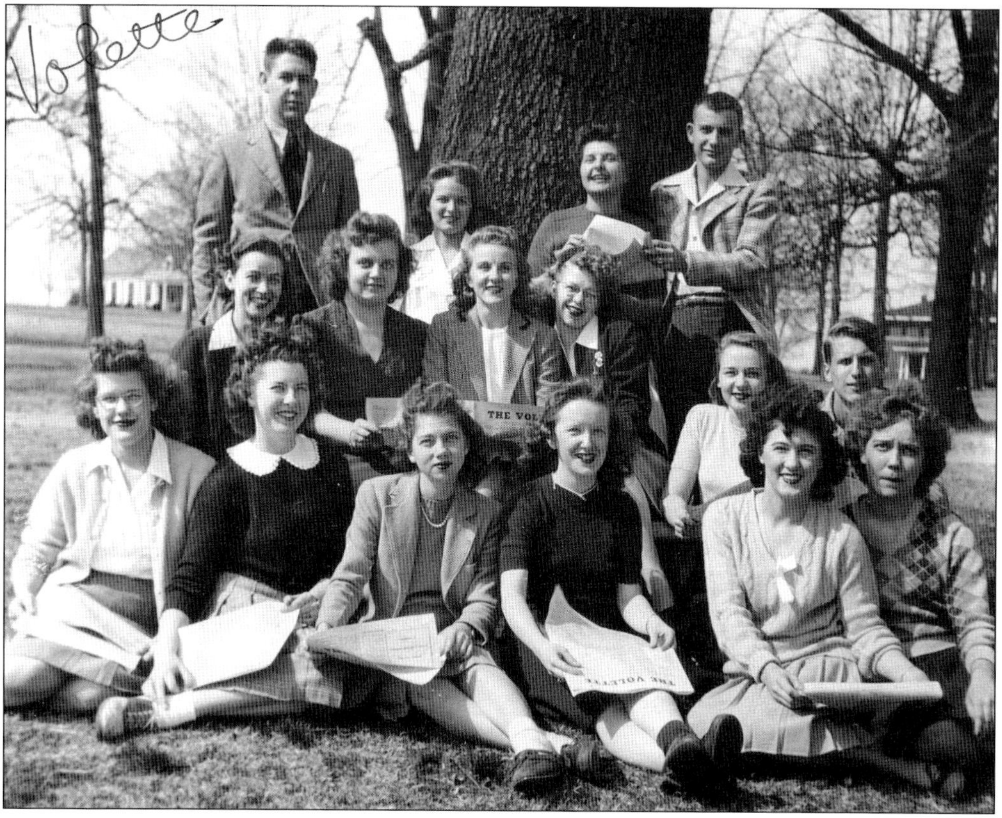

The 1946 *Volette* staff is pictured in the Quad. Staff members are, from left to right, (first row) Shirley Walker, unidentified, Dottie Lowe, Judy May, Elsie Christenbury, and Anne Hopson; (second row) Sue King, Aneta Galey, Kathryn Rose Thomas, Marisue Adams, Peggy Goodwin, and E.T. Brann; (third row, standing) Harry Harrison Kroll Jr., Erie Kate Porter, Betty Rae, and Joe Ham. The University of Tennessee at Martin's student newspaper has evolved over nearly a century, beginning in 1928 with the *Checkerboard*, quickly followed by the *Volette*—named through a student contest—and finally becoming the *Pacer* in 1971, a nod to the university's then athletics nickname. Early editions of the *Volette* included campus news, faculty updates, sports coverage, humorous columns, and even personal student tidbits like weekend travel and library misbehavior rules. As the university grew, so did the paper's role in reflecting campus life. The name "the *Pacer*" was retained even after UTM's mascot changed to the Skyhawk in 1995, with staff emphasizing the paper's commitment to being a pacesetting, independent voice for students. The *Pacer* remains a source of campus news and commentary to this day.

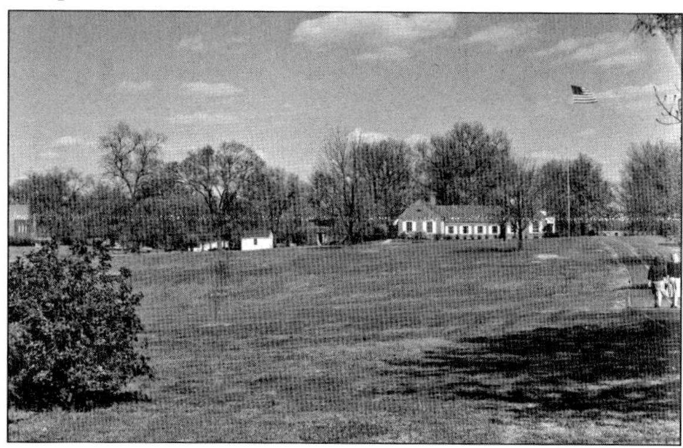

This eastward view of the campus during the 1940s features the Home Economics Building on the right and the Physical Education Building and gymnasium on the left. These structures played a central role in student life and academic instruction during this era. The image reflects the university's early architectural development and its commitment to practical and physical education.

Three

The University of Tennessee Martin Branch 1952–1967

In 1951, House Bill 264 was passed by the state legislature and signed into law by Gov. Gordon Browning, granting the school the authority to offer four-year degrees in agriculture and home economics. This marked its official designation as a university and led to its renaming as the University of Tennessee Martin Branch (UTMB). The focus on agriculture highlighted the significance of farming in the northwest region and reflected ongoing advancements in agricultural practices.

In April 1952, the University of Tennessee Board of Trustees convened for the first time as a full body on the UTMB campus, emphasizing the institution's growing importance. By the decade's end, enrollment had surpassed 1,000 students. This period also saw the completion of two major construction projects: the Agriculture-Biology-Library Building (now Brehm Hall) in 1951 and the Administration Building in 1959, which was later renamed Hall-Moody in 1968 to replace the original aging structure.

The 1960s brought significant expansion, with student enrollment soaring from 1,123 in 1960 to 4,197 by 1969. This rapid growth necessitated a broader curriculum and the most extensive construction phase in the school's history. To accommodate the increasing demand for student housing, the university acquired Carter's Motor Inn in Martin—later known as Shannon Hall—as temporary lodging for male students until new dormitories were built. Additionally, the campus saw the construction of multiple dormitories and apartments, the Engineering-Physical Science Building, the Physical Education and Convocation Center, the Paul Meek Library, and the Holt Humanities Building.

As the student body expanded, UTMB underwent transformative changes, evolving into a comprehensive university. In 1960, the board of trustees approved the establishment of fraternities and sororities. A year later, with the end of segregation, Jessie L. Arnold became the first African American student admitted. In 1965, Paul Meek, who had led the institution for over 31 years, was elevated to vice president of the University of Tennessee and chancellor of the Martin Branch, further cementing UTMB's growing prominence within the UT System.

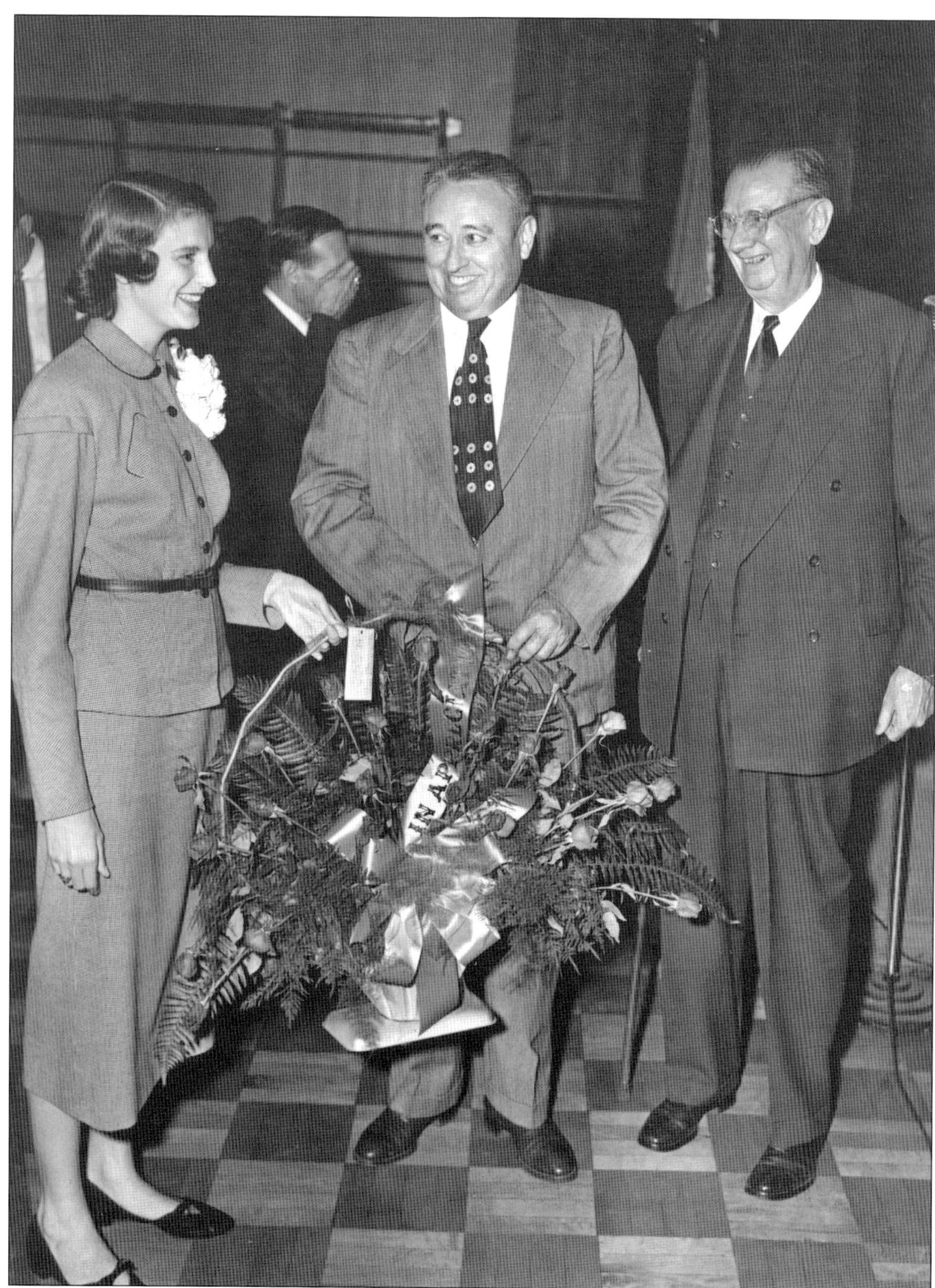

Gov. Gordon Browning (center), who served as Tennessee's governor from 1937 to 1939 and again from 1949 to 1953, made a visit to UTJC. During his visit, he was presented with flowers by Janice Miles and Charlie Tomerlin, representatives of the Union City Chamber of Commerce. The event was part of a broader effort to gain the governor's support for elevating UTJC to four-year status. Browning's endorsement proved instrumental in the successful transition of UTJC into the University of Tennessee Martin Branch.

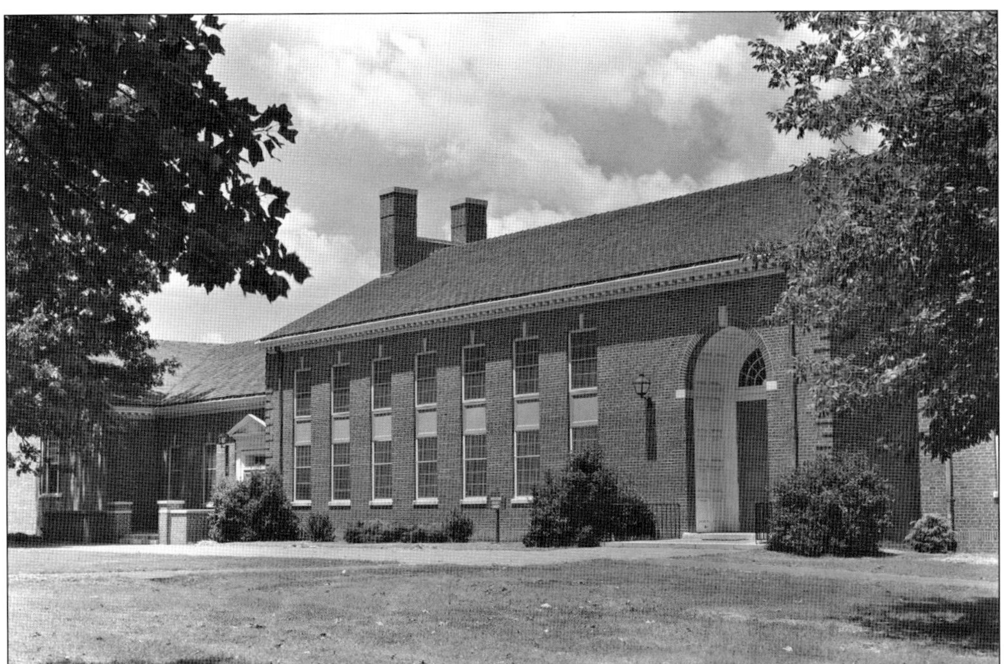

Due to a growing need for classrooms, the university decided to construct a new building that would house the agriculture and biology departments as well as the campus library. Completed in 1951, the university simply named the structure the Agriculture-Biology-Library (ABL) Building. In 1967, needing more space, the library moved into its own building. The agriculture and biology departments have continued to operate in the building.

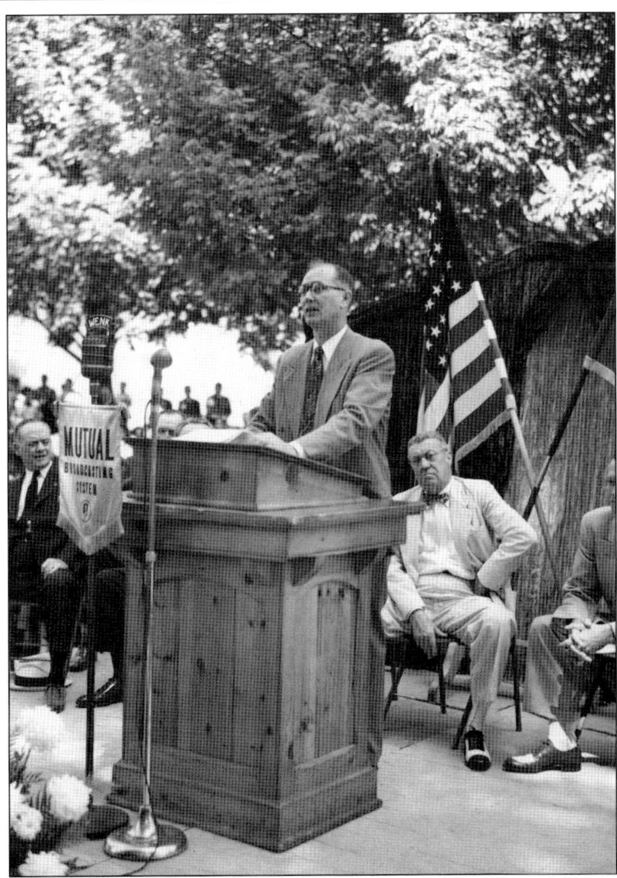

On October 23, 1970, the structure was renamed Brehm Hall in honor of Dr. Cloide Everett "C.E." Brehm, president of the University of Tennessee (1946–1959). Pictured is Dr. Paul Meek speaking at the ribbon cutting of the ABL Building in 1951. Brehm is seated behind Meek.

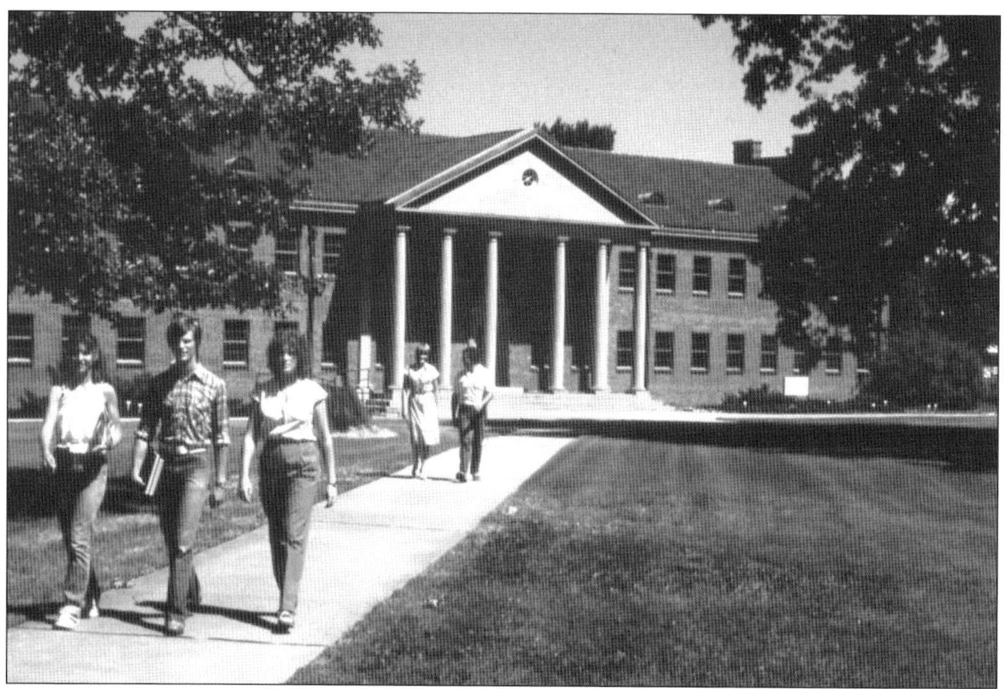

Constructed in 1951 to meet the growing demand for student housing after World War II, a new men's residence hall was built with space for 150 students. It also featured the Student Recreation Center, popularly known as "the Wagon Wheel." The original architectural plans included symmetrical wings at both ends, but only part of the north wing was completed. On December 5, 1966, the building was officially named Browning Hall in tribute to Gov. Gordon Browning. From 1967 to 1973, it operated as a coed dormitory, housing both male and female students. In 1975, the hall was converted into office and classroom space, and by 1990, it was renamed the Business Administration Building, now home to the College of Business and Global Affairs.

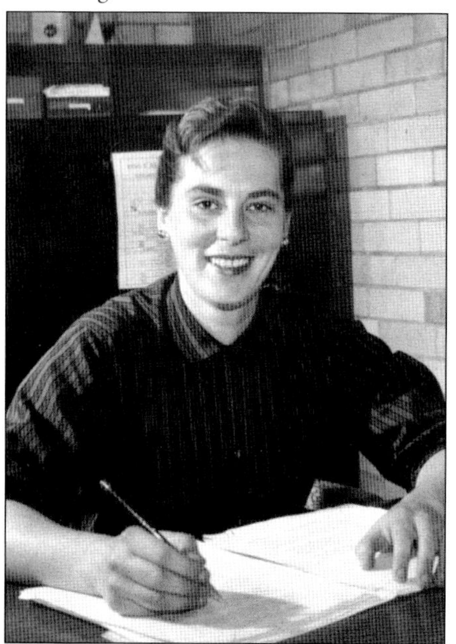

Bettye Giles arrived at UTMB in 1952 as a physical education instructor when no varsity sports existed for women, only intramural options. Drawing from her own experiences in athletics, she pioneered women's sports at the university, launching its first women's varsity tennis team and advocating for greater opportunities. In 1969, she cofounded the Tennessee College Women's Sports Federation, which helped lay the foundation for Title IX, the law prohibiting sex-based discrimination in education. Giles became UTM's first and only director of women's athletics, serving until 1994 and leaving an enduring legacy. Honored in multiple Halls of Fame, her name is now etched on the university's softball field and a female athlete award, recognizing her lifelong dedication to advancing women's sports.

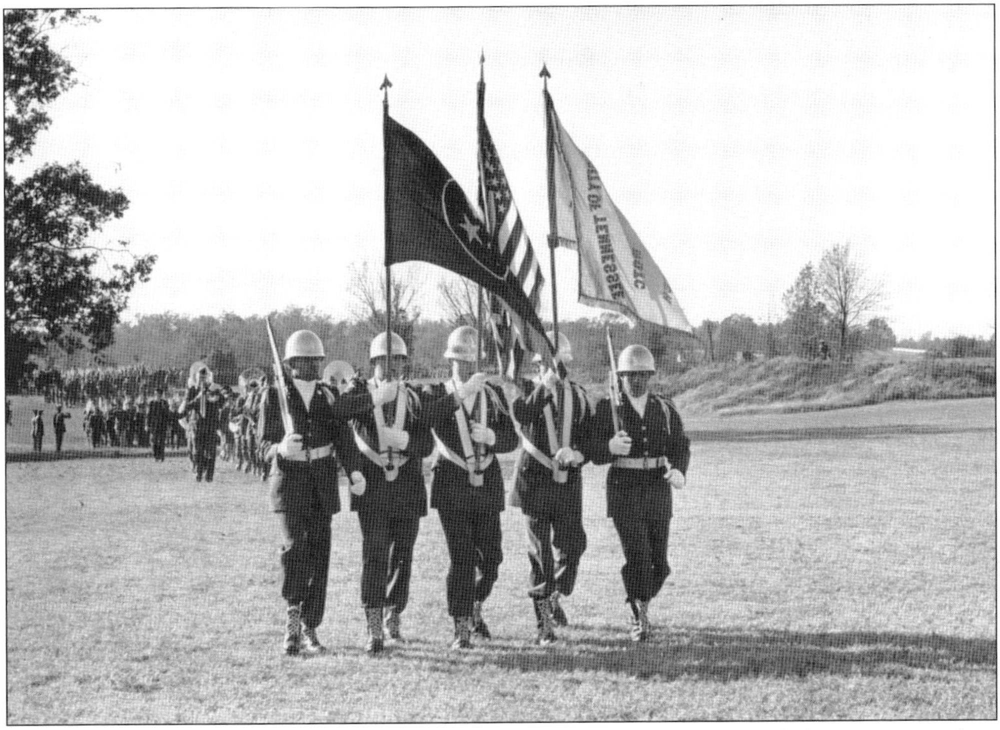

UTMB's ROTC program began in fall 1952 as part of the university's physical education curriculum and was required of all male students. The program offered basic military science courses covering leadership, drill, and national defense, with the goal of developing "the qualities of leadership required in both military and civil enterprises," according to Dean Paul Meek. Now known as the Skyhawk Battalion, the program includes cadets from six regional colleges and universities and continues to prepare future Army officers through academic instruction and field training.

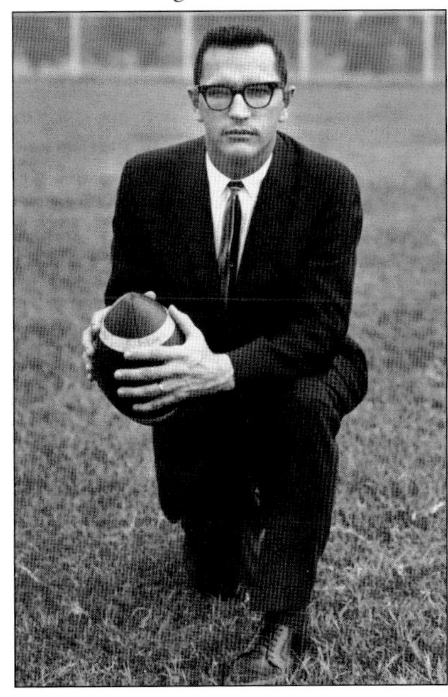

Bob Carroll began his journey at UTJC as a student and football player, earning a two-year degree in 1954 before completing his bachelor's degree at the University of Wyoming. In 1957, he was appointed head football coach at UTMB, a role he held until 1974, finishing with a record of 83 wins, 82 losses, and 4 ties. One of the highlights of his coaching career came in 1967 when he led the team to a 10-1 record and a victory over West Chester State in the Tangerine Bowl. Carroll earned his master's degree in history and political science from the University of Mississippi in 1962 and later joined the history department as a faculty member. Before retiring in 1997, he also served as vice chancellor for alumni affairs. With over 40 years of dedicated service to UTM, Bob Carroll left a lasting legacy upon his retirement.

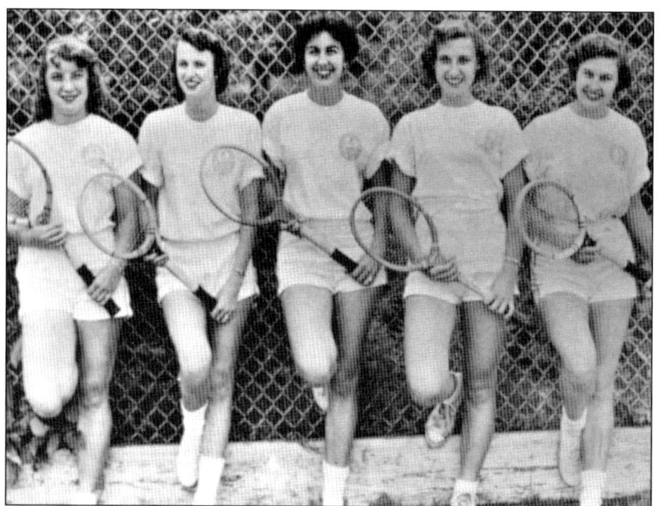

From left to right are Mary Meals, Roberta Brakefield, Shirley O'Neal Adams, Doris May, and Shirley Sharp. Tennis, recognized as a spring interscholastic sport, garnered considerable interest among UTMB students. This enthusiasm reached new heights in 1955 when the women's tennis team completed an undefeated season. The team's remarkable success—winning all nine of their matches without a single loss—was due in large part to the skilled coaching of Bettye Giles.

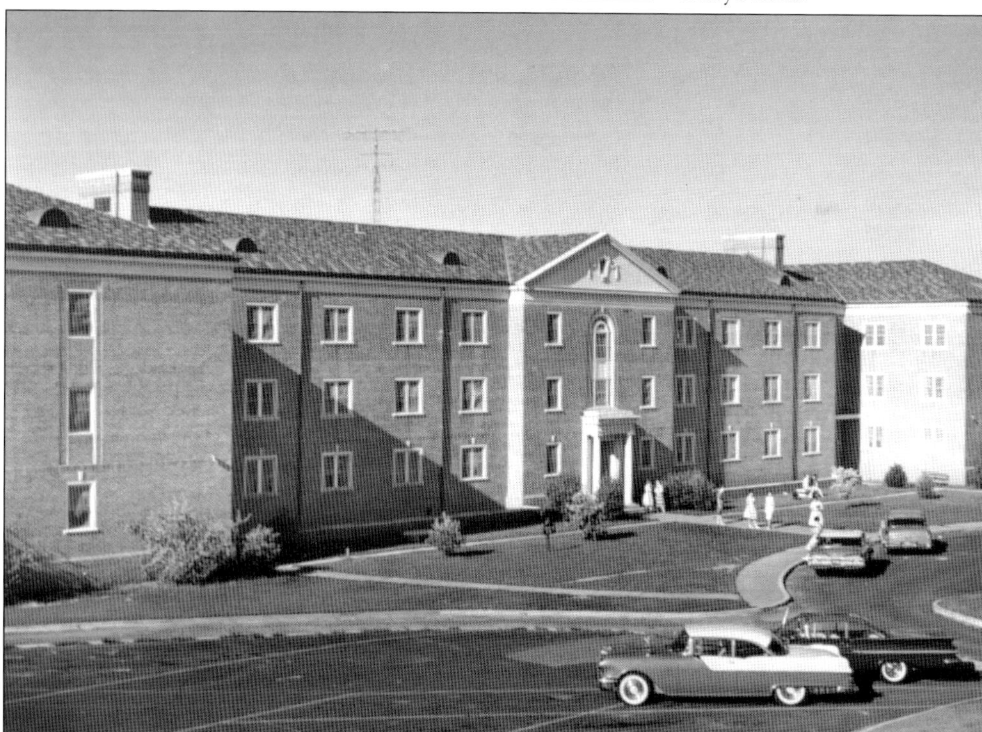

As student enrollment rose throughout the 1950s, the demand for housing—particularly dormitories for women—grew significantly. The "Wooden Box," a temporary men's residence, was dismantled, and construction of Clement Hall began in 1956. Built for 236 students, a 1963 expansion increased its capacity to over 450. On February 11, 1966, it was officially named Clement Hall in honor of Gov. Frank G. Clement. Over the years, it has served as flexible space for offices and classrooms during campus renovations. From 1993 to 1995, it temporarily housed library collections during the Paul Meek Library renovation and later served as home for the agriculture and biology department offices during Brehm Hall renovations. Today, Clement Hall is largely used for office space, with some areas closed for renovations. It now houses the Office of Housing, Student Success Center, testing services, Skyhawk Mail Services, and digital printing services.

The 1956 homecoming parade featured Harry Jetton's entry, themed "Plow Through Arkansas State," which won the decorated car division. In the homecoming game, the Arkansas State Indians triumphed over UTMB with a score of 20-12. The UTMB football team concluded the season with an even record of four wins and four losses.

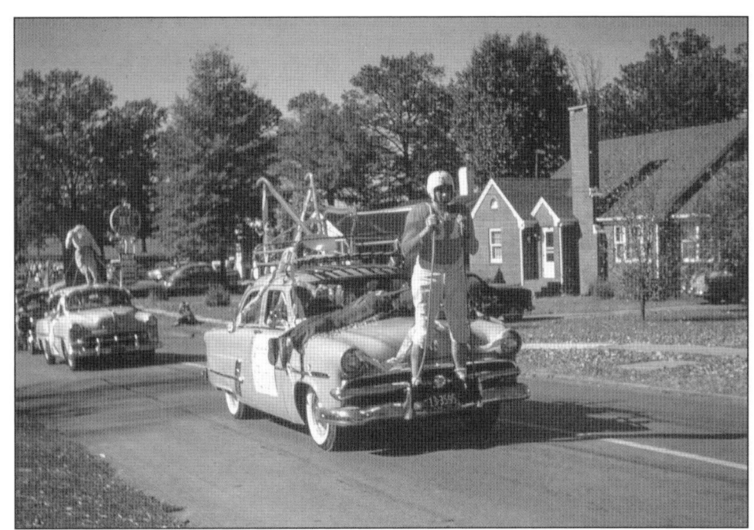

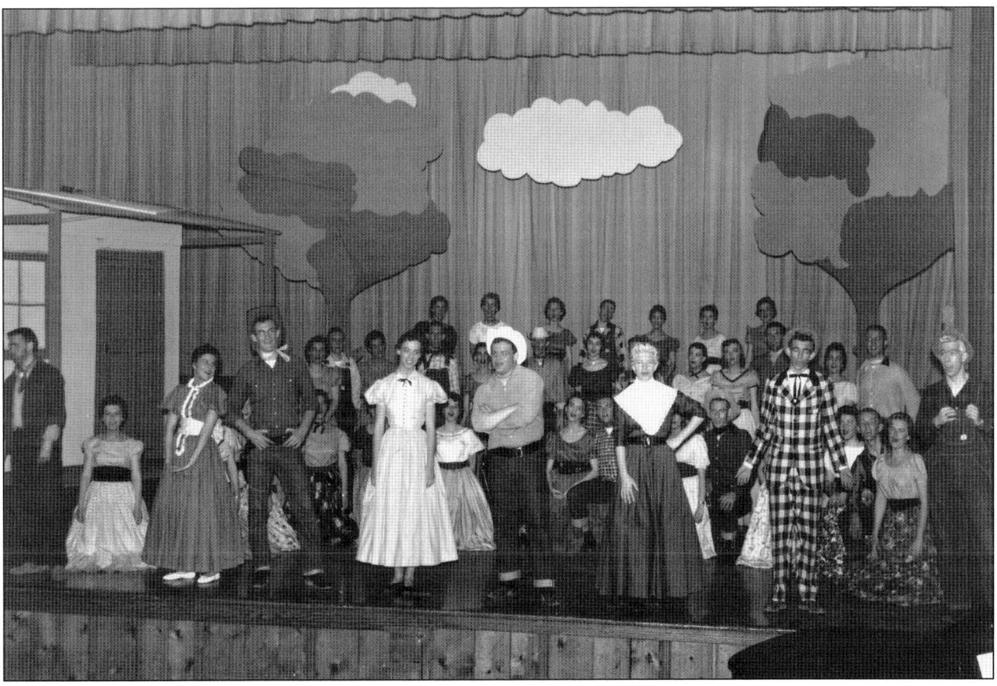

By 1958, in just its third year, the Vanguard Theatre had already become a leading presence on campus. That winter quarter, it partnered with the UTMB chorus to stage *Oklahoma!*, its first musical production. Presented over two nights, the show was a tremendous success, drawing acclaim for its outstanding quality. Audiences enthusiastically praised the production, noting the impressive talent and dedication that brought the beloved Broadway classic to life. The cast included, from left to right (standing, first row) Jud Fry (Royce Ray), Ado Annie (Peggy Morris), Will (Adam Scott), Laurey (Beth Goff), Curly (Stan Patterson), Aunt Eller (Elizabeth Grabiel), Ali Hakim (Jimmie Dallas), and Andrew Carnes (Bobby Bradshaw).

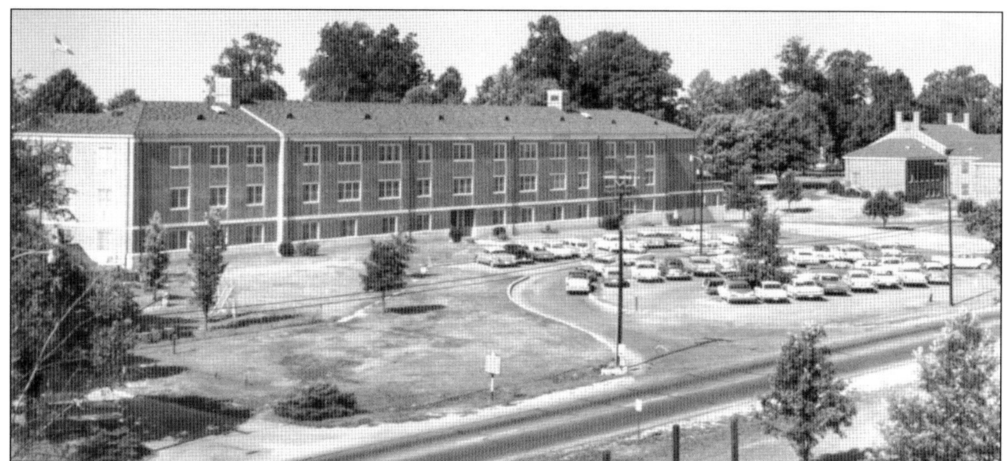

By the 1950s, the university's administrative division had outgrown the Administration Building, originally constructed in the early 1900s for the Hall-Moody Institute. A new Administration Building was completed in 1959 to house administrative offices and academic departments. On February 2, 1968, it was renamed the Hall-Moody Administration Building to honor the university's predecessor, the Hall-Moody Institute, and its alumni were recognized as UTM alumni. In 1974, the building underwent modernization and remodeling. The building has since played a central role in the university's administration and academic functions.

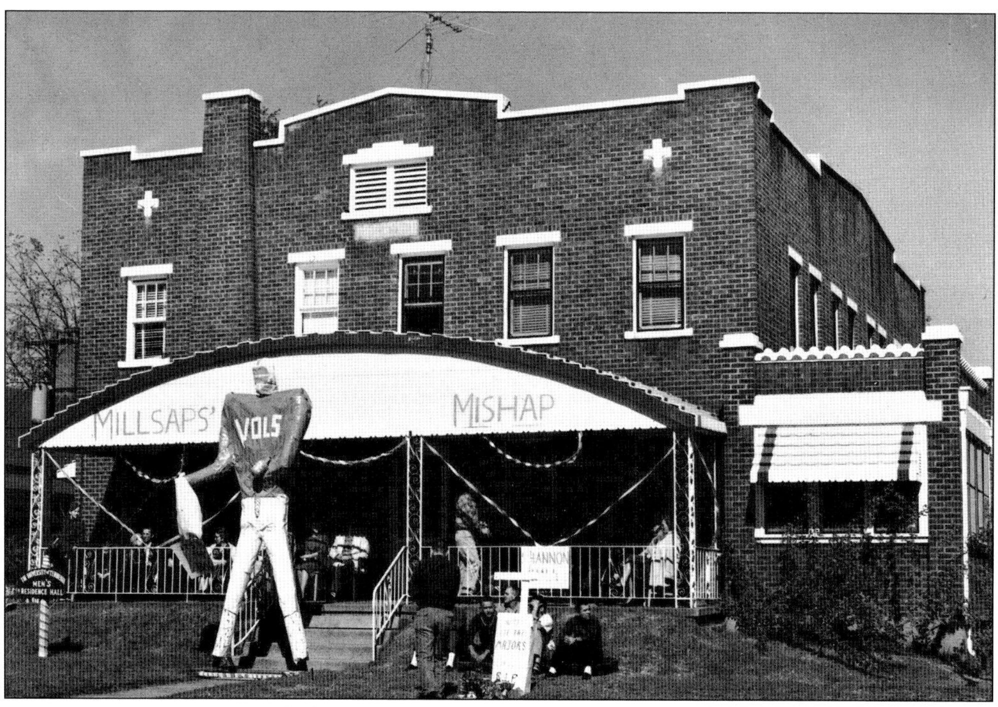

Carter Motor Inn was originally built as a privately owned hotel and had been operating in Martin since the 1930s. In 1959, the university acquired the building to serve as student housing. By the fall of 1960, it accommodated 45 male students. Renamed Shannon Hall in 1963, the building was later sold by the university in 1967 as new dormitories were being built south of campus. Eventually, the structure was demolished. It was located just off campus on the north side of University Street, east of the University Street and Lovelace Avenue intersection.

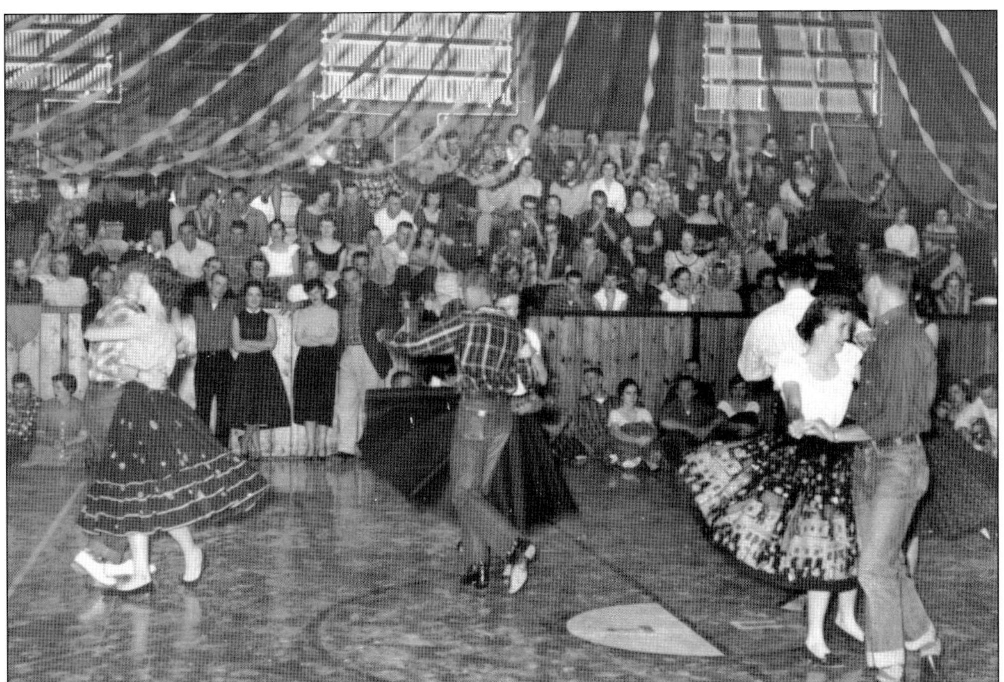

Another important social event on the UTMB campus was the Barnwarming Dance. Barnwarming was organized by the agriculture department. There were regular student activities that took place annually. Donning proper attire, UTMB students attended dances like the Barnwarming, Winter Wonderland, the Engineering Ball, and the Christmas Dance. Like Barnwarming, many of these events crowned kings and queens.

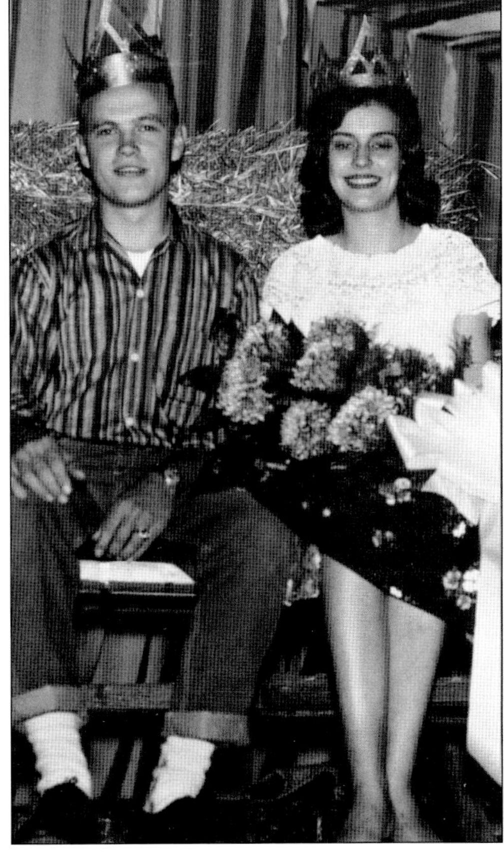

Pictured are the 1960 Barnwarming king and queen, Bobby Duck and Martha Cloar.

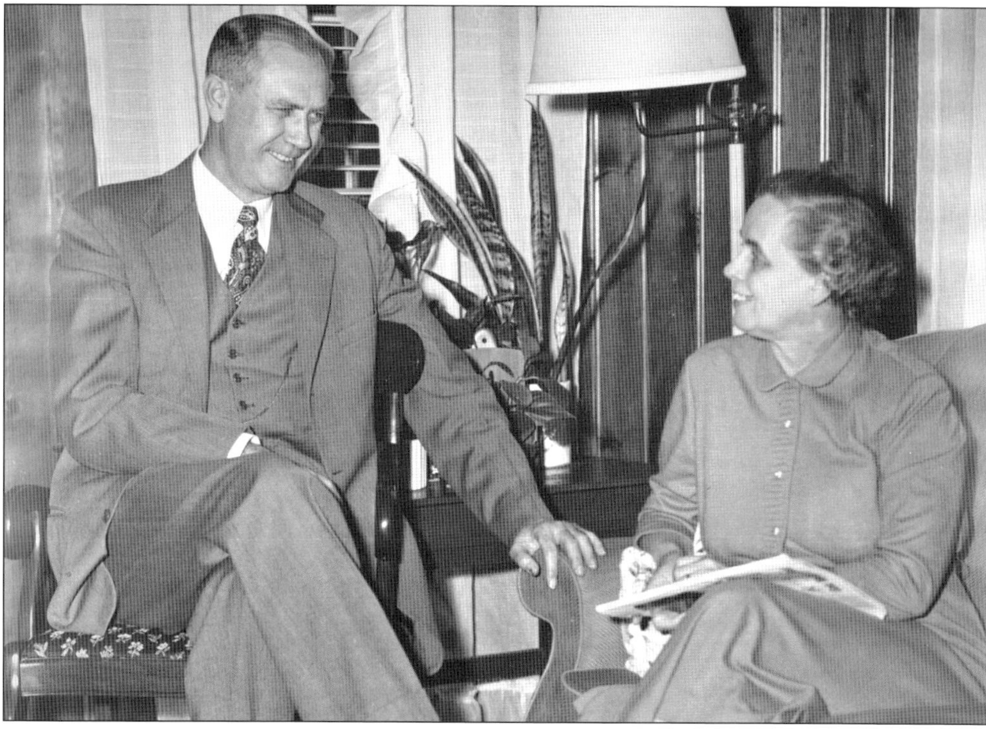

Dr. Paul Meek and his wife, Martha, are seated in their home during the 1960s. The Meeks were deeply respected and cherished by the entire community. Born and raised in Weakley County, Paul Meek met Martha Campbell while they were students at the University of Tennessee. During their time at UT, Paul served as senior class president, while Martha held the position of treasurer. The couple married in 1922.

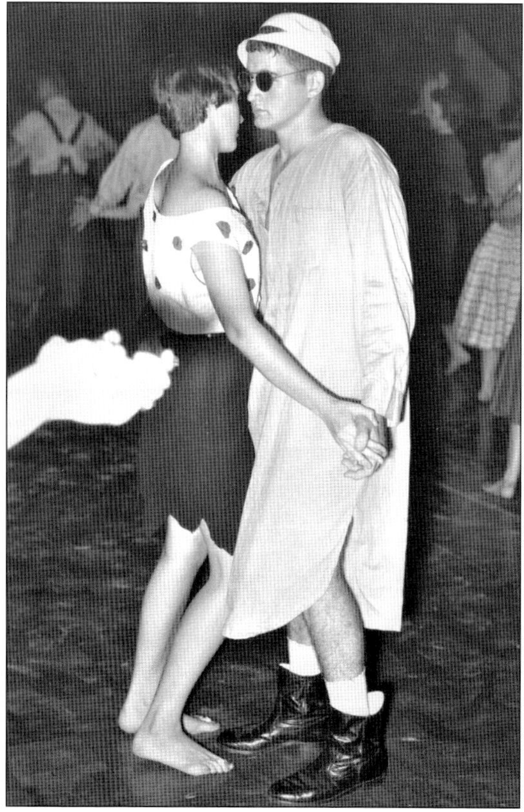

The annual Sadie Hawkins dance, a traditional fall quarter event, was sponsored by the Veterans Club. During the dance, a student dressed as the mayor of Dogpatch crowned a couple as "Little Abner and Daisy Mae." The Veterans Club was established in 1948 through the merger of the Army Club and the Bluejackets Club. Membership was open to any UTMB student who had served at least 90 days of active duty in any branch of the US armed forces and had been honorably discharged or released. The club aimed to foster camaraderie and connection among its members and the wider student body. It held meetings twice a month and organized a major social event each quarter.

Beginning in 1934, one of the most eagerly awaited annual events during the UTJC era was Carnicus. Sponsored by the physical education department, Carnicus showcased tumbling exhibitions, dance routines, comedic skits, and clown performances and included the crowning of a queen (Carni) and king (Cus). The event's name was a blend of the words "carnival" and "circus." A highlight of the 1960 Carnicus was a remarkable bicycle act performed by Ray Pollard and Monte Bayless, who demonstrated impressive feats of skill and balance.

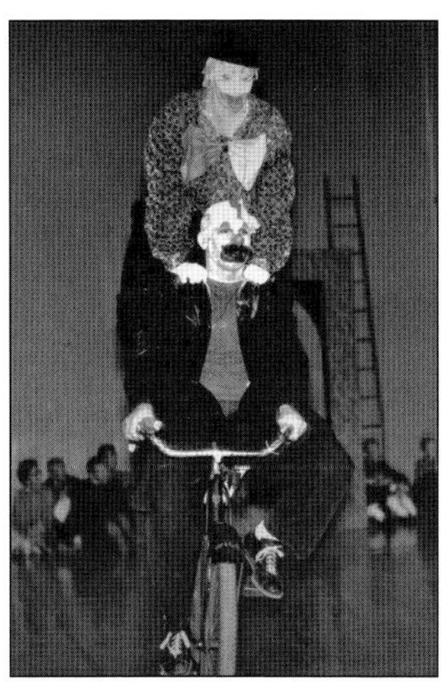

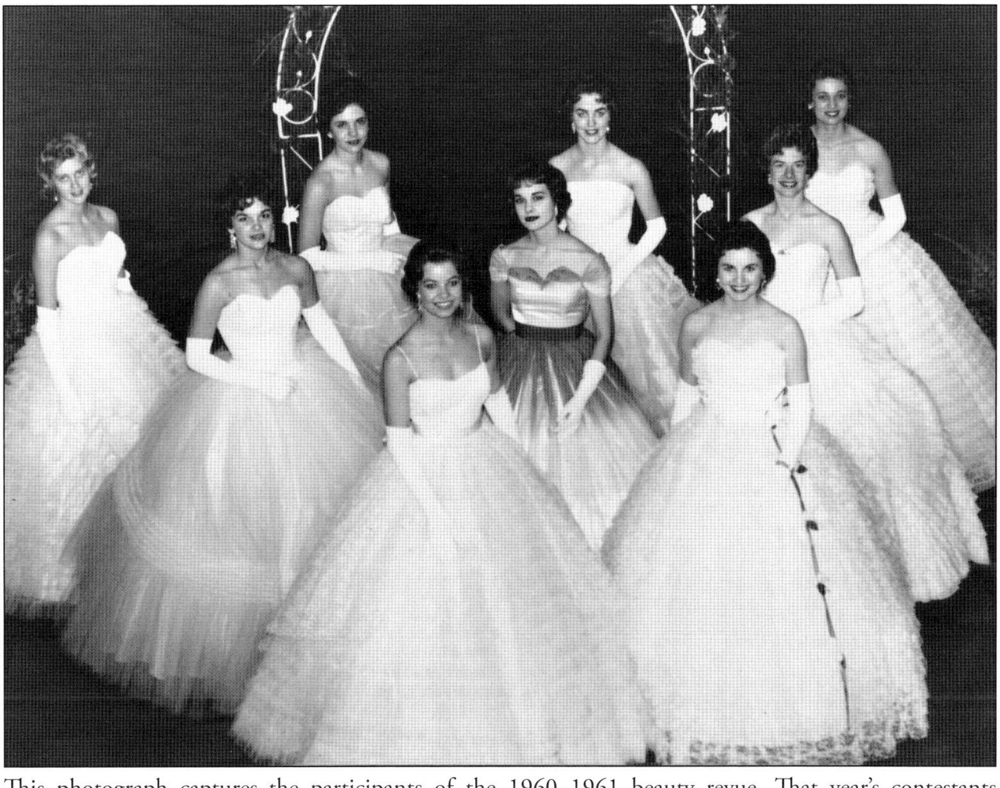

This photograph captures the participants of the 1960–1961 beauty revue. That year's contestants included, from left to right, (first row) Carol Melton and Mary Arnold; (second row) Jennie Lou Hall, Camille Sammons, and Alice Clare Freeman; (third row) Amanda Lashlee, Ann Rowsey (queen), Letty Taylor, and Sandra Westbrook. Established in 1959 by the All-Student Club in response to increased student interest, the beauty revue quickly became a featured event in the university's yearbook. Contestants competed in formal wear, swimsuit, and talent segments, with a question-and-answer portion added in 1960 to enhance the competition. The event spanned two nights and included representatives sponsored by various campus clubs and organizations. On the first night, nine finalists were chosen to advance to the final round, culminating in the crowning of the queen, who would go on to represent UTMB in events throughout the year.

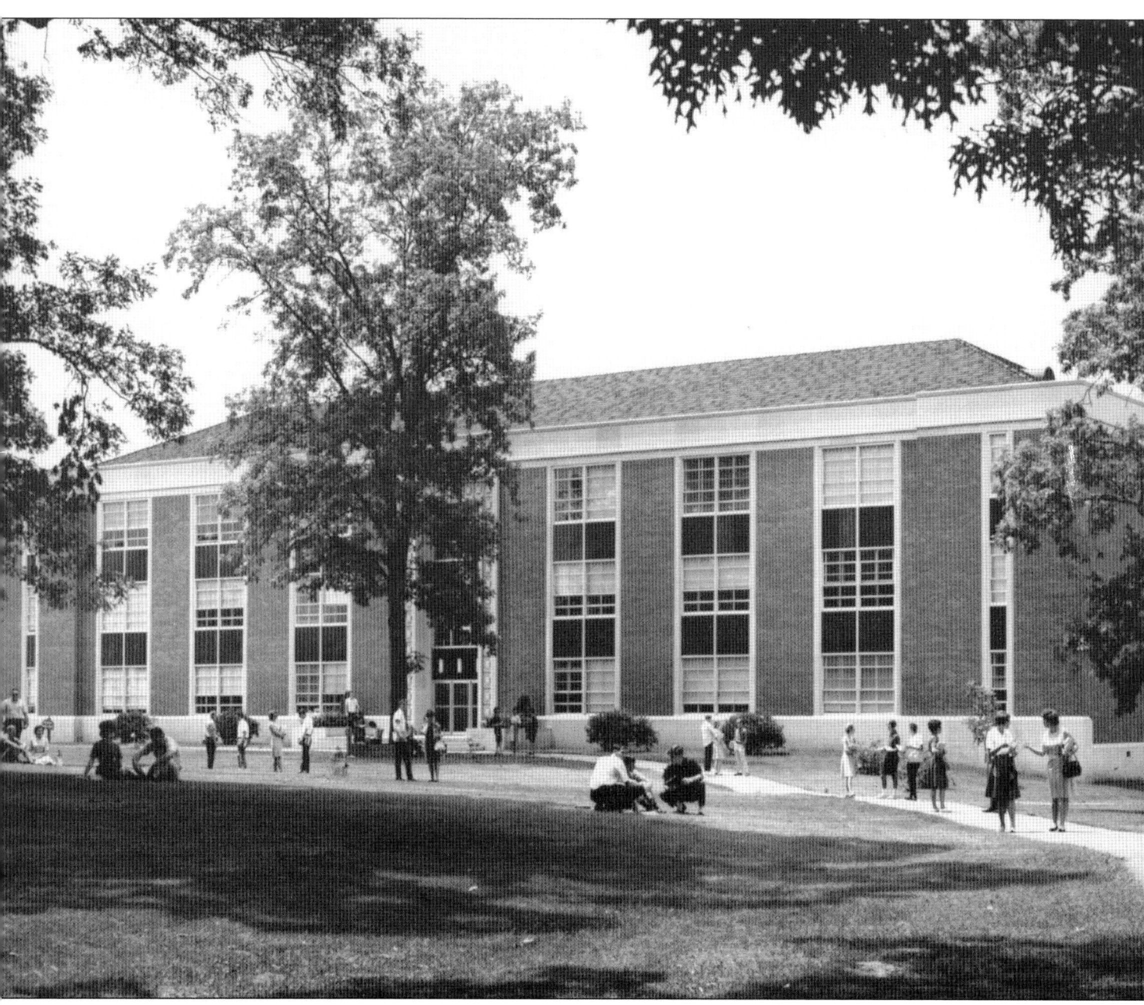

Following the rapid growth of the engineering department in the years after the war, the university recognized the need for a larger and more modern facility to replace the outdated Mechanical Arts Building. In 1960, construction commenced on the new Engineering-Physical Sciences Building, which was completed the following year. A significant addition to the rear of the structure began in 1969, nearly doubling the available office and classroom space. As its name suggests, the building houses offices and classrooms for both the engineering and physical sciences departments. In 1999, the building was renamed in honor of Joseph E. Johnson, 19th president of the University of Tennessee.

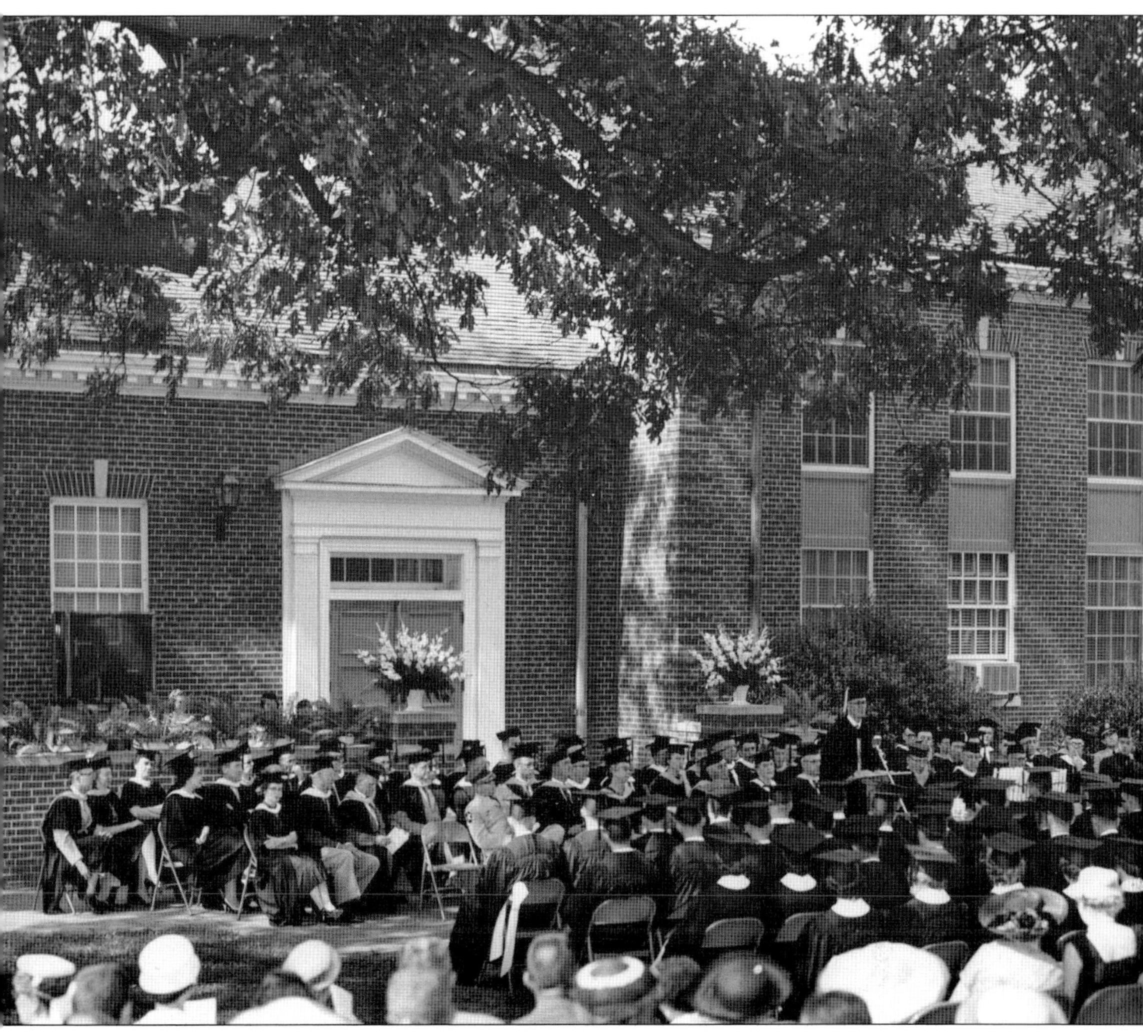

The commencement ceremony was held outside the ABL Building in June 1965. This outdoor setting provided a dignified backdrop for celebrating the academic achievements of the graduating class. Family members, faculty, and university officials gathered in attendance, marking the conclusion of another successful academic year.

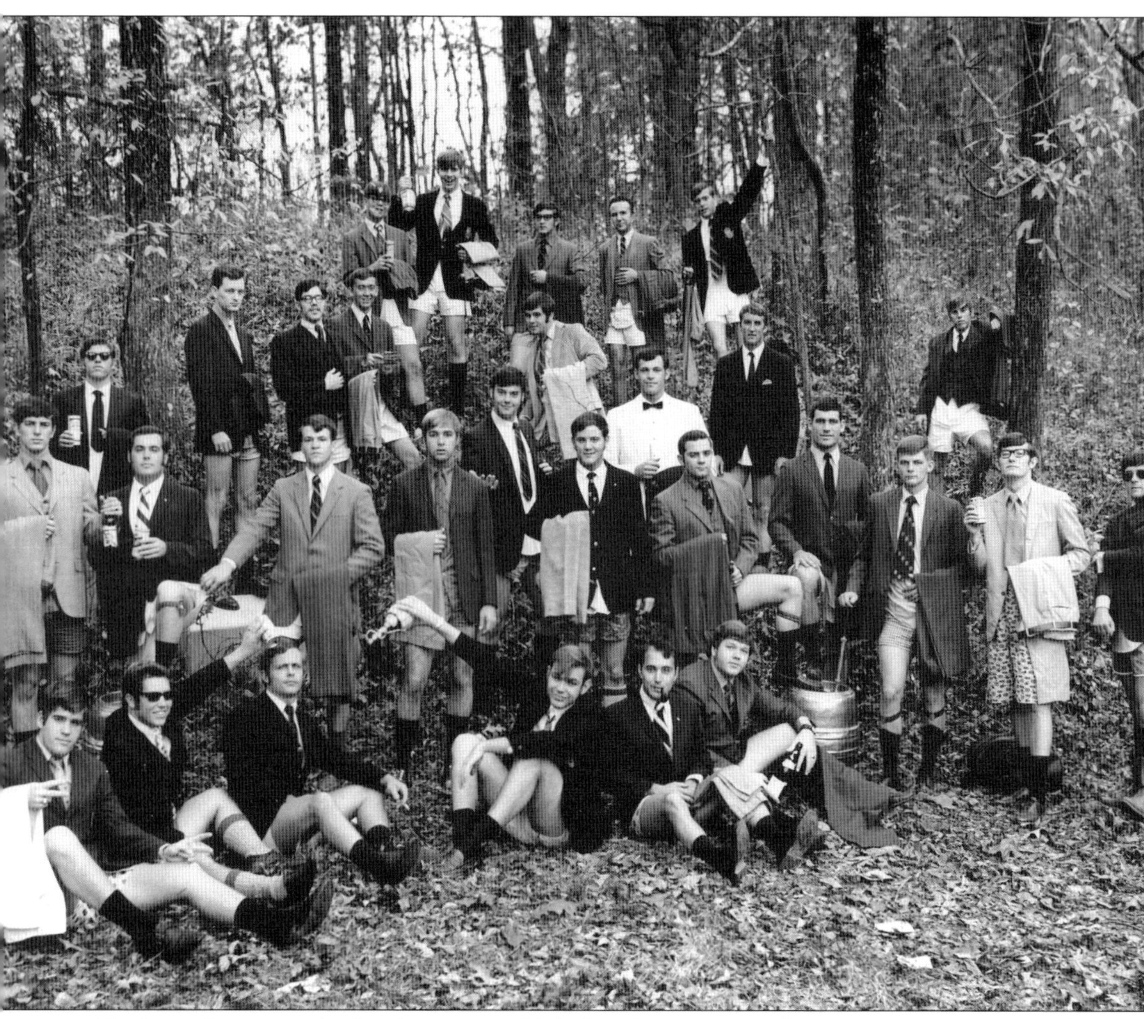

Phi Sigma Kappa was the first fraternity established at the University of Tennessee at Martin, originally receiving its charter in 1960. Although the chapter was briefly inactive after disbanding in 2016, it made a return to campus from 2018 to 2019. Founded in 1873 at the University of Massachusetts, Phi Sigma Kappa was created to foster morality, learning, and social culture. The UTM chapter, known as Tau Tetarton, has upheld these principles through its active involvement in campus life and community service. According to UTM, the fraternity promotes a lifelong brotherhood committed to personal growth, leadership development, academic achievement, service, cultural awareness, and integrity—working to better individuals, the university community, and the world.

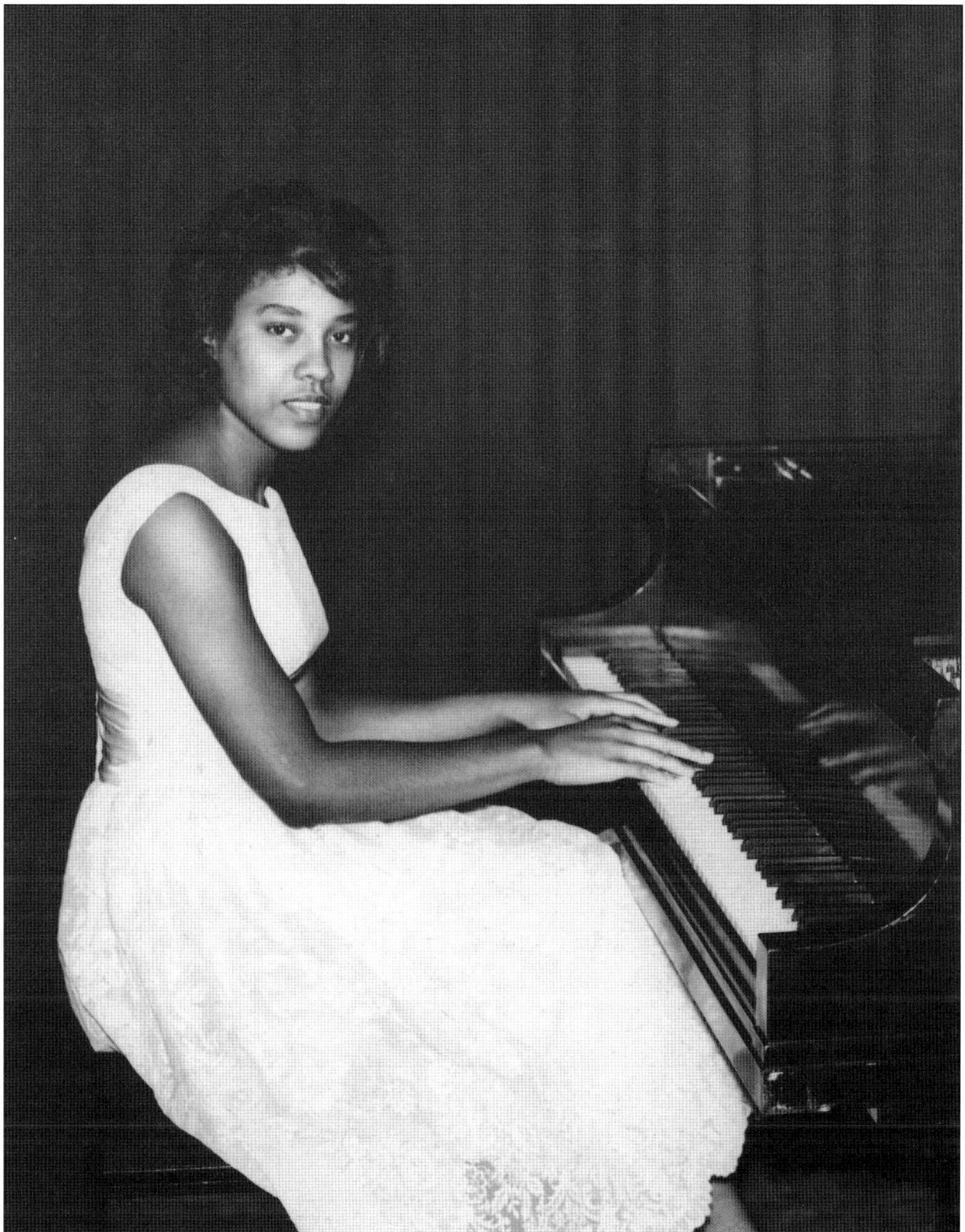

Unlike many campuses in the South, UTMB experienced a relatively quiet and gradual integration, which contributed to increased enrollment over time. In 1961, the same year Black undergraduates enrolled at UT Knoxville, Jessie L. Arnold from Martin, Tennessee, became UTMB's first Black student. During her time at UTMB, Arnold was an active member of the Student National Education Association and the university chorus.

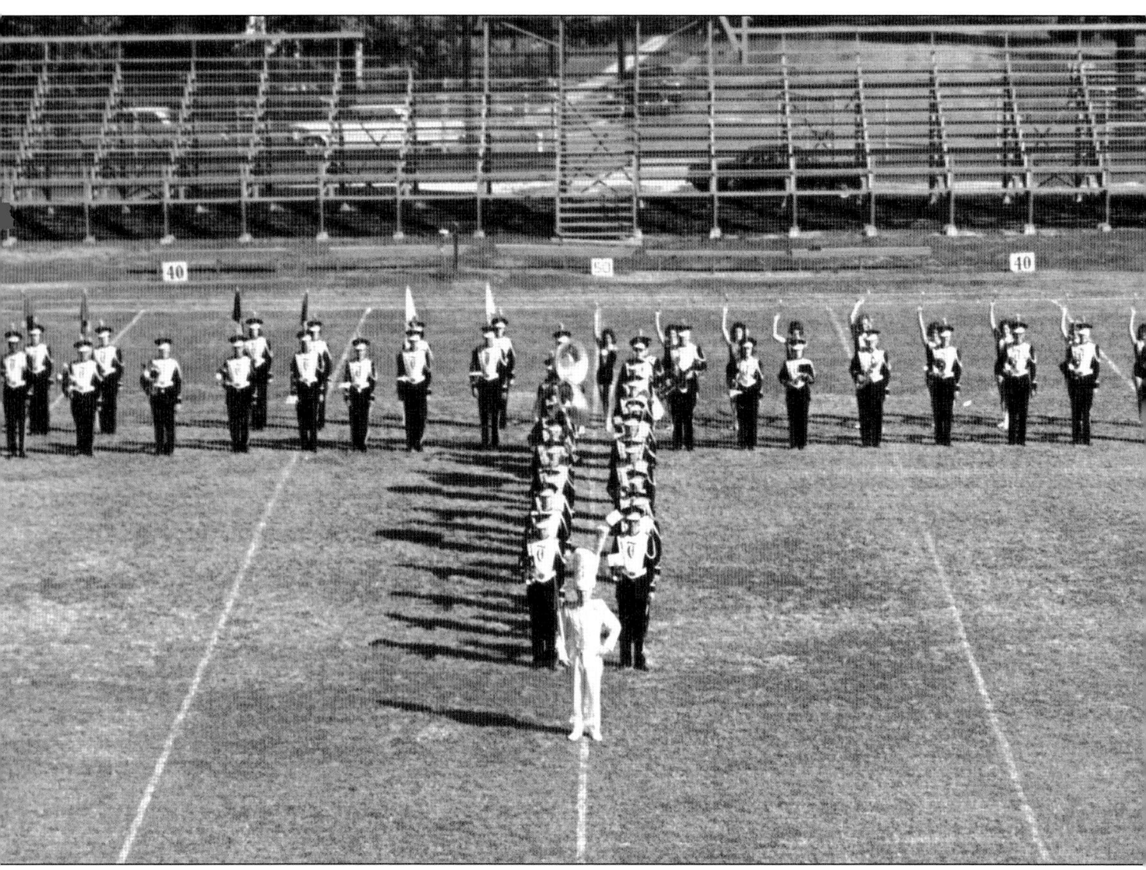

Pictured, the 1964 UTM marching band, now known as the Aviators Marching Band, has its roots in the Hall-Moody Institute, where music was an essential part of campus life. As the institution transitioned from UTJC to UTM, the band grew in size and significance, becoming a proud symbol of university tradition. Over the years, it evolved from a small ensemble with military-style uniforms and a brass focus to a diverse, full-instrumentation group. Today, the Aviators Marching Band performs at athletic events, parades, and community gatherings while offering students valuable musical education. It continues to represent the spirit, pride, and tradition of UTM.

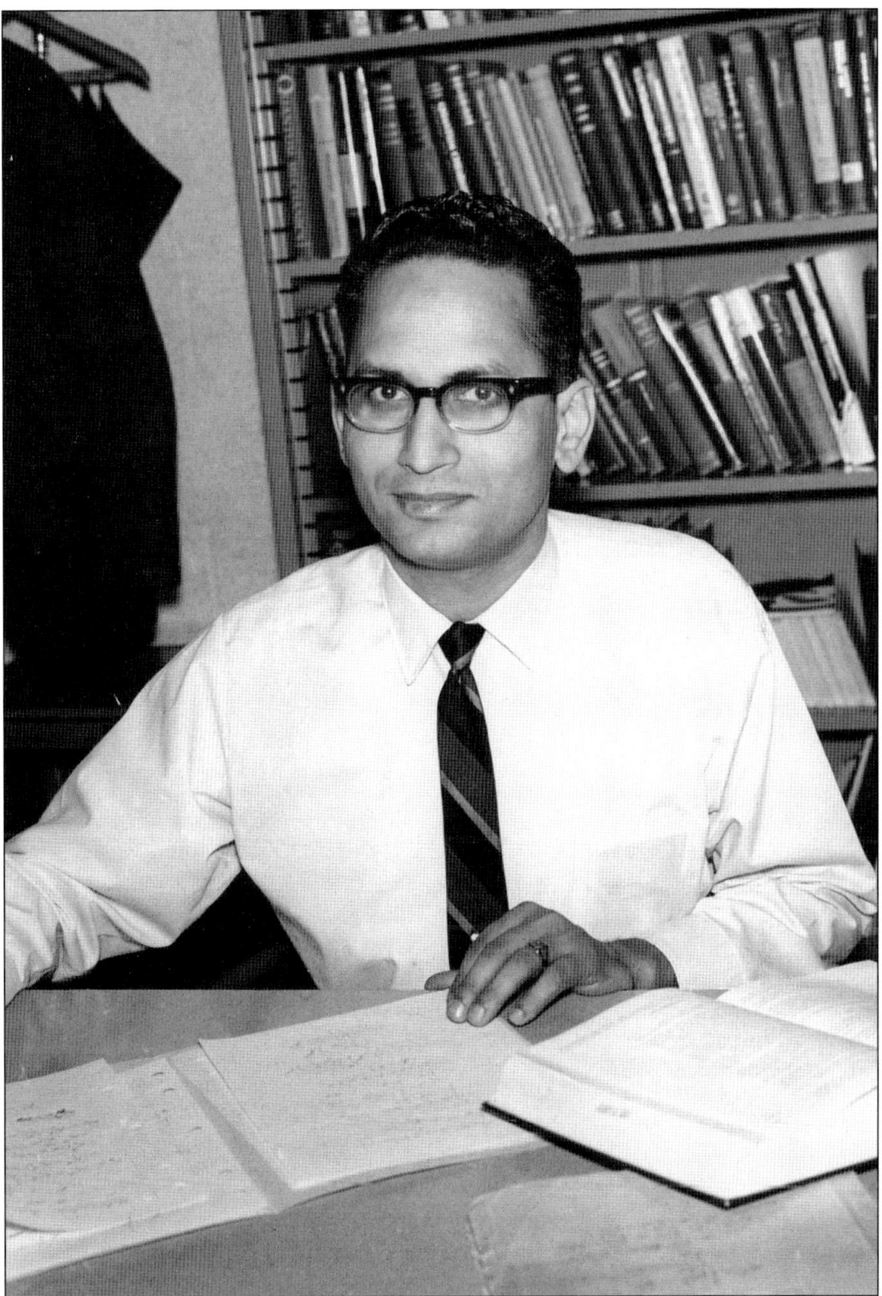

Dr. Shakti Kumar "S.K." Airee, a chemistry professor at UTM, retired after an impressive 54-year teaching career, making him the longest-serving faculty member in the university's history. He joined UTMB in 1965 as an assistant professor and played a pivotal role in advancing the chemistry program, helping it gain American Chemical Society accreditation. Beyond teaching, Airee was active in university governance through the Faculty Senate and served as curator of the university museum. In 1971, he founded the university's chapter of the Student Affiliates of the American Chemical Society, which became the nation's most highly decorated chapter. His six-decade involvement with the American Chemical Society included leadership roles and coediting a regional newsletter that served five states.

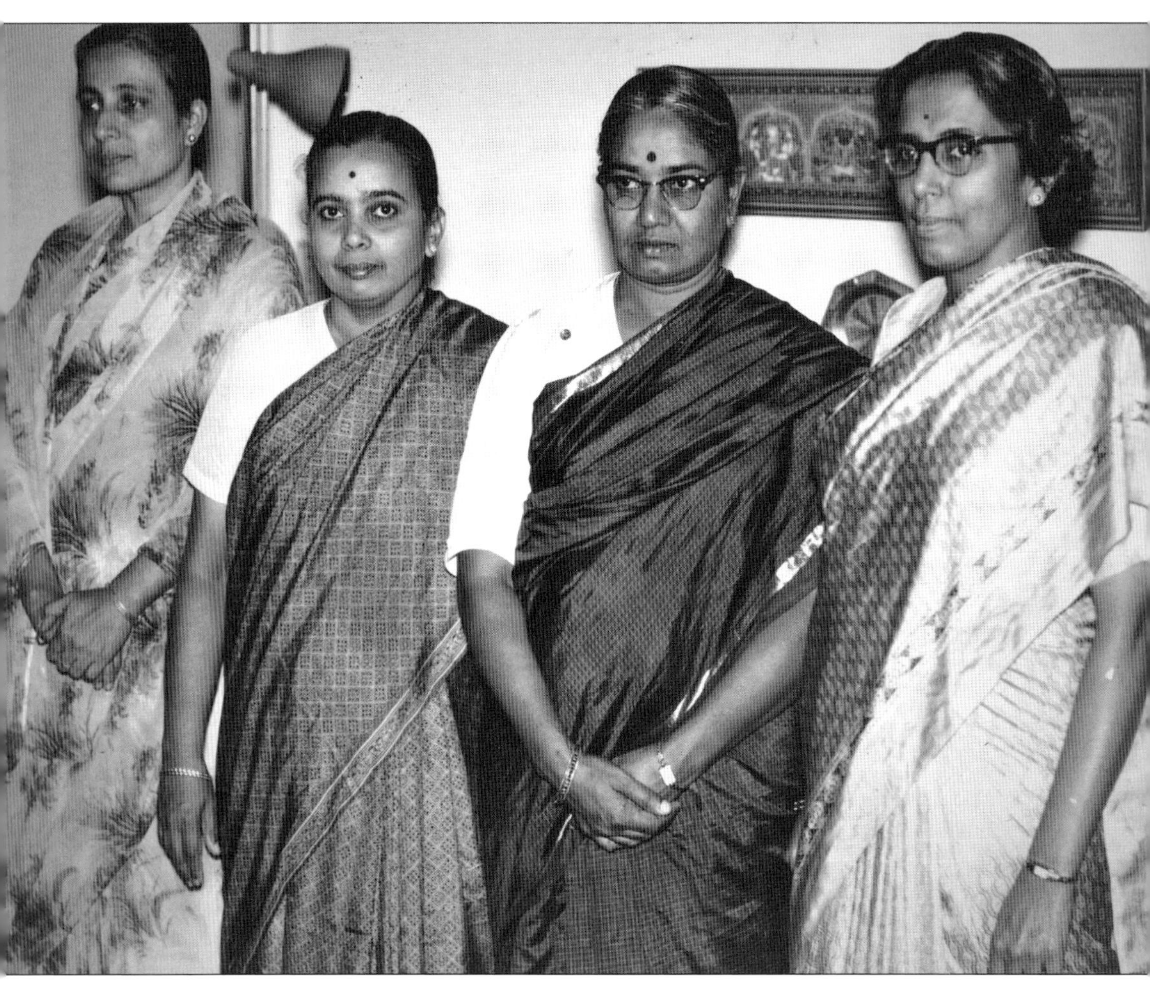

One of the primary goals of the Home Economics Club is to instill professional pride in young women. Membership is open to all girls enrolled in the Department of Home Economics, providing them with opportunities to connect with others who share an interest in the art of homemaking. In 1961, the club placed a special focus on international relations, incorporating this theme into many of its meeting programs. Visitors from various countries shared insights into their family traditions, cultural customs, and educational systems. A notable highlight was the visit of four women from India, who contributed to the club's efforts in promoting the International Federation of Home Economics.

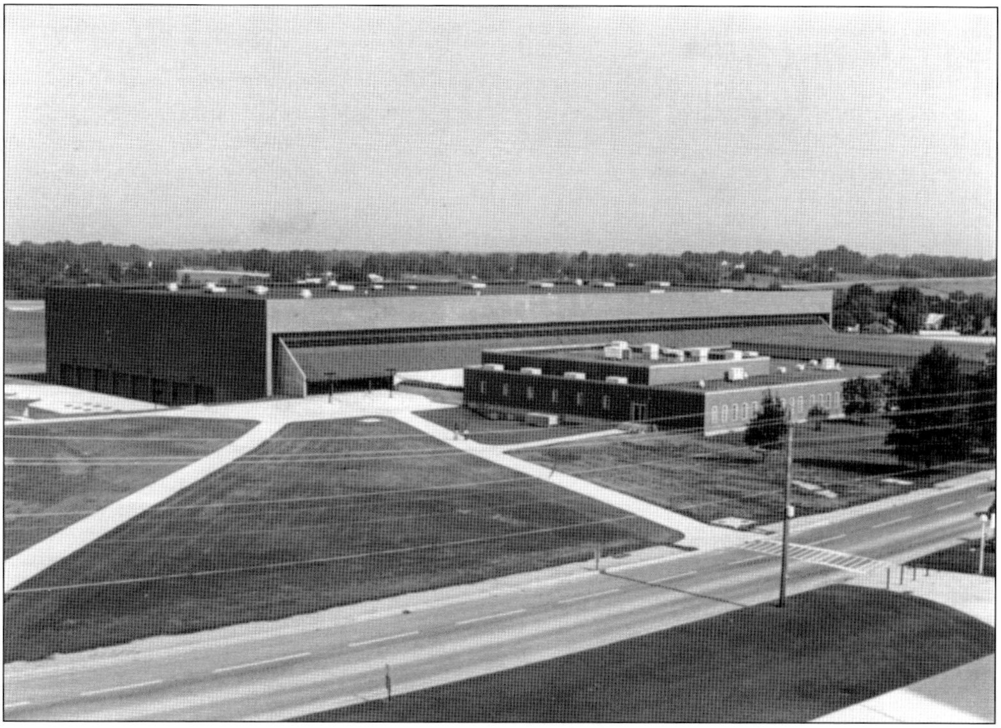

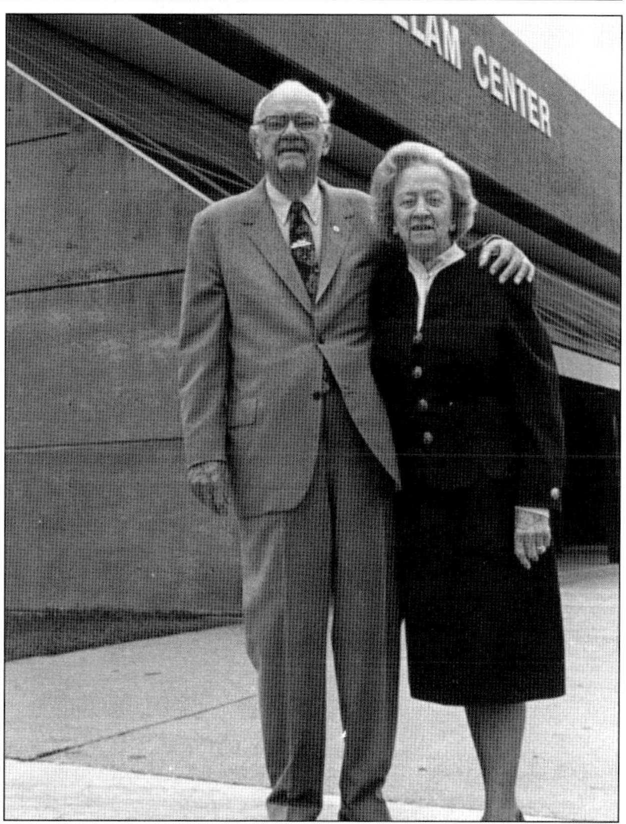

By the 1950s, university growth had rendered the original Physical Education Building inadequate. To accommodate the expanding campus, construction of a new facility began in 1962 on the west side of Mount Pelia Road. Completed in the summer of 1963, the new complex included classrooms, offices, locker rooms, two activity rooms, and a gymnasium with a seating capacity of 3,500. Throughout the 1960s and 1970s, it primarily served the physical education and athletics department and hosted most major campus events such as Carnicus, commencements, basketball games, concerts, and more. In 1973, the facility was expanded with the addition of a neighboring field house. This field house was officially named the Kathleen and Tom Elam Center in 1994. The Elams are pictured in front of the building.

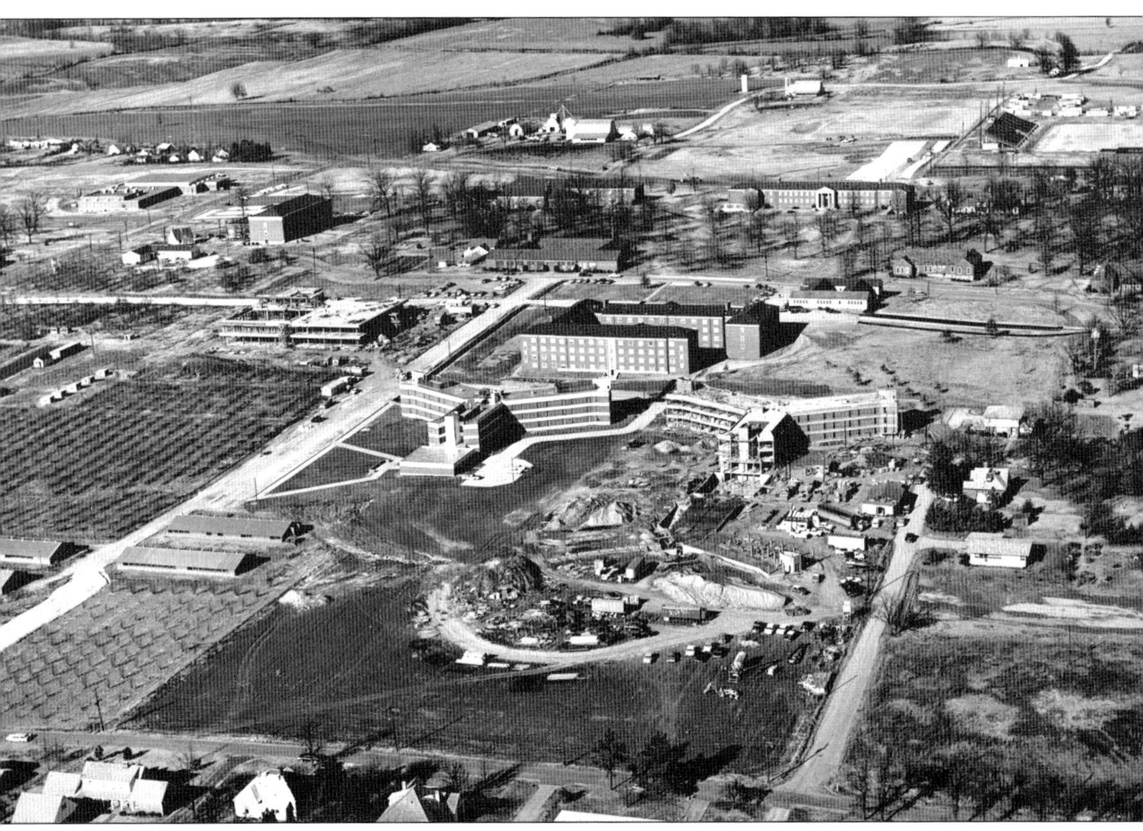

An aerial view taken in 1966 captures the rapid expansion of UTMB, which, at the time, was the fastest-growing institution of higher education in the state. As enrollment surged, numerous construction projects were underway. The Dr. Edward J. and Carolyn P. Boling University Center and several Y-shaped dormitories were nearing completion. In addition to these developments, plans and funding were already in place for more dormitories, a fine arts building, and a library.

Four

The University of Tennessee at Martin 1967–Present

In 1967, the institution was officially renamed the University of Tennessee at Martin (UTM), marking a pivotal moment in its history. That same year, the football team achieved a remarkable 10-1 season, culminating in a Tangerine Bowl victory, and Miss UTM earned the title of Miss Tennessee. The era also saw a lasting tribute to decades of leadership with the naming of the Paul Meek Library in 1968. Another groundbreaking milestone in 1967 was the appointment of Harold Conner Sr. as the university's first African American administrator, who played a central role in founding the Black Student Association and establishing freshman studies, later receiving the BSA Legacy Award for his contributions.

In the early 1970s, enrollment stabilized around 5,000 students as the university broadened its academic programs. This growth was matched by significant campus development, including the completion of the Fine Arts Building in 1971 and Gooch Hall in 1973, which housed key academic departments. A residential swimming pool added in 1975 enhanced student life. Among the students who arrived during this era was standout athlete in basketball and volleyball Pat Head, who would go on to win a silver medal at the 1976 Olympics and become one of the most celebrated coaches in collegiate sports history.

The 1980s were marked by efforts to attract high-achieving students and strengthen academics through initiatives like the University Scholars Program and the Governor's School for the Humanities. In 1983, the university launched its first major fundraising initiative, The Campaign for Quality, successfully reaching its $2 million goal a year early. This decade also saw two historic appointments: the system's first female chancellor, Dr. Margaret Perry, and UTM's first African American vice chancellor of academic affairs, Dr. Frank Black. Support for nontraditional students grew with the opening of the Child and Family Resource Center, and the West Tennessee Agricultural Pavilion and Stalling Facility was constructed, later named for Gov. Ned Ray McWherter.

The 1990s brought expanded academic offerings, including four-year degrees in nursing and engineering and graduate business programs, along with national recognition for campus beauty and safety. Enrollment surpassed 6,000 by 1997. The 2000s and 2010s saw continued growth, modernization, and athletic achievement. In 2023, the university appointed its first African American chancellor, Dr. Yancy Freeman, marking a new chapter defined by record retention, increased access, and transformative investments in science, agriculture, and engineering.

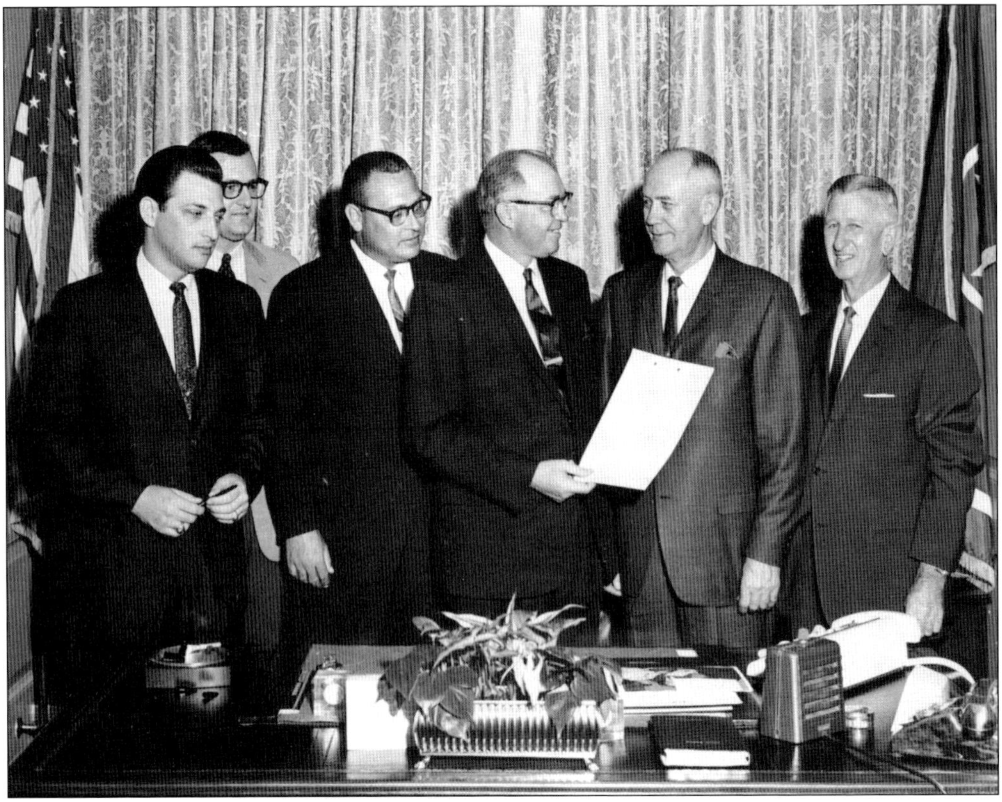

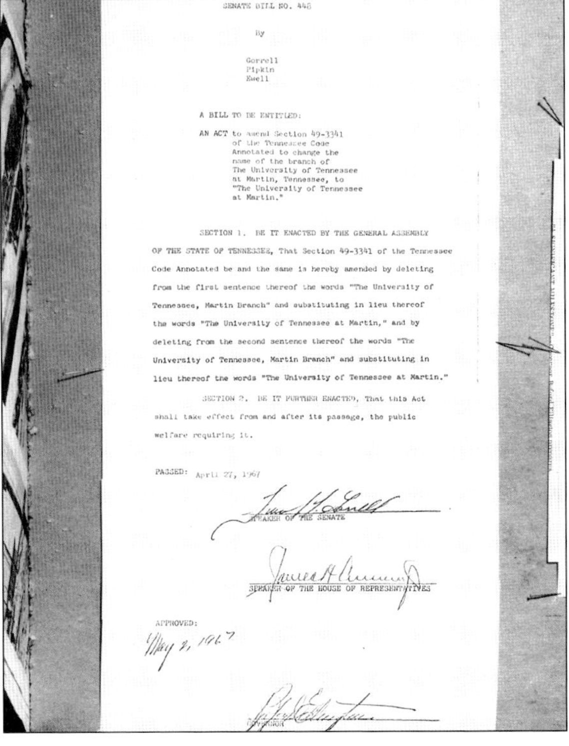

SENATE BILL NO. 448

By

Gorrell
Pipkin
Ewell

A BILL TO BE ENTITLED:

AN ACT to amend Section 49-3341 of the Tennessee Code Annotated to change the name of the branch of The University of Tennessee at Martin, Tennessee, to "The University of Tennessee at Martin."

SECTION 1. BE IT ENACTED BY THE GENERAL ASSEMBLY OF THE STATE OF TENNESSEE, That Section 49-3341 of the Tennessee Code Annotated be and the same is hereby amended by deleting from the first sentence thereof the words "The University of Tennessee, Martin Branch" and substituting in lieu thereof the words "The University of Tennessee at Martin," and by deleting from the second sentence thereof the words "The University of Tennessee, Martin Branch" and substituting in lieu thereof the words "The University of Tennessee at Martin."

SECTION 2. BE IT FURTHER ENACTED, That this Act shall take effect from and after its passage, the public welfare requiring it.

PASSED: April 27, 1967

SPEAKER OF THE SENATE

SPEAKER OF THE HOUSE OF REPRESENTATIVES

APPROVED:

May 2, 1967

GOVERNOR

On May 2, 1967, the University of Tennessee Martin Branch officially became the University of Tennessee at Martin with the signing of Senate Bill No. 448 by Tennessee governor Buford Ellington, marking the beginning of a new era for the institution. Dr. Paul Meek (second from right) is pictured with Ellington (center) and Dr. Andy Holt (right of Meek) at the signing of the bill. Pictured at left is the bill in its entirety with the signatures of Frank C. Gorrell, Speaker of the House; James H. Cummings Jr., Speaker of the House of Representatives; and Gov. Buford Ellington. In Section 1 of the bill, it says, "Be it enacted by the General Assembly of the State of Tennessee, That Section 49-3341 of the Tennessee Code Annotated be and the same is hereby amended by deleting from the first sentence thereof the words 'The University of Tennessee, Martin Branch' and substituting in lieu thereof the words 'The University of Tennessee at Martin.'"

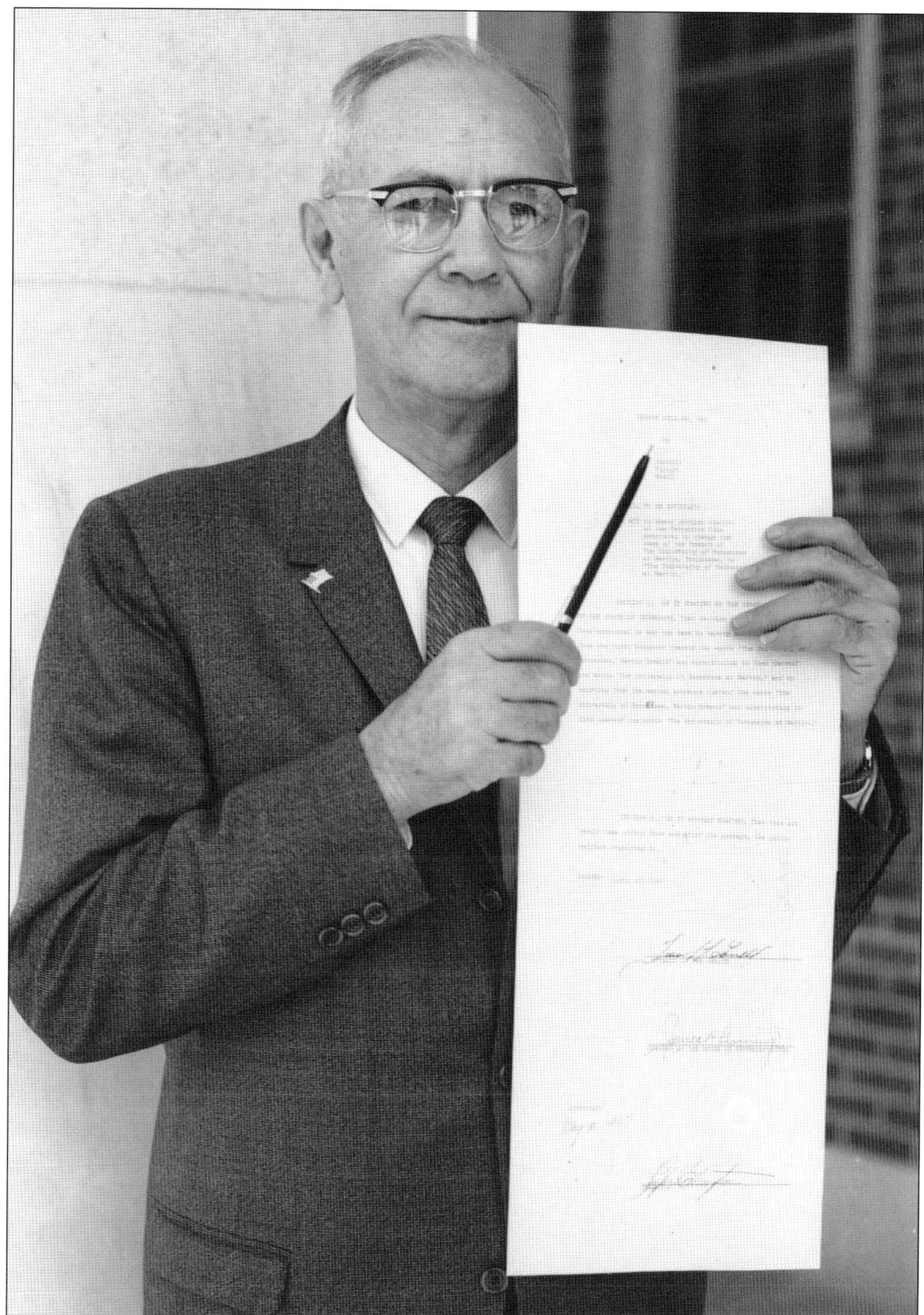

After returning from his trip to Nashville, Meek poses for a photograph and proudly points to Senate Bill No. 448 with the pen Ellington used to sign it. This photograph was later used in the *Vollette* on May 4, 1967, with an article about the name change titled "Gov. Signs Name Change, University Adopts New Title."

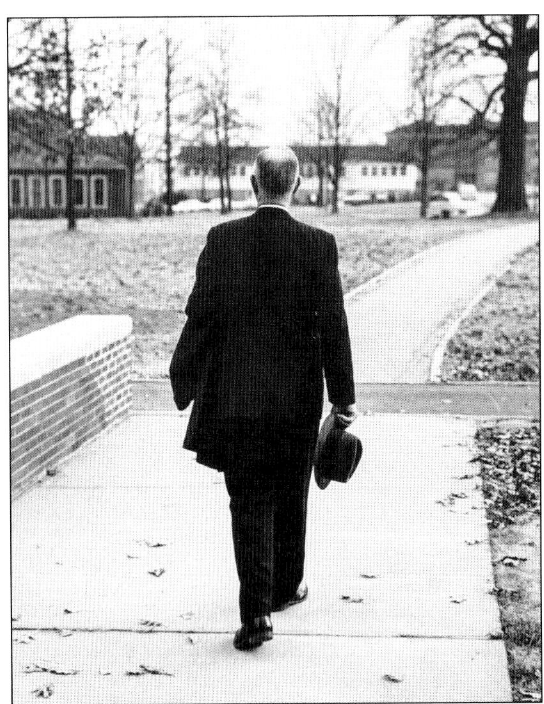

Dr. Paul Meek, who had been the guiding force of the institution since 1934, retired on September 1, 1967, marking the conclusion of a distinguished career in higher education. Throughout his 30-year tenure, Meek led the school through the challenges of the Great Depression, the uncertainties of World War II, and the rapid growth of the 1950s and 1960s. In recognition of his extraordinary service, the institution honored him by naming its newly constructed library after him in 1968. Andy Holt, president of the UT System, said, "The heart of any campus is the library, and that's why it is named after Paul Meek."

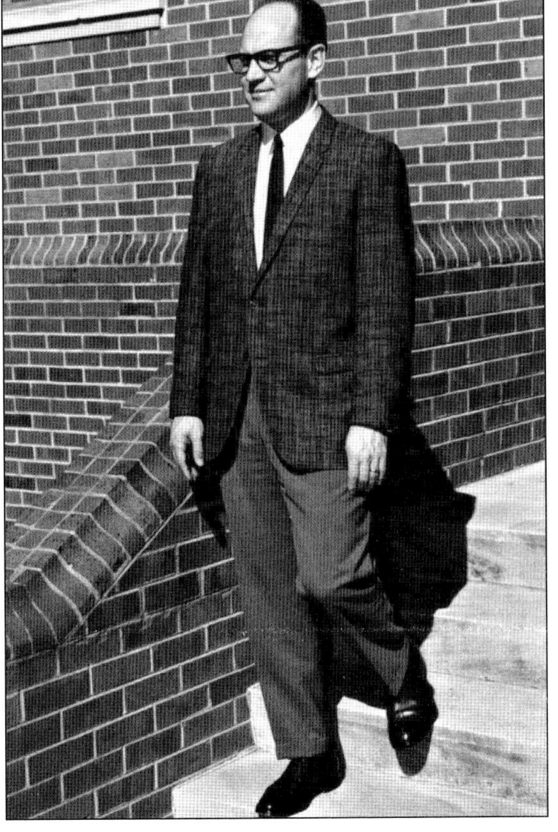

Dr. Archie Reece Dykes served as the third executive officer of UTM from 1967 to 1971. He assumed the chancellorship following the retirement of Dr. Paul Meek and held the position for three years before returning to Knoxville in 1971. At the time of his appointment, he was the youngest chief executive of a higher education institution in the state. During his tenure as chancellor, Dykes oversaw the continued growth and expansion of the campus as it entered a new era as the University of Tennessee at Martin.

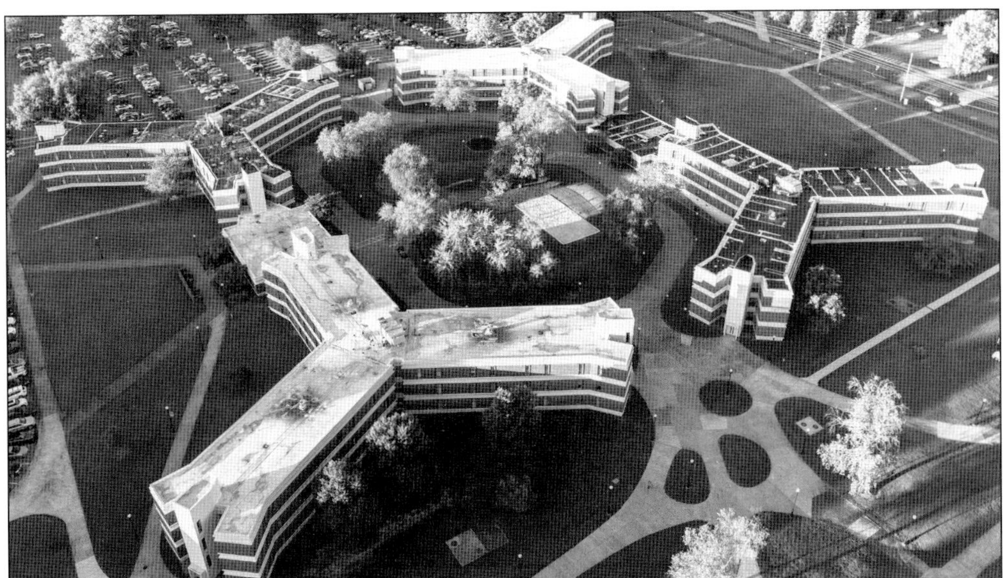

With the surge in student enrollment during the mid-1960s, housing remained a significant concern at UTM. In response, several student housing projects were undertaken, including the construction of four dormitories—McCord, Austin Peay, Ellington, and Browning—designed in a distinctive double-Y pattern. To expedite availability, construction was divided into two phases. The first phase, completed in the fall of 1965, provided accommodations for 264 single female students. The second phase, finalized in 1967, added another 264 units. In 2025, only Ellington and Browning Halls remain. Ellington Hall, completed in the fall of 1967, was officially named on April 17, 1969, in honor of Gov. Buford Ellington. Browning Hall, the last of the Y-type dormitories, was finished in 1970. Located farthest west among the group, it was originally known as the G-H Dormitory before being renamed in 1990 to honor Gov. Gordon Browning. This facility was designed to house 468 single students.

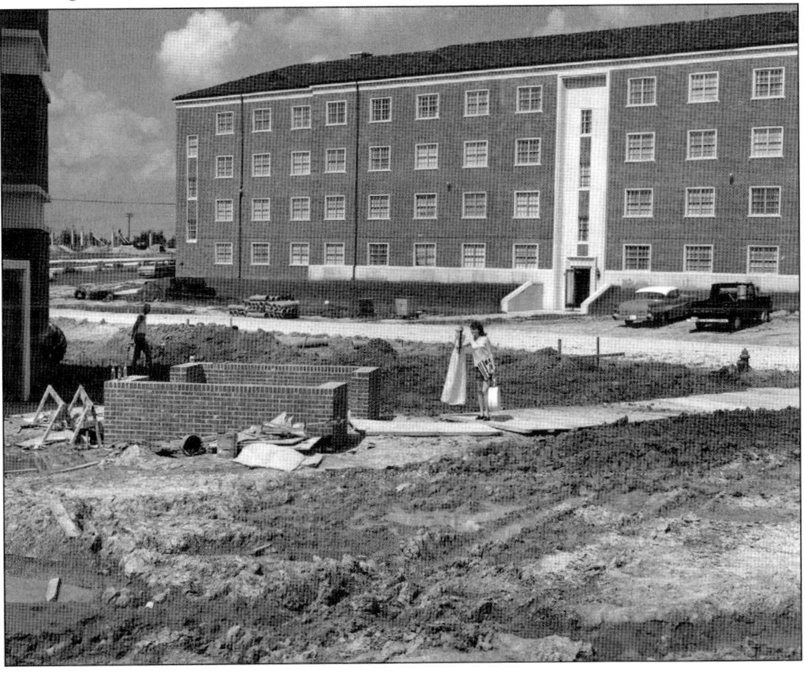

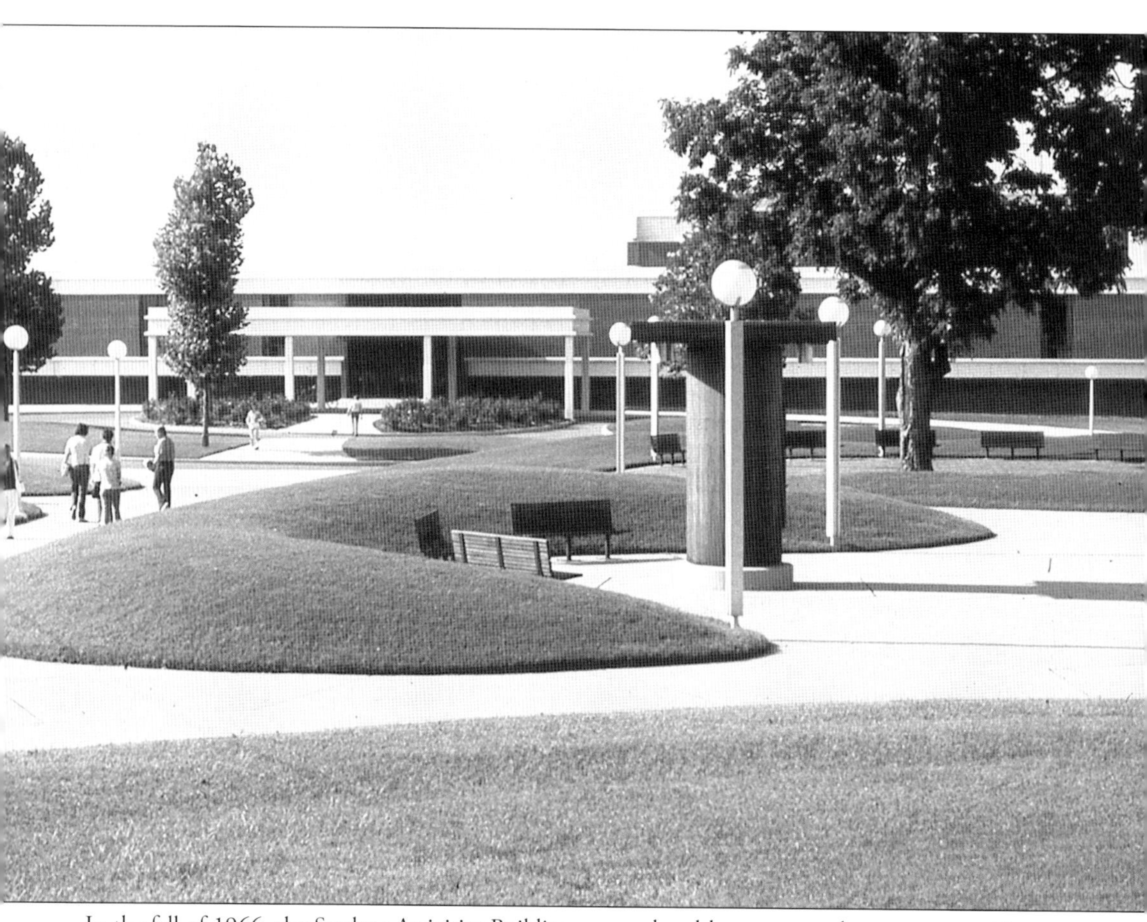

In the fall of 1966, the Student Activities Building was replaced by a new student center, marking one of the final major projects in the college's period of significant physical expansion. Initially, the building covered 59,600 square feet and included the cafeteria, snack bar, game rooms, bookstore, post office, and ballroom. A larger cafeteria and food services expansion followed in 1983, bringing the total square footage to 87,734. In 1993, the building was named in honor of Dr. Edward Joseph Boling, who served as president of the University of Tennessee from 1970 to 1988, and his wife, Carolyn P. Boling. Additional improvements in 1997 included space for a post office, auditorium, and extra meeting rooms on the north side. The area between the university center and Paul Meek Library was also lowered and leveled to create the new Centennial Circle.

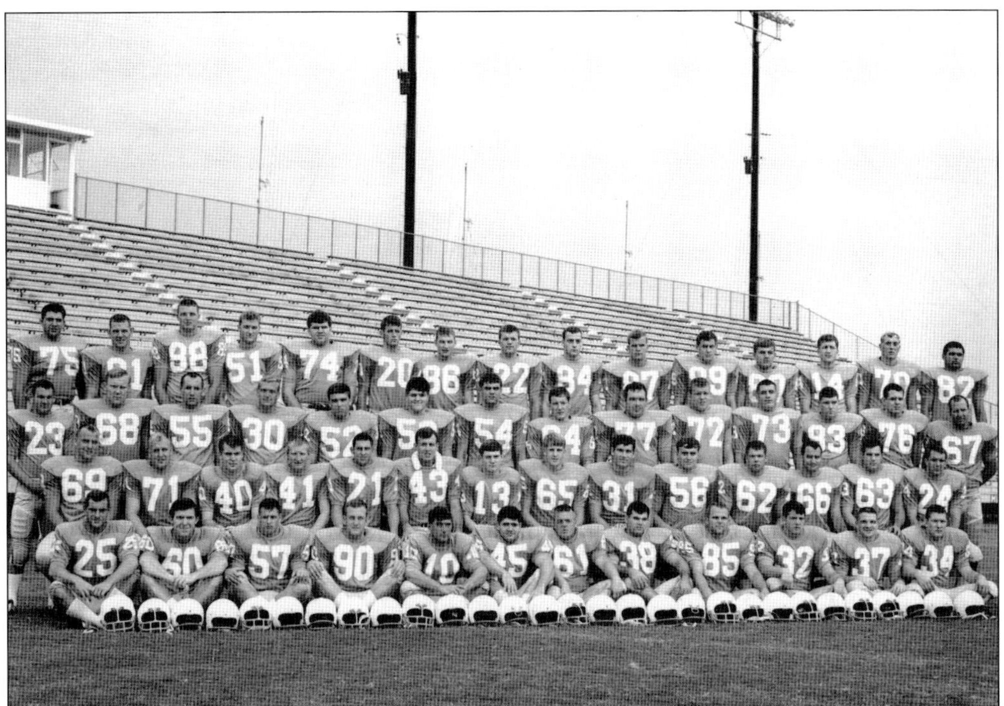

In the fall of 1967, UTM's football team achieved an impressive 8-1 season, earning a spot in a major NCAA bowl game. Despite being underdogs, the team defeated West Chester State 25-8 in front of 5,500 fans to win the Tangerine Bowl in Orlando, Florida. This historic win helped secure UTM's reputation as the top small college team in the eastern United States. Five players from the team went on to sign professional contracts, and 15 were later inducted into the UTM Athletics Hall of Fame. The team's 10 wins remain the second highest in the university's football history, and their success was celebrated with a headline in the *Orlando Sentinel* declaring, "Tangerine Bowl Proves A Tennessee Waltz." Coach Bob Carroll is pictured celebrating with his team after the big win.

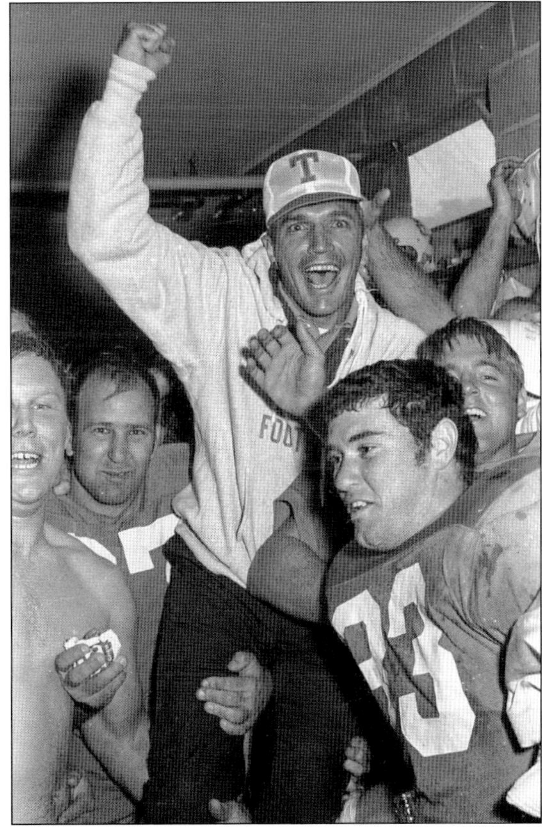

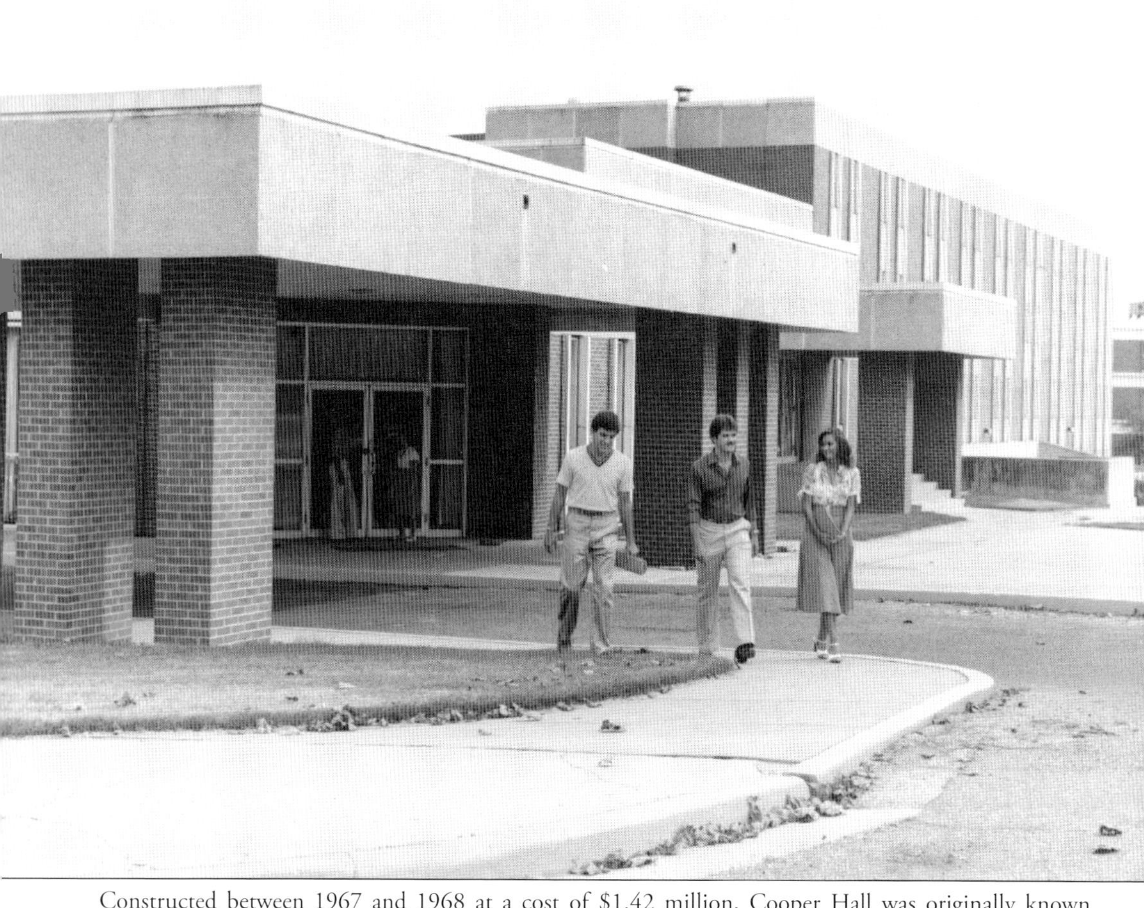

Constructed between 1967 and 1968 at a cost of $1.42 million, Cooper Hall was originally known as the Atrium Dormitory and featured an experimental architectural design. The four-story structure was built around a central courtyard, with eight-unit suites designed to promote community living—an innovative concept at the time. Completed in the fall of 1968, the residence hall housed up to 316 students and quickly became known for its distinctive layout. On December 7, 1995, the building was renamed Cooper Hall in honor of former Tennessee governor Prentice Cooper. Today, Cooper Hall serves as a coeducational residence hall and home to several of UTM's Living Learning Communities, including preprofessional health, engineering, agriculture, music, education, criminal justice, ROTC, university scholars, and Call Me MiSTER. The hall features suite-style accommodations, community rooms with social and study spaces, and remains a hub for academic and social engagement.

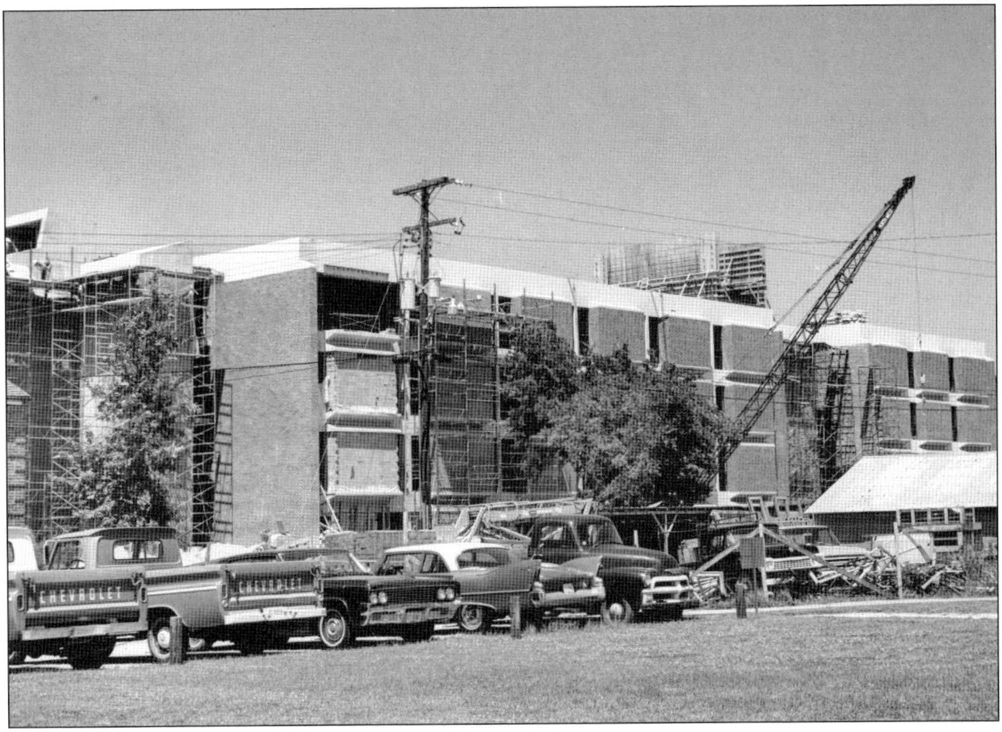

The Holt Humanities Building was finished by the fall of 1968 to address the campus's urgent need for office and classroom space. Spanning 65,072 square feet, the building was designed to include 31 classrooms, 90 offices, a large auditorium-style lecture hall, and laboratories for psychology and foreign languages. Today, it houses most of the university's liberal arts programs, including the departments of history and philosophy, English, and modern foreign languages as well as the dean of humanities and fine arts.

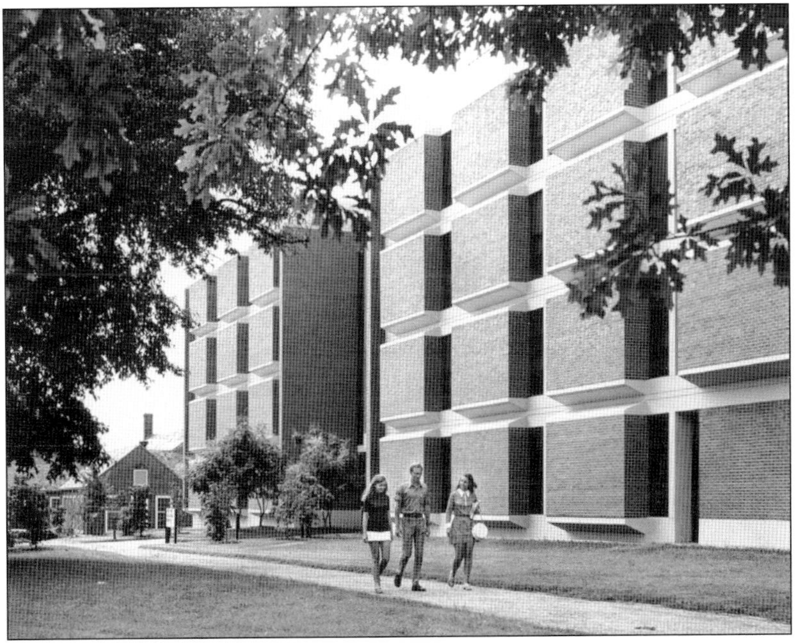

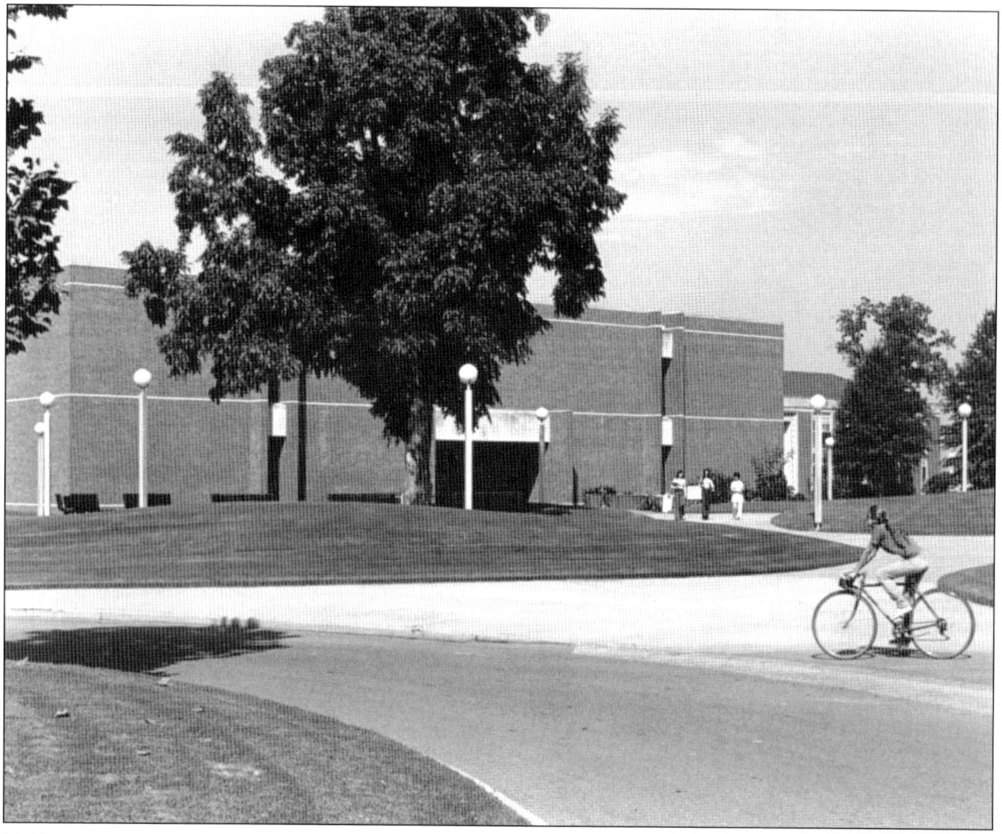

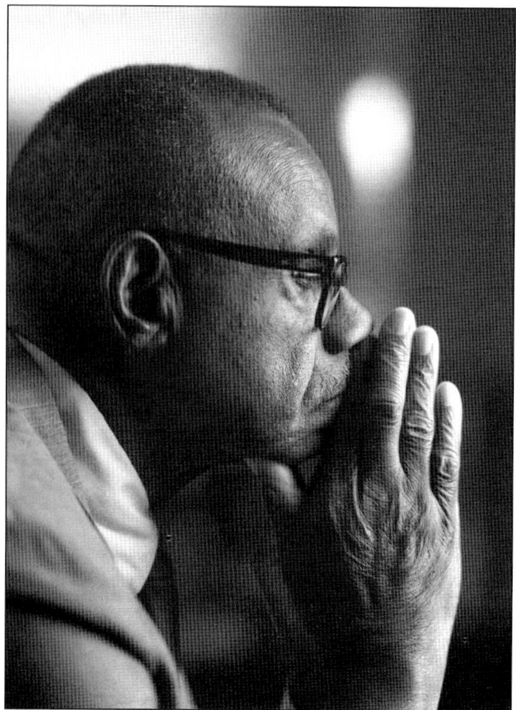

By the early 1960s, the campus library, originally located in the ABL Building, had outgrown its space. Construction on a new library building began in the spring of 1966 and was finished by spring 1968. The 60,000-square-foot facility was designed to accommodate 200,000 books, along with other library-related media materials. The building was named in honor of Dr. Paul Meek, who served as chancellor of the University of Tennessee at Martin and its predecessors from 1934 to 1967.

In 1969, Rev. Harold Conner Sr. made history as the first African American administrator hired at UTM. Beloved by students, he initially served as assistant dean of students before advancing to assistant vice chancellor for student affairs. During his tenure, Conner played a key role in founding the Black Student Association (BSA) and freshman studies. In recognition of his contributions, he became the first recipient of the BSA's annual Legacy Award. Conner retired from UTM in 1981.

From 1969 to 1978, Nadine Gearin served as the coach of UTM's first intercollegiate women's basketball team, playing a pivotal role in establishing UTM as a trailblazer in women's athletics. Under her leadership, the team won the 1970–1971 Tennessee College Women's Sports Federation title and secured three Western Division championships. Gearin compiled an overall coaching record of 104-86. Beyond basketball, she also coached the women's volleyball team (1969–1973) and the UTM badminton club (1968–1970). Dedicated to the university for 40 years, she officially retired on June 30, 1997, and was honored with induction into the UTM Athletics Hall of Fame in 1988. From 1970 to 1974, she coached the legendary Hall of Fame coach Pat Head Summitt in both basketball and volleyball.

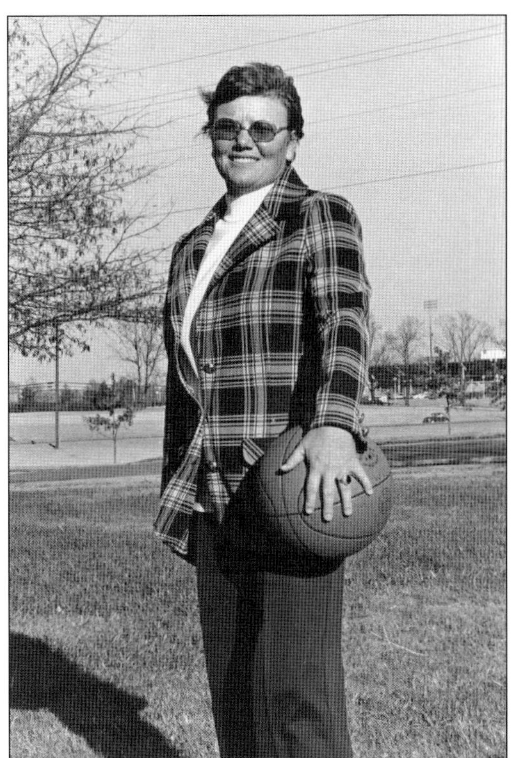

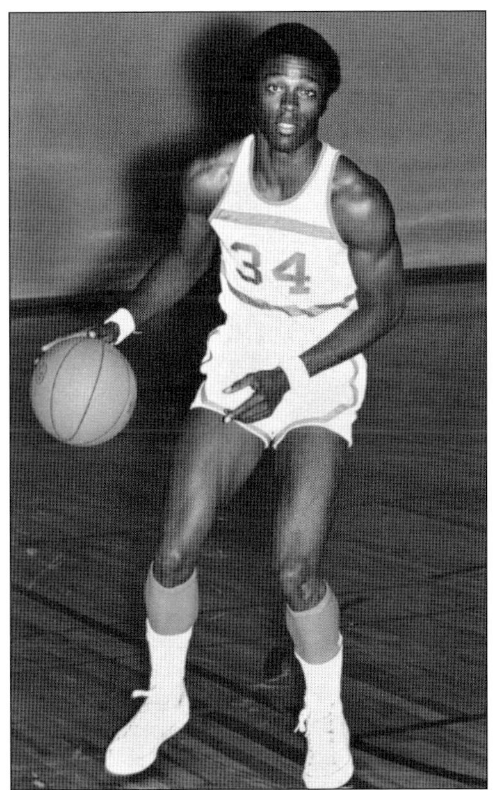

In 1969, Leonard Hamilton became the first African American basketball player at UTM. Serving as team captain, he displayed strong leadership on and off the court. During his senior season at UTM, he was named the team's Most Valuable Player and Best Defensive Player, averaging 11.7 points per game and setting a school record with 206 career assists. His outstanding performance earned him all-conference first-team honors, a spot on the Tennessee-Kentucky All-Star team, and the title of "Mr. UTM" from the student body. Beyond his playing career, he built a remarkable four-decade coaching legacy, earning multiple Coach of the Year awards, leading teams to eleven NCAA Tournament appearances and fourteen 20-win seasons, and achieving 660 career wins.

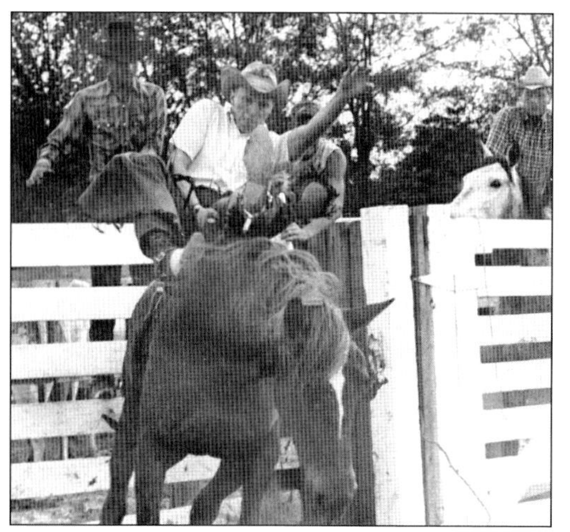

The first rodeo was held in 1969, with UTM claiming victory over three other in-state colleges. Over time, the program continued to thrive, moving to new locations and gaining enthusiastic support from students, faculty, and the local community. By 1980, the launch of the Rodeo Booster Club transformed the event into a weeklong celebration, embedding it even deeper into campus tradition. Soon, the stands were packed with energized fans cheering on cowboys and cowgirls through every thrilling ride. Each spring, thousands of attendees suit up in their Western finest—complete with hats, boots, and big belt buckles—and head to the Ned McWherter Agricultural Complex for a one-of-a-kind rodeo experience.

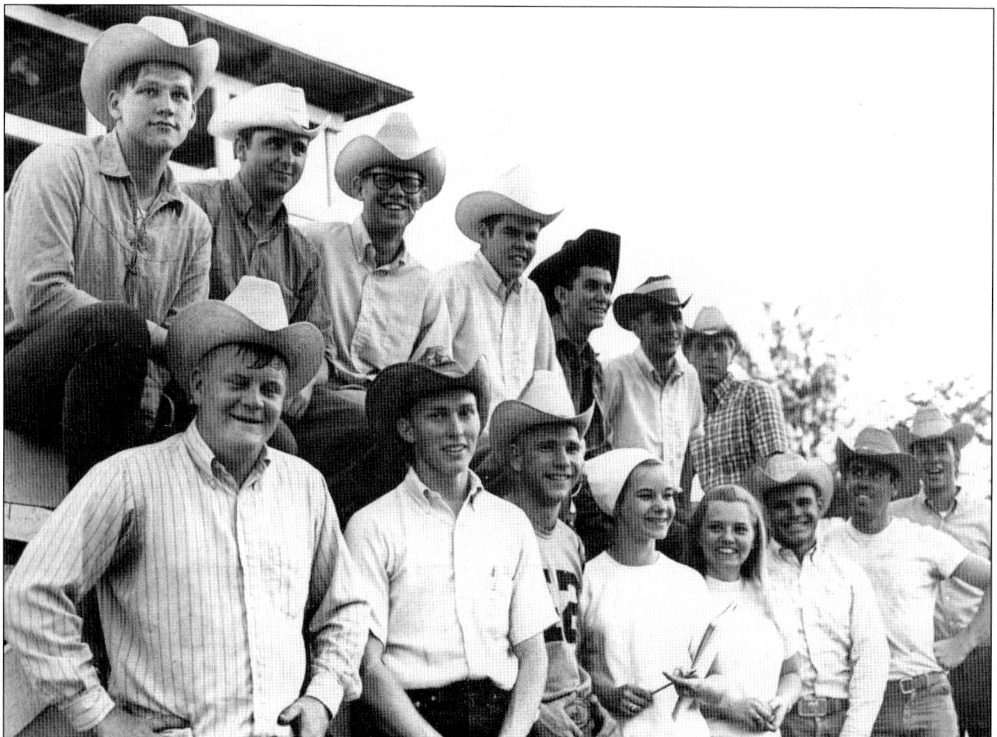

Pictured is UTM's inaugural rodeo team, founded in 1969. The university launched its rodeo program just a year earlier, in 1968, which has since evolved into Tennessee's only collegiate rodeo team—a proud tradition that endures to this day. It all started with a modest $600, raised by selling a Shetland pony, and a deep-rooted passion for rodeo. In 1973, UTM joined the National Intercollegiate Rodeo Association, and the following year, they made history as the first team east of the Mississippi River to qualify for the National Intercollegiate Rodeo Association National Finals. That early success continued into the late 1970s, highlighted by national champions Skip Emmett in 1975 and Tony Coleman in 1977, cementing UTM's reputation as a collegiate rodeo powerhouse.

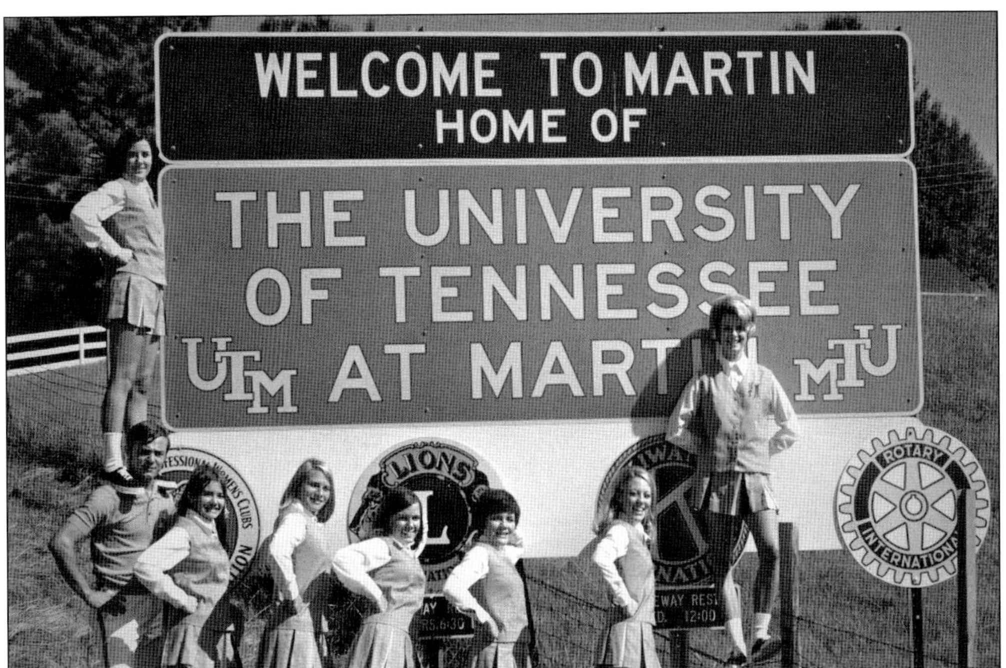

The 1969–1970 cheerleading squad included James Pruett, Daryl Brandenburg, Cheryl Snyder, May Check, Marcia Hanna, Debbie Browning, Peggy Guthrie, Bonnie Samuels, and Barbara Moody. UTM cheerleaders are essential to the university's athletic program, promoting school spirit and supporting sports teams. Chosen every spring, they take on roles that go beyond leading cheers at games. Their duties include organizing pep rallies, creating spirit signs, and energizing crowds during local parades. Dressed in UTM's signature blue, orange, and white, they connect enthusiastic fans with the teams through their polished performances. From bonfires to parades, their dedication ensures that UTM's spirited traditions remain strong.

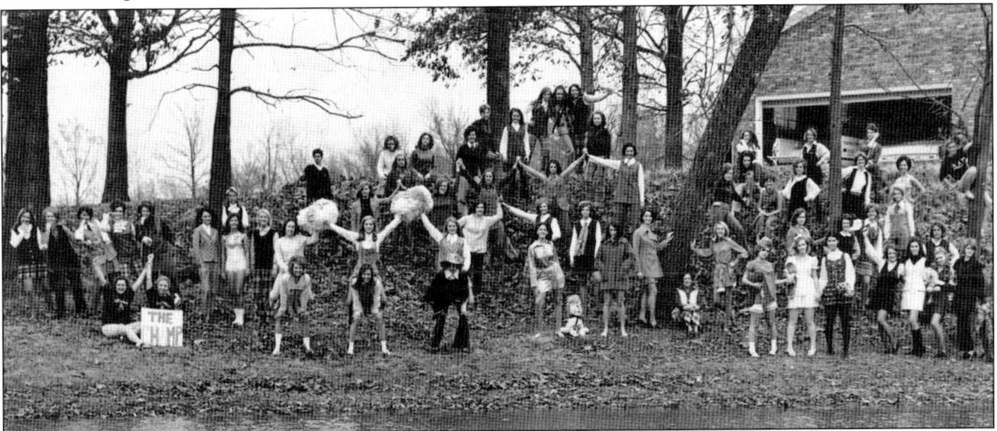

Being part of the fraternity and sorority community at UTM provides students with opportunities to build meaningful relationships, pursue their interests, engage in service, and uphold shared values. The UTM community emphasizes brotherhood/sisterhood, service, and academic excellence both in and out of the classroom. With 19 organizations governed by three councils, they cultivate a supportive and dynamic environment. Pictured is the 1969–1970 Alpha Delta Pi Sorority, committed to fostering a strong sisterhood that supports the physical, intellectual, social, and spiritual growth of its members. Their mission is to create lifelong friendships and promote collaboration among students and faculty.

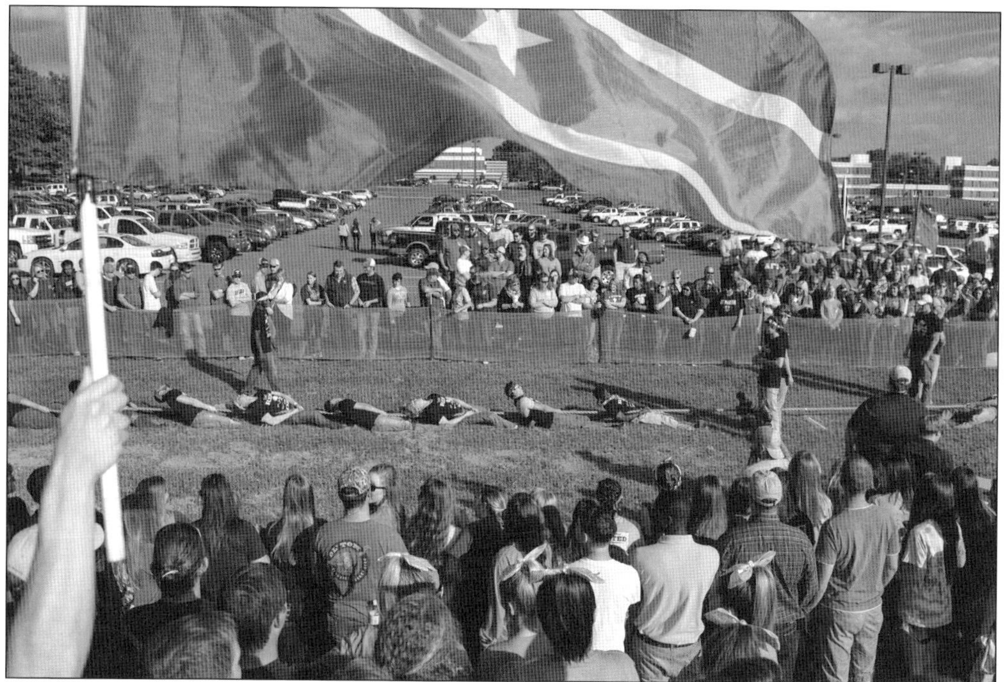

Rope Pull is one of UTM's longest-standing and most beloved traditions among Greek organizations, with origins tracing back to the 1930s as a simple intramural sport known then as "Tug-o-War." By the late 1950s and early 1960s, the event had become part of homecoming festivities under the name Interfraternity Council (IFC) Tug-o-War and was held behind the Phi Sigma Kappa house, marking the first recorded mention of the iconic mud pit and the rise of Alpha Gamma Rho's long-standing dominance. An October 1961 issue of the *Volette* notes that freshman initiation "virtually came to a close" with the tug-of-war match held at halftime of the UTMB-Missouri Miners football game, showing the contest's early integration into campus culture. Today, Rope Pull is held near Pacer Pond and features intense competition between fraternity and sorority teams, with weeks of training leading up to the event. More than just a tug-of-war, Rope Pull embodies teamwork, tradition, and Skyhawk spirit.

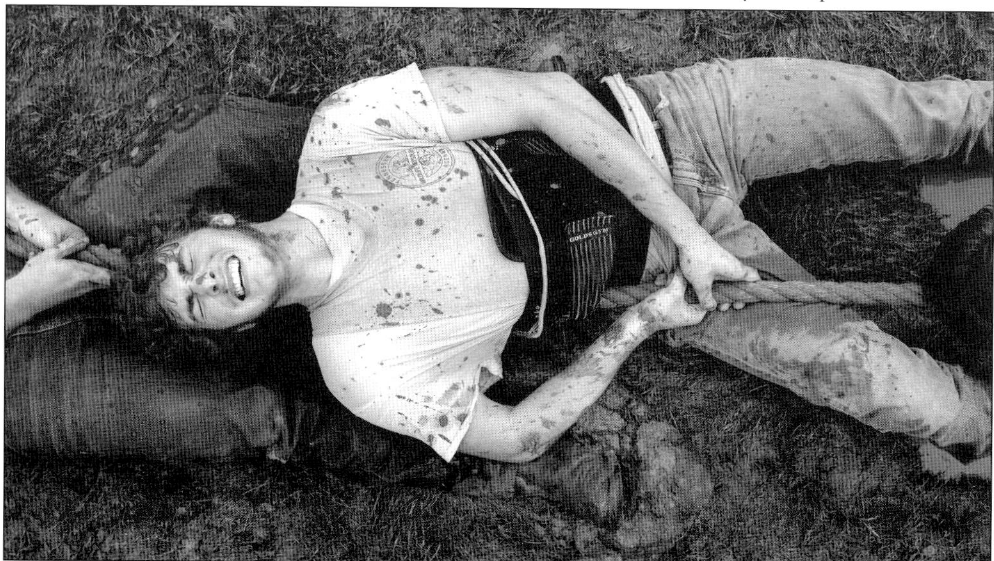

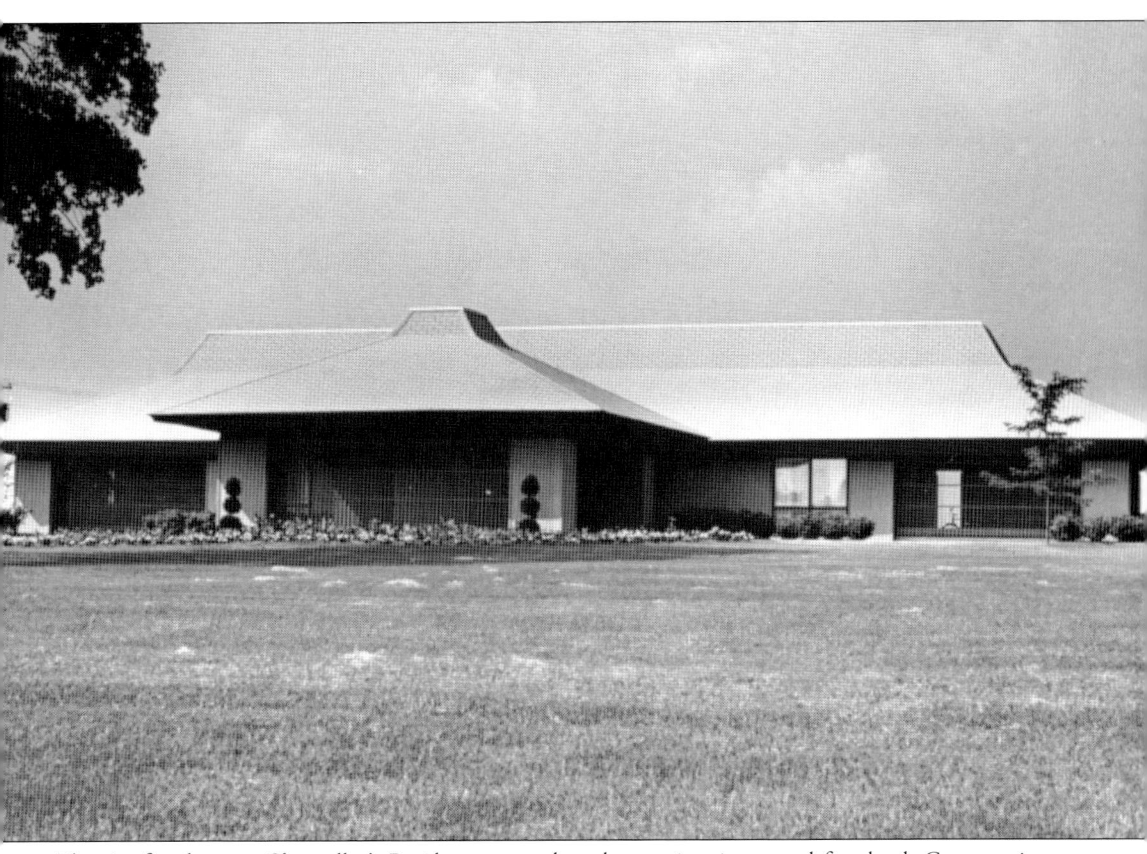

The site for the new Chancellor's Residence was selected on university-owned farmland. Construction began in 1969 and was completed by the fall of 1970. Serving as the official residence of the university's executive officer, it also functions as a reception center. On October 15, 2010, the UT Board of Trustees named the UTM Dunagan Alumni Center in honor of Nick and Cathy Porter Dunagan for their outstanding service to the University of Tennessee at Martin. As chancellor and first lady, the Dunagans were dedicated partners in leadership. The Dunagan Alumni Center now houses the Office of Alumni Relations and Annual Giving and serves as a gathering space for alumni and campus organizations. It also includes the Chancellor's Suite, where the UTM chancellor hosts guests and events on behalf of the Office of the Chancellor.

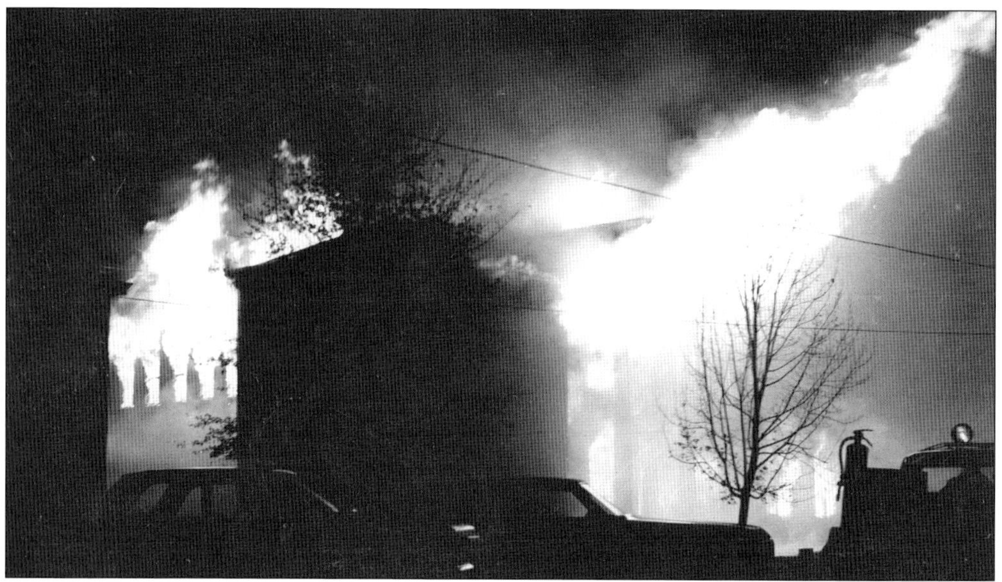

In the early hours of Thanksgiving Day in 1970, a fire destroyed the old Hall-Moody Administration Building. The alarm was first reported around 1:30 a.m. by the Martin City Police to campus officials. After the new Administration Building was completed in 1959, the Hall-Moody Building served various functions, including storage, and later became home to the music and drama departments. Once the Fine Arts Building was constructed, the Hall-Moody Building was marked for demolition and had been vacated, leaving it empty at the time of the fire.

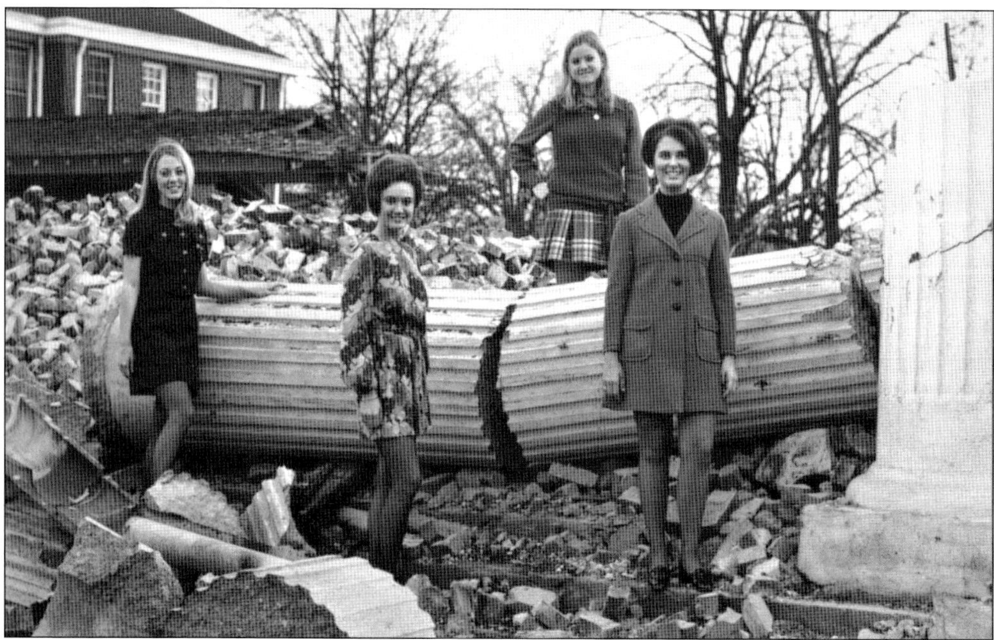

Four students, from left to right, Donna Smith, Donna Reece, Kay Kittrell, and Rebecca Russell, stand for a photograph amid the remains of the former Hall-Moody Administration Building, which had been destroyed by fire. Once a prominent fixture on campus and a symbol of the university's early history, the building had already been slated for demolition. The students' presence captures a moment of reflection and resilience during a time of change.

Dr. Larry Thomas McGehee served as the fourth chancellor of the University of Tennessee at Martin from 1971 to 1979. Born on May 18, 1936, in Paris, Tennessee, he began his academic career at the University of Alabama in 1966, advancing to executive vice president by 1969. After UTM, he became special assistant to the president at UT Knoxville, then joined Wofford College in 1982 as vice president of planning, marketing, and evaluation, serving until his death in 2008. He gained national recognition in 1972 for a concise, two-and-a-half-minute, 250-word commencement speech at the University of Alabama.

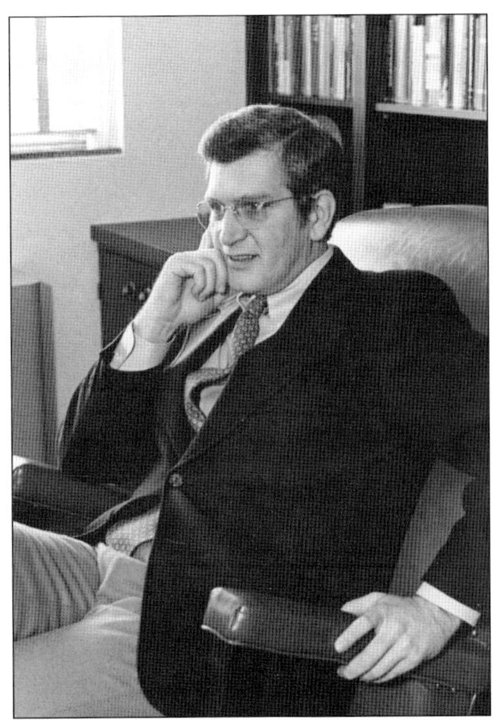

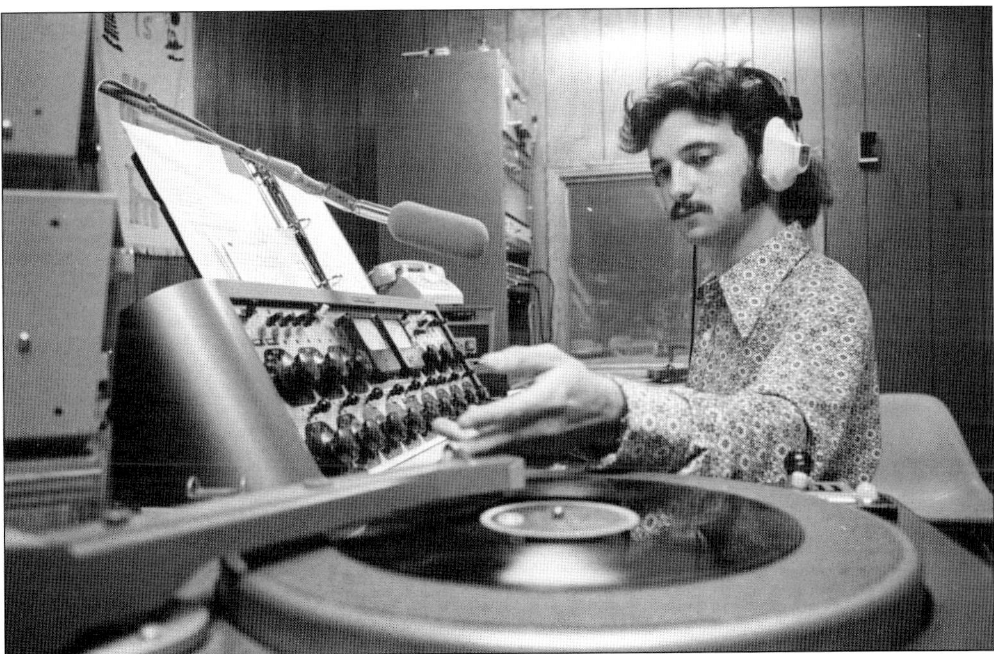

WUTM 90.3 "The Hawk" began broadcasting on September 15, 1971, from a small building on Hurt Street. Originally aiming for 90.1 FM, UTM shifted to 90.3 after Murray State claimed the first frequency. With only 10 watts and borrowed equipment, English professor Robert Todd and students launched the university's first student-run radio station. Now part of the Department of Mass Media and Strategic Communication, WUTM has thrived under Dr. Richard Robinson since 2001, earning over 300 national awards and expanding into streaming and sports. In 2021, it proudly celebrated 50 years on air.

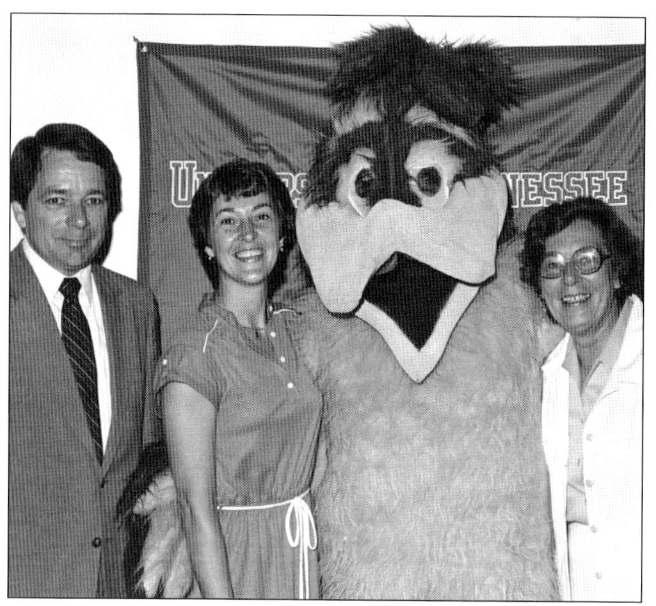

In 1971, the university sought to establish a new identity to differentiate itself from UT Knoxville. Several names were considered, including Takers, Cobras, Pioneers, Pacers, Commanders, and interestingly, Hawks. After conducting a student poll, Pacers was chosen, and a decade later, the first mascot characters were introduced. In January 1981, Pacer Pete, a six-foot blue-and-orange roadrunner, made his debut among students and fans. A few years later, a female counterpart, Pace-Her Polly, was created. Pictured are, from left to right, chancellor Charles Smith, coach Anne Strusz, Pacer Pete, and Bettye Giles.

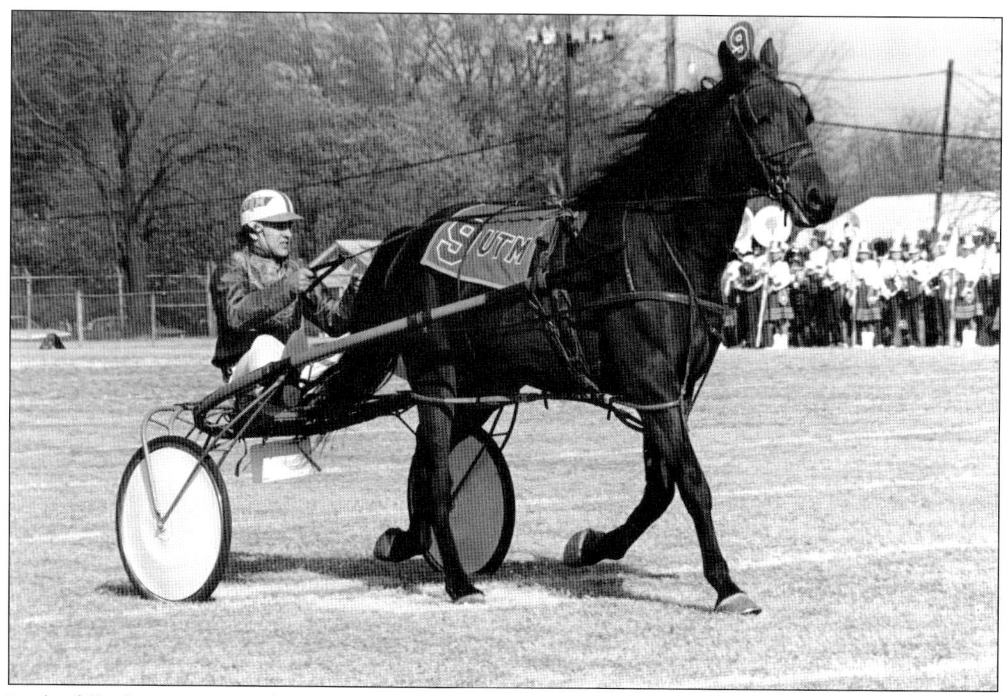

In the fall of 1971, a pacer horse named Chuckie, along with a sulky driven by Curtis Sullivan, became the official mascot and symbol of the Pacers. Pacer horses are mainly used in harness racing, where they pull a lightweight, tow-wheeled vehicle called a sulky. Alongside Pacer Pete and Pace-Her Polly, this trio represented the Pacers until 1995, when the university adopted its current nickname, the Skyhawks, and introduced the mascot Captain (Skyhawk).

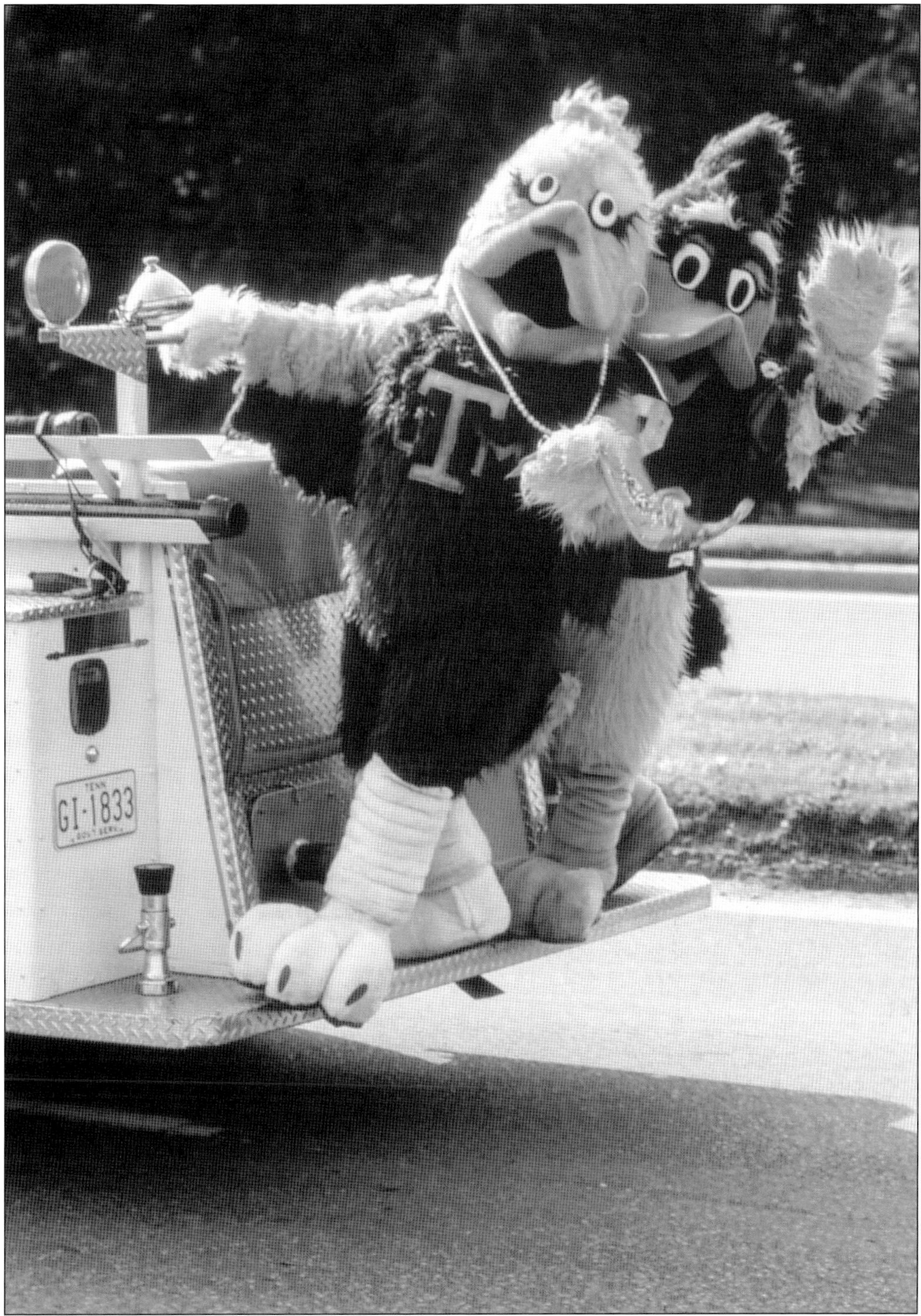

In addition to Pacer Pete and Chuckie, a third mascot named Pace-Her Polly was introduced at the request of Bettye Giles, then the director of women's athletics, who wanted a female counterpart to Pacer Pete. This trio of mascots represented the university until 1995, when the institution adopted its current nickname, the Skyhawks.

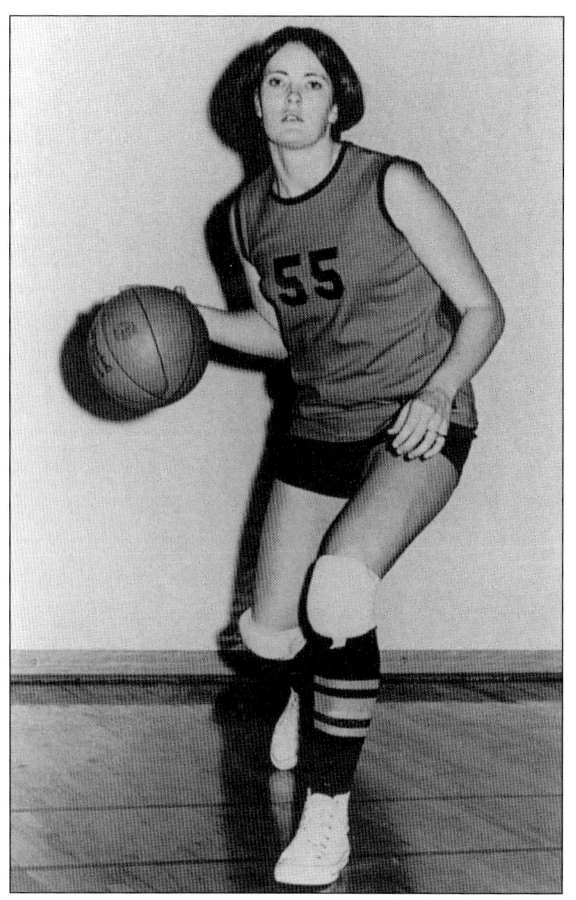

Pat Head (later Summitt) attended the University of Tennessee at Martin from 1970 to 1974, earning All-American honors while playing under UTM's first women's basketball coach, Nadine Gearin. She later cocaptained the US women's national basketball team at the inaugural women's tournament in the 1976 Summer Olympics, where she helped secure a silver medal. In 1984, she made history by coaching the US women's team to Olympic gold, becoming the first US Olympian to both win a basketball medal as a player and coach a medal-winning team. Shortly after earning her degree in physical education from UTM, she was appointed head coach of the University of Tennessee women's basketball team. Over 38 seasons, Summitt led the Lady Vols to eight NCAA Division I championships and retired with 1,098 wins—the most in college basketball history at the time of her retirement. Pictured below are Head (Summitt, left) and Gearin (right) during Head's (Summitt's) jersey retirement ceremony, February 19, 1974. Head (Summitt), who suffered a season-ending knee injury earlier in the year, became the first woman at UTM to be honored in this way.

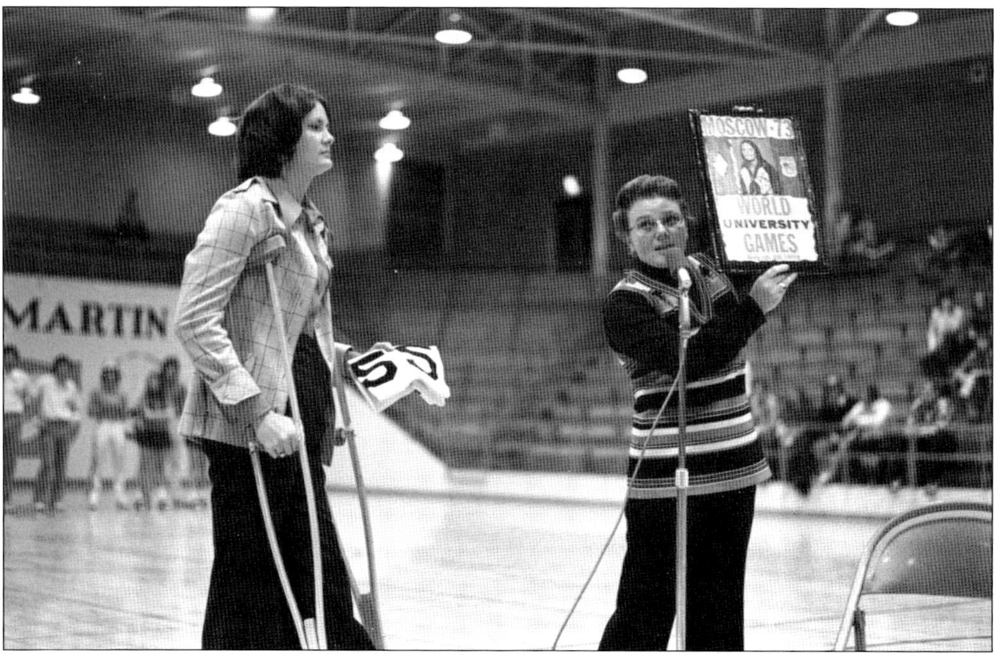

In January 1971, the Harlem Globetrotters, known for their flashy style and nearly unbeatable record, experienced a rare defeat at UTM's new field house. Before a crowd of about 3,000, the New Jersey Reds—also known as the Washington Generals or New York Nationals—pulled off the upset when Red Klotz sank a last-second shot. Meadowlark Lemon missed a final attempt, sealing the loss. Klotz later quipped, "It was like we had just killed Santa Claus." Though it occurred during winter break with little official record, the game remains a vivid and legendary moment in UTM history.

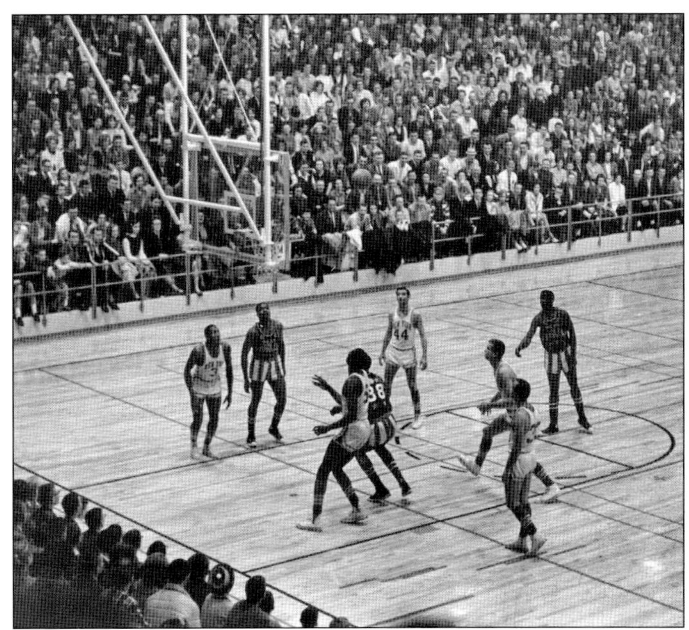

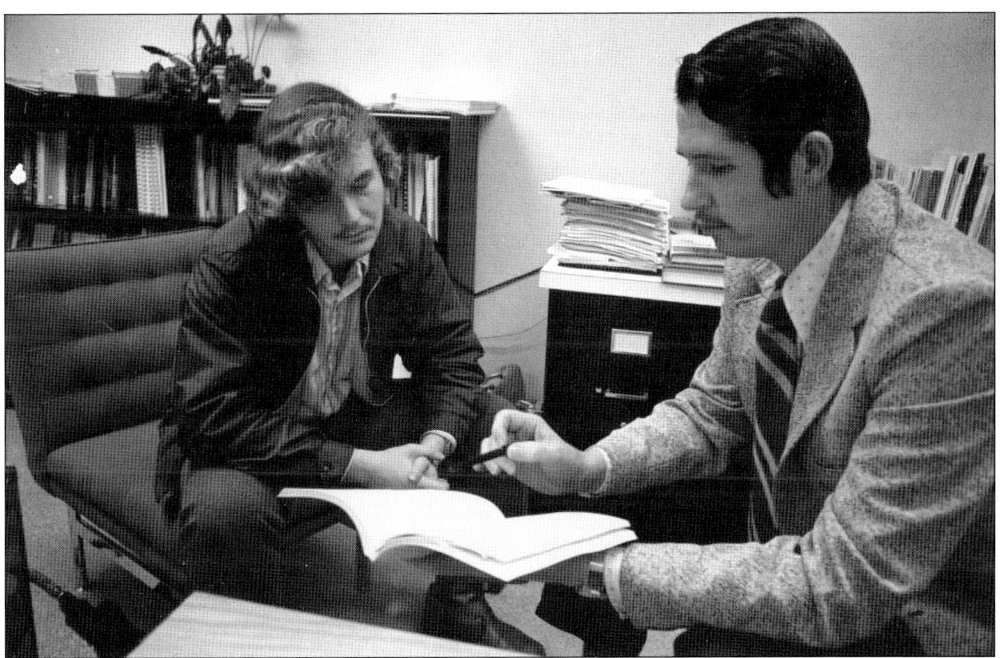

Dr. Phillip W. Watkins began serving as UTM's first vice chancellor for student affairs in 1973 after more than a decade on campus as a professor and administrator. A 1956 UTMB graduate and former SGA president, Watkins returned to his alma mater in 1964 and quickly became a guiding force in student life. By the early 1970s, he had already helped establish the Office of Student Life and laid the foundation for programs that would shape the student experience for decades to come. In recognition of his enduring impact, the auditorium in the Boling University Center was later named in his honor.

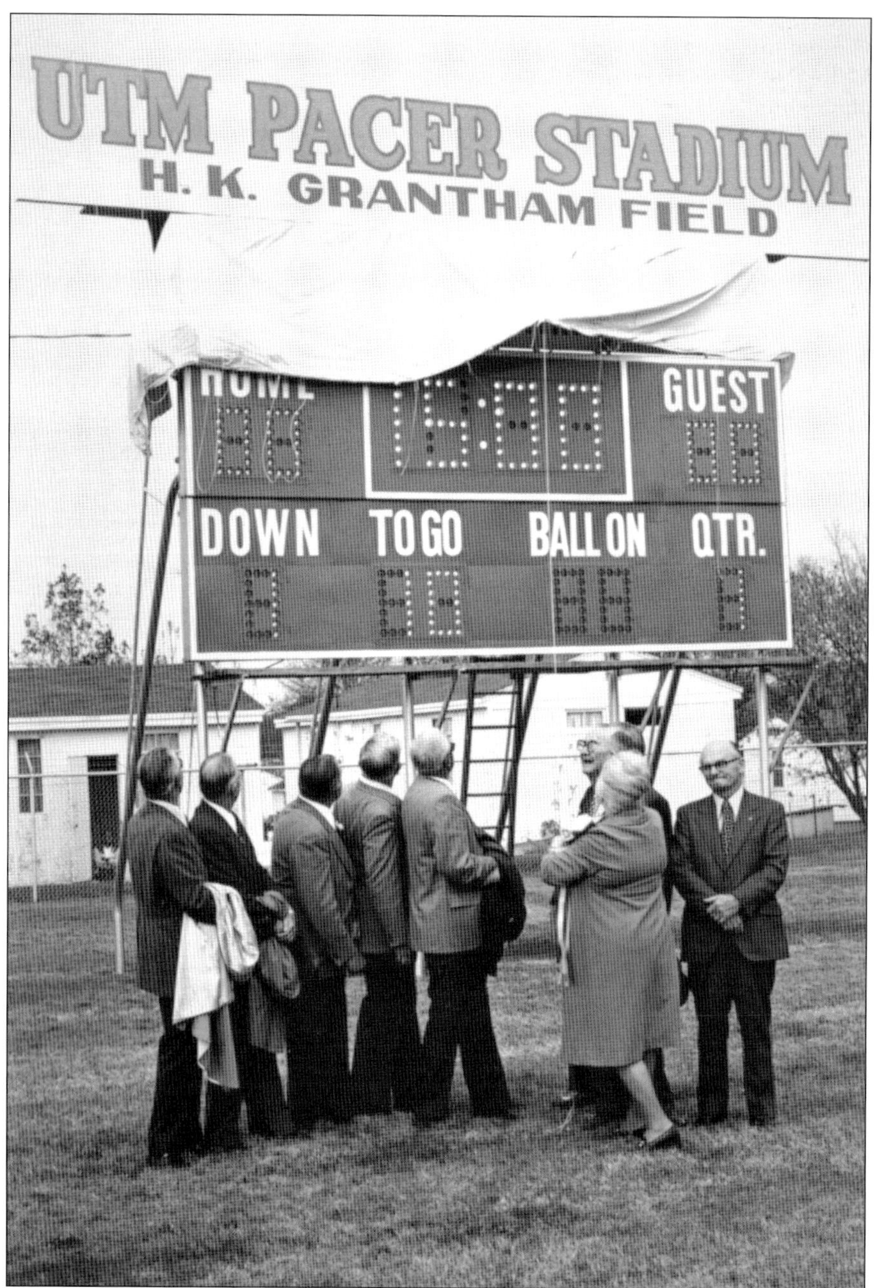

Originally built in 1930, the football field was among the first stadiums in West Tennessee to feature lighting for night games. When it opened that year, large crowds gathered not only to cheer on a talented team but also to experience the novelty of evening football under the lights. In 1974, the field at UTM was officially named H.K. Grantham Field in honor of Coach Grantham, thanks to strong support from his former players. Grantham was instrumental in the field's design and left a significant legacy in UTM athletics. He served as head coach for football, baseball, and men's basketball, while also overseeing the physical education department and directing the athletics program. During the dedication ceremony, Lucille Grantham and many of Grantham's former players were present to witness the unveiling of the new sign at Pacer Stadium—later renamed Hardy M. Graham Stadium.

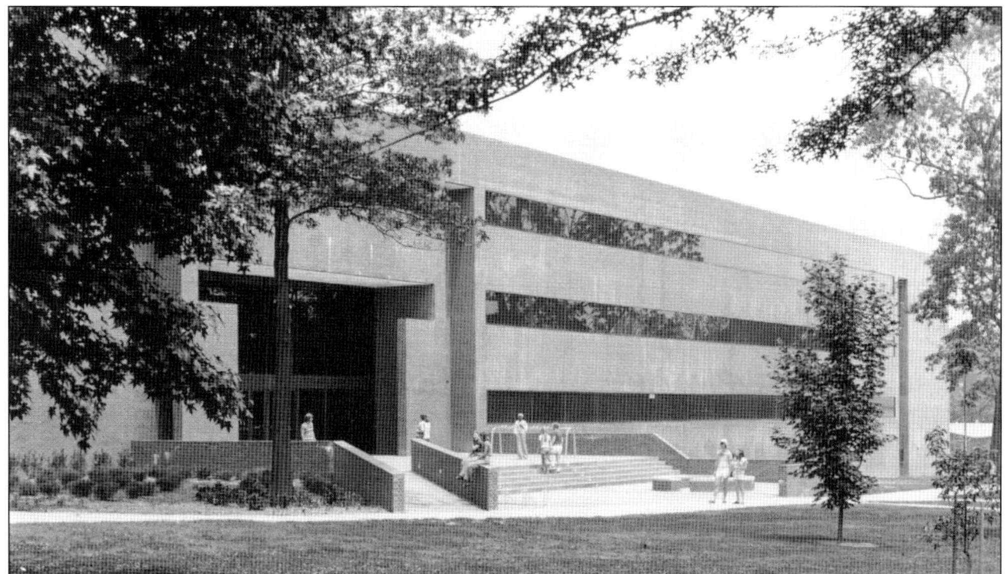

The Home Economics, Education, and Nursing Building was finished in 1974 and was officially renamed on September 9, 1976, in honor of Cecil M. and Boyce A. Gooch, significant benefactors of the university. Now known as Gooch Hall, the building spans 118,288 square feet and features a 182-seat auditorium, along with several classrooms and offices. Currently, Gooch Hall accommodates the offices and classrooms for the educational studies and education administration programs, the communications department, and the nursing department.

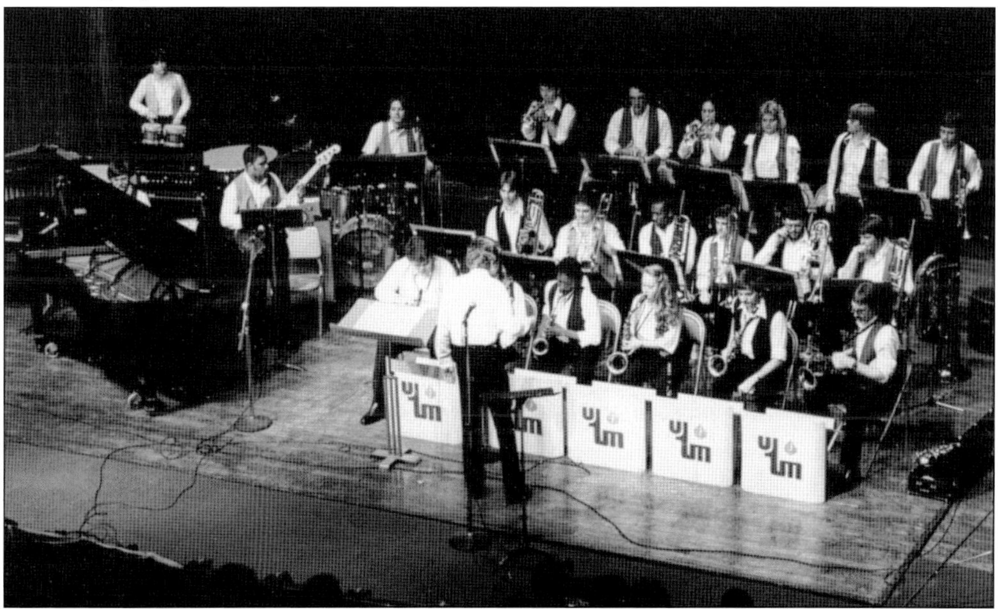

The UTM Jazz Band consists of select musicians from the UTM Band, dedicated to honing their skills in the art of jazz improvisation. Showcasing the richness, energy, and creativity of jazz—widely regarded as America's premier art form—the group performs in the traditional jazz band style. UTM Jazz Band concerts highlight classic swing and jazz standards by legends like Duke Ellington and Count Basie, alongside modern works, Latin jazz, and funk. The ensemble also hosts jam sessions that welcome both UTM students and members of the public.

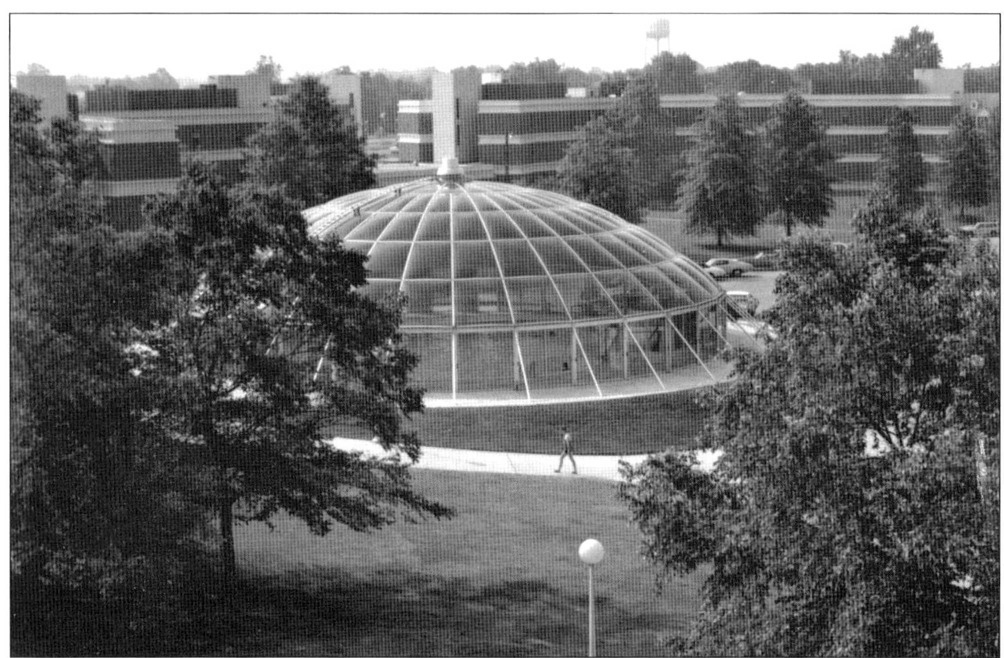

Constructed in 1975, the Dome Swimming Pool was designed as a recreational facility for students residing in the dorms. It remained in use until 1999, when it was demolished and replaced with outdoor volleyball pits.

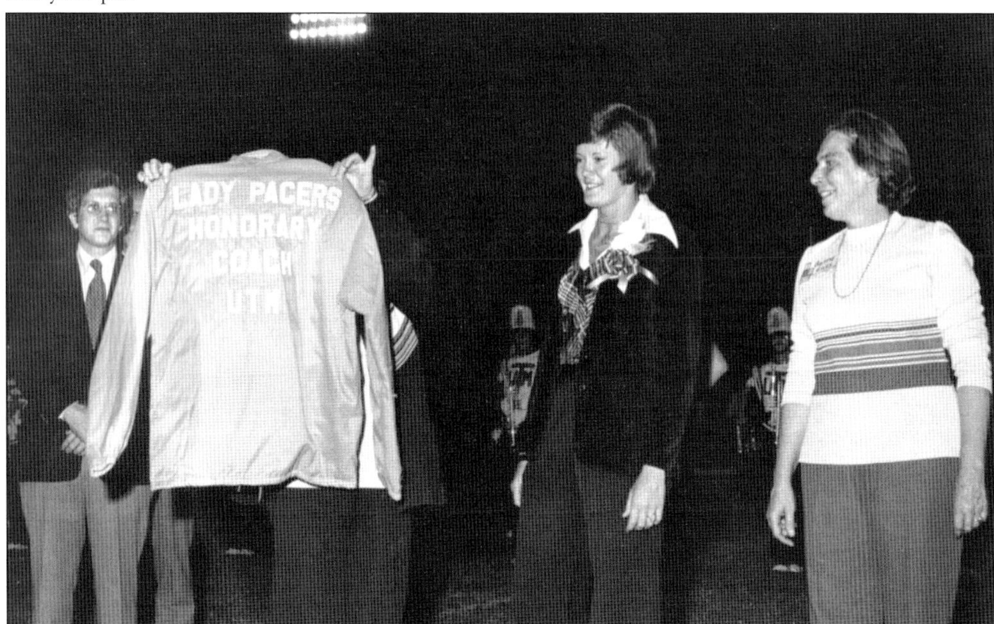

On September 25, 1976, Pat Head (later Summitt) was honored with a designated Recognition Day. A cocaptain of the silver medal–winning US women's basketball team at the 1976 Summer Olympics, she was recognized by the university during halftime of the UTM versus Jackson State football game. As part of the tribute, she received a coat and the basketball goal she had used during her freshman year at UTM. Pictured are, from left to right, chancellor Larry McGehee, unidentified, Pat Head (Summitt), and Bettye Giles.

On Friday, October 15, 1976, the comedy duo Cheech and Chong—featuring American Cheech Marin and Canadian Tommy Chong—performed a homecoming concert. Originally founded in Vancouver, the pair gained widespread commercial and cultural success throughout the 1970s and 1980s with their stand-up routines, studio albums, and films. The event was organized by the Student Government Association.

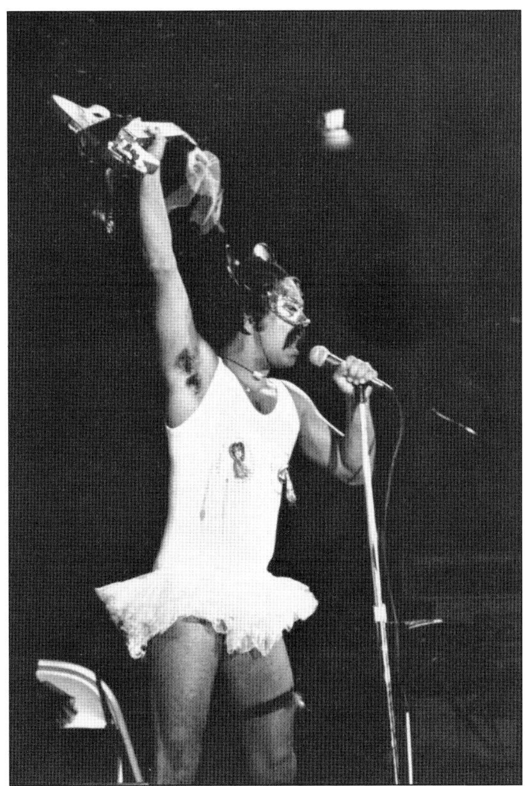

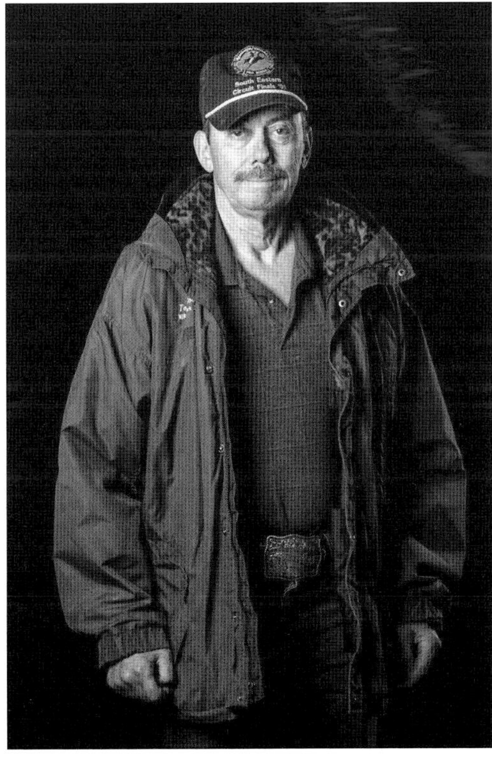

In 1977, Tony Coleman became the school's second national champion by capturing the all-around title at the NIRA National Finals. This achievement came just a year after UTM Rodeo secured its first Ozark Region team championship. In 1978, Coleman took on the role of the program's first part-time coach, coinciding with the relocation of UTM Rodeo to a newly established outdoor arena on the north end of campus the following year. The formation of the Rodeo Booster Club in 1980 helped transform UTM Rodeo into a weeklong celebration featuring a variety of events leading up to the competition. Coleman was later appointed UTM's first full-time rodeo coach in 1991, a position he held with distinction until 1997.

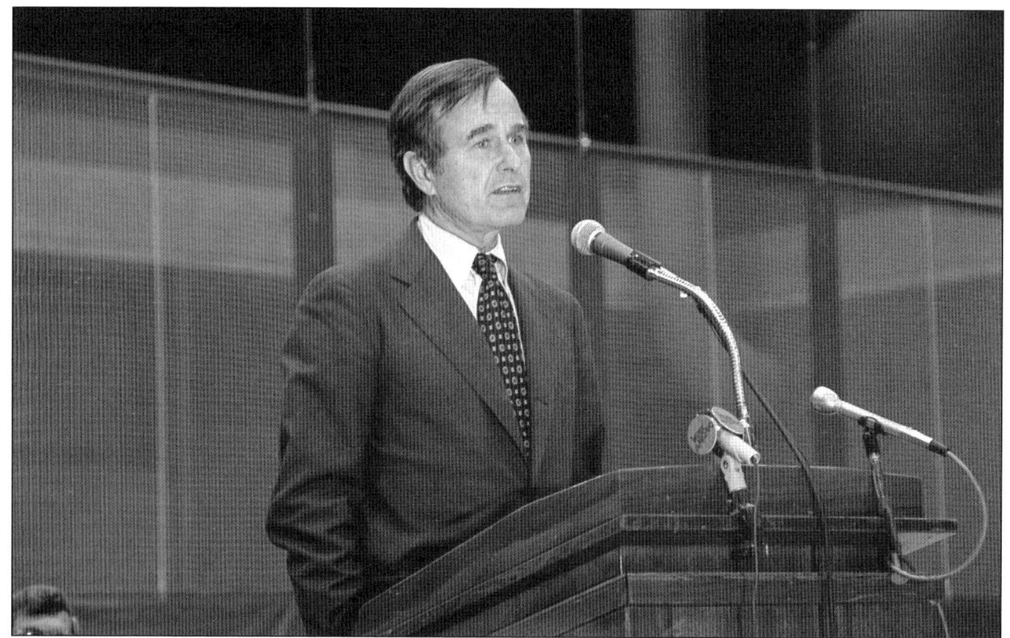

On November 17, 1978, former CIA director and future vice president and president George H.W. Bush, speaking to a crowd at the Convocation Center (now the Kathleen and Tom Elam Center), highlighted concerns over Cuba's imperialistic actions and emphasized the importance of strengthening US-China relations.

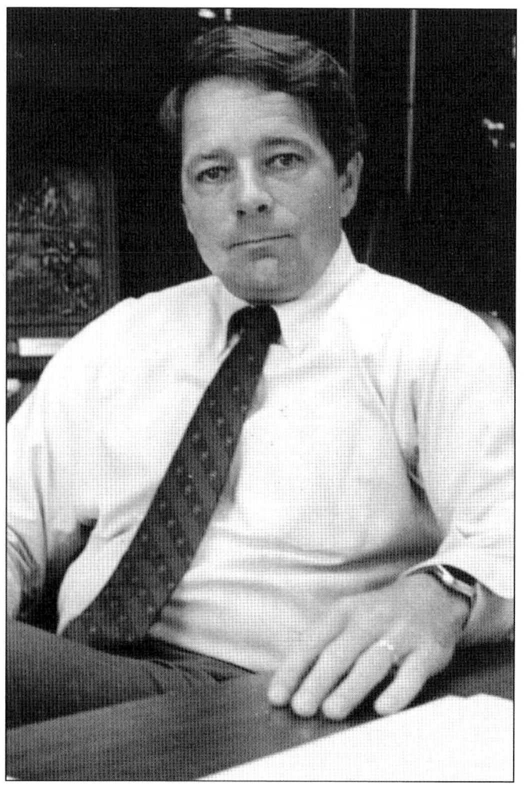

Dr. Charles Smith became the fifth UTM chancellor in 1980, succeeding Larry McGehee, and served until 1985. A native of White County, Tennessee, he earned degrees in journalism, English, and higher education from the University of Tennessee, Knoxville, and George Peabody College. He began his career as a journalist before transitioning into public relations and administrative roles in higher education, eventually serving as chancellor at both UT Nashville and UTM. At UTM, he prioritized recruiting top students from northwest Tennessee and established programs like the University Scholars, Honors Seminar, and Governor's School for the Humanities. After leaving UTM, Smith became vice president of the UT System, later serving as Tennessee's commissioner of education before retiring in 2000.

On September 22, 1981, Bobby Knight, head basketball coach at Indiana University, served as the keynote speaker at UTM's season ticket rally. The event, attended by around 300 people, was organized by Pacer athletic director and former University of Tennessee men's basketball coach Ray Mears. At the time, Knight's Indiana Hoosiers were the reigning national champions, having also achieved an undefeated season and the 1976 NCAA title under his leadership. Known for his candid and colorful personality, Knight entertained the crowd with humorous stories from his coaching career. Amid the laughter, he shared a more serious message, emphasizing that preparation is the cornerstone of success. "Basketball has taught me—and others—something about winning," he said. "There's a difference between winning and losing, and that difference is preparation."

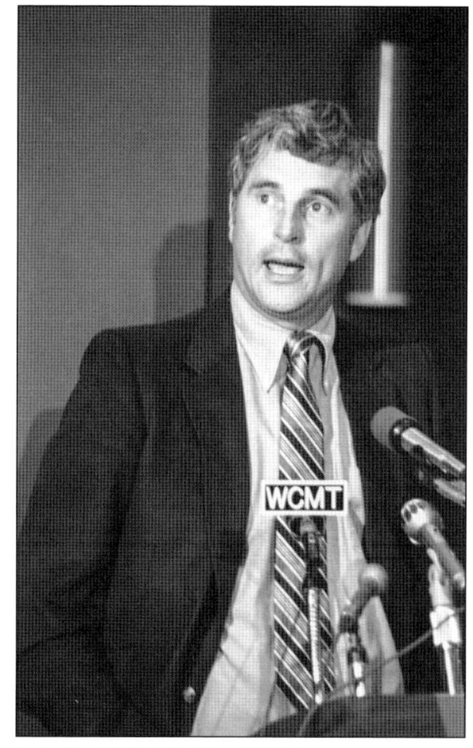

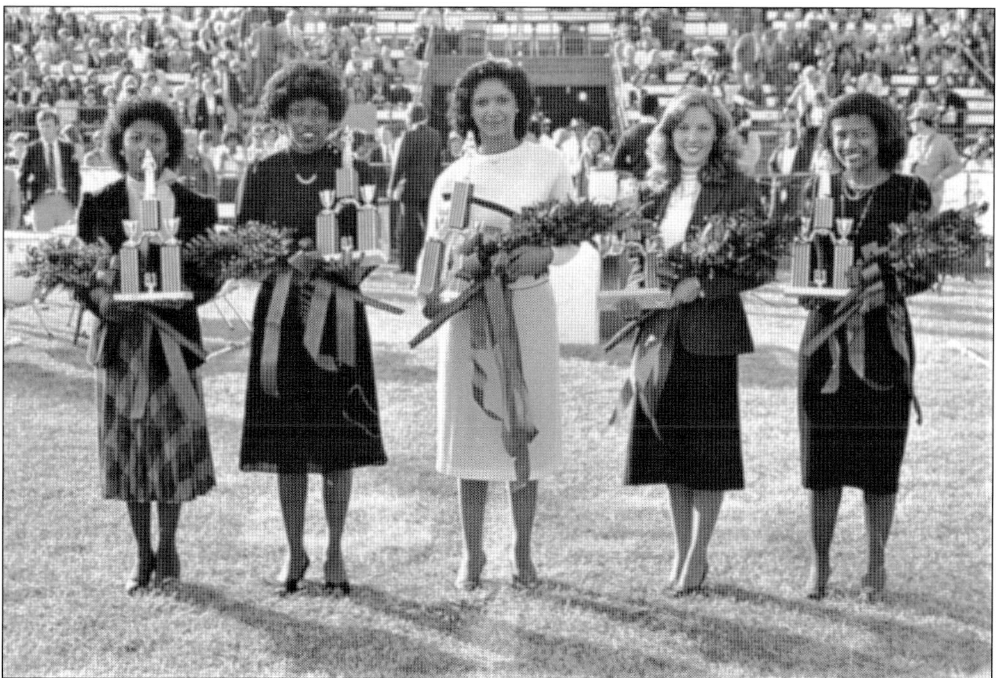

Brenda Brown, a freshman representing Clement Hall, made history in 1981 as UTM's first Black homecoming queen. She was crowned during halftime of the homecoming football game, where UTM secured a 34-25 victory over Delta State. The 1981 homecoming court included, from left to right, Debra Messenger, Debra McCray, Queen Brenda Brown, Dana Barber, and Cheryl Anthony.

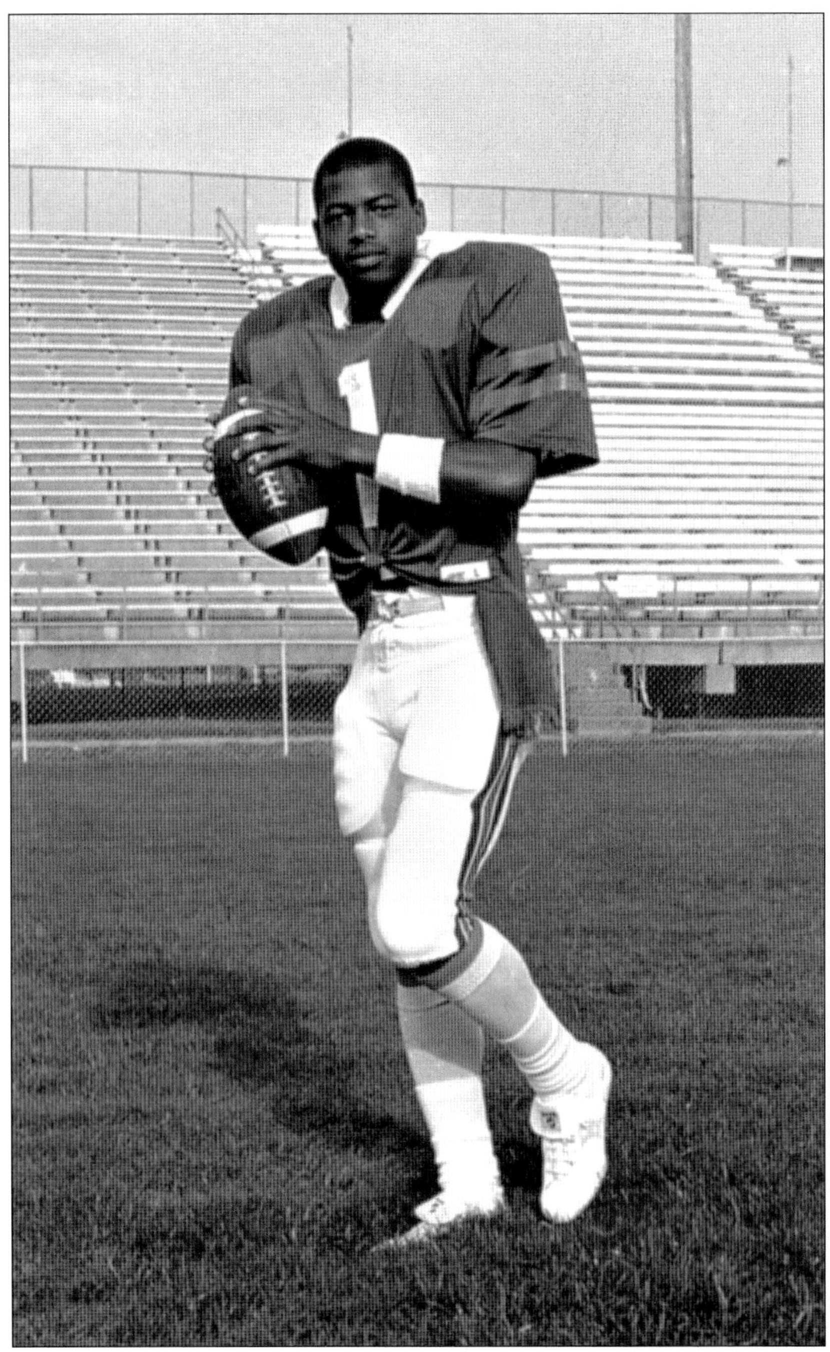

Jerry Reese, from Tiptonville, Tennessee, is a former American football executive, player, and coach, widely recognized for his 23-year career with the New York Giants. He served as the team's general manager from 2007 to 2017, during which he guided the franchise to two Super Bowl victories. He played football and earned his bachelor's degree at UTM, where he gained recognition as one of the university's top defensive backs and earned a reputation as one of the hardest hitters in the Gulf South Conference. During his sophomore year, Reese led the conference in interceptions and was named to the second All-GSC Decade Team for the 1980s. In 2009, Reese was inducted into the Tennessee Sports Hall of Fame.

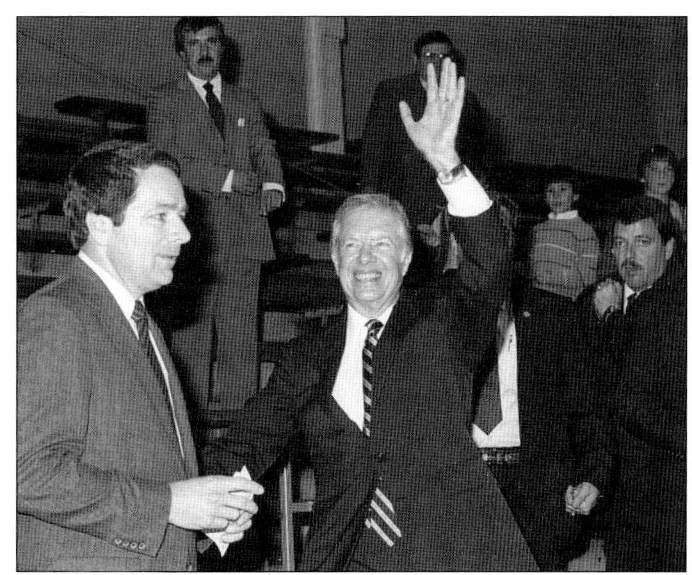

On December 4, 1982, former president Jimmy Carter attended an appreciation dinner held at UTM in honor of Tennessee House Speaker and future governor Ned Ray McWherter. The event welcomed several notable guests, including Gov. Lamar Alexander and Sen. Jim Sasser. A native of Dresden in Weakley County, McWherter was a strong advocate for UTM. His daughter, Dr. Linda Ramsey, also had close ties to the university as a professor of physical education.

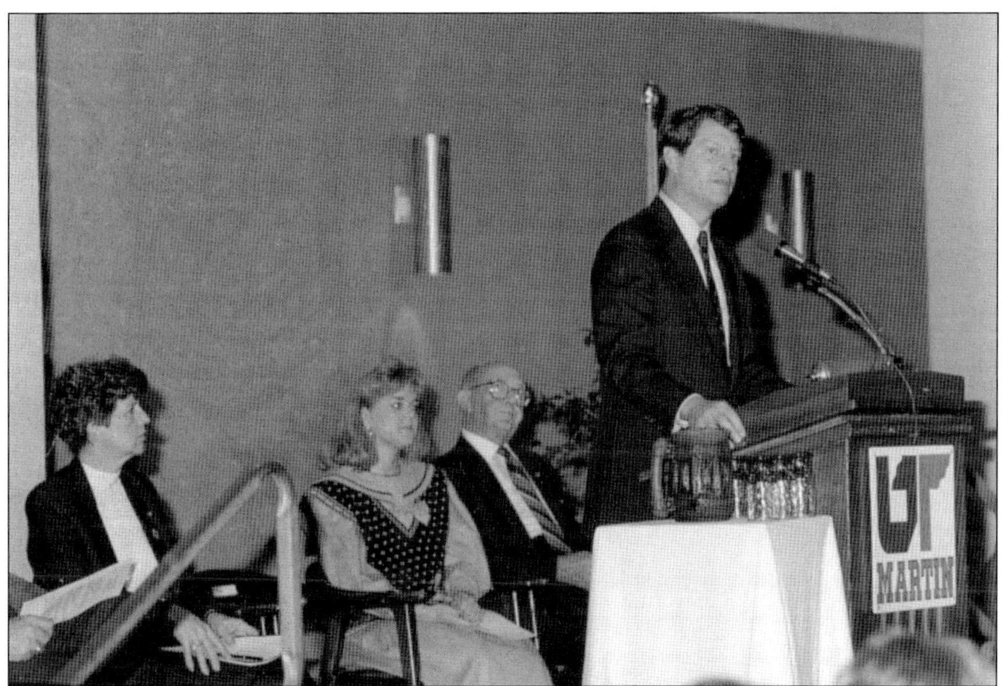

On October 15, 1984, Democratic Senate candidate Albert Gore Jr. visited UTM to speak with students and faculty. Gore, who later served as the 45th vice president of the United States under Pres. Bill Clinton and became a leading environmental advocate, emphasized his commitment to grassroots democracy and promised to hold town meetings across all 95 counties in Tennessee if elected. Accompanied by state campaign coordinator and Congressman Ed Jones, Gore shared his personal ties to the region, noting his mother's roots in Palmersville and his wife Tipper's family ties to Martin. Pictured here, Gore spoke about his dedication to UTM's growth and addressed key issues such as the Equal Rights Amendment, affirmative action, and the national debt. Over his time in Tennessee politics, Gore visited UTM several times. In this photograph, Gore speaks during an event on November 27, 1989.

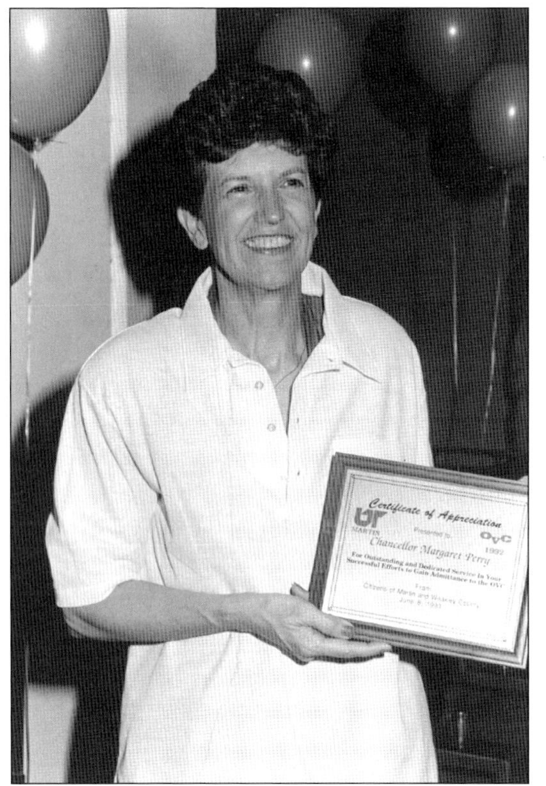

Dr. Margaret N. Perry served as the sixth chancellor of UTM from 1986 to 1997 and was the first woman in an executive role within the UT System and at any four-year public university in Tennessee. A Waynesboro native born in 1940, she earned three degrees in home economics and nutrition from UT. She guided UTM through late-1980s financial challenges and 1990s expansion, overseeing campus improvements, academic growth, Division I athletics, and the Skyhawks mascot rebranding. Known for her student-centered leadership, Perry was named chancellor emeritus upon retiring after 11 years of distinguished service.

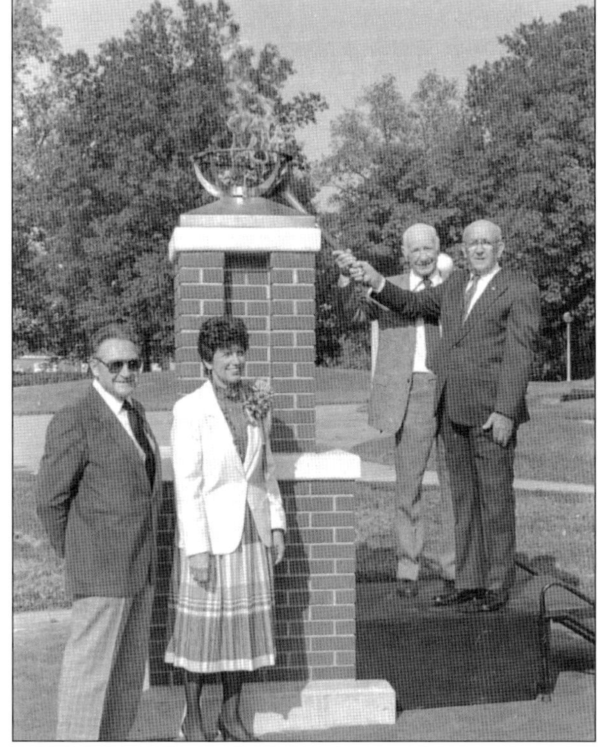

UTM's "eternal flame" was first lit in 1986 during a UT National Alumni Association ceremony honoring the three UT campuses. Installed outside the Paul Meek Library after a torch relay across Tennessee, the flame—carried by UTM professor Phil Davis—became a campus landmark. In 2000, chancellor Phillip Conn had the flame removed. After Conn's departure, staff members Larry Holder, Karen Elmore, and Tim Nipp recovered parts of the flame and began restoration efforts. With support from chancellors Nick Dunagan and Tom Rakes, a permanent indoor tribute featuring the original torch and bowl was installed in the library in 2007.

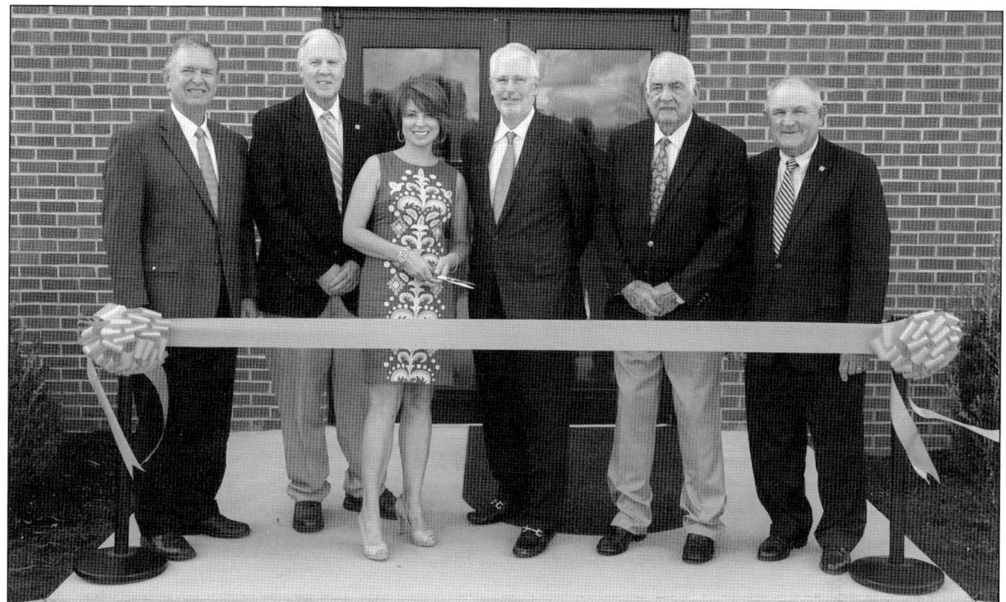

A standout on the UTM golf team and 1987 Academic All-American, Bill Rhodes (center) combined athletic discipline with academic achievement to build a successful business career. A Memphis native and four-year letterman, he captained the Pacers as a senior and earned honorable mention All-America honors before earning an accounting degree. After completing his master of business administration at the University of Memphis, he joined Ernst & Young and later rose at AutoZone, becoming the youngest CEO of a Fortune 500 company at age 39. Rhodes, who stepped down in 2024, credits UTM and mentors like coach Grover Page for shaping his values.

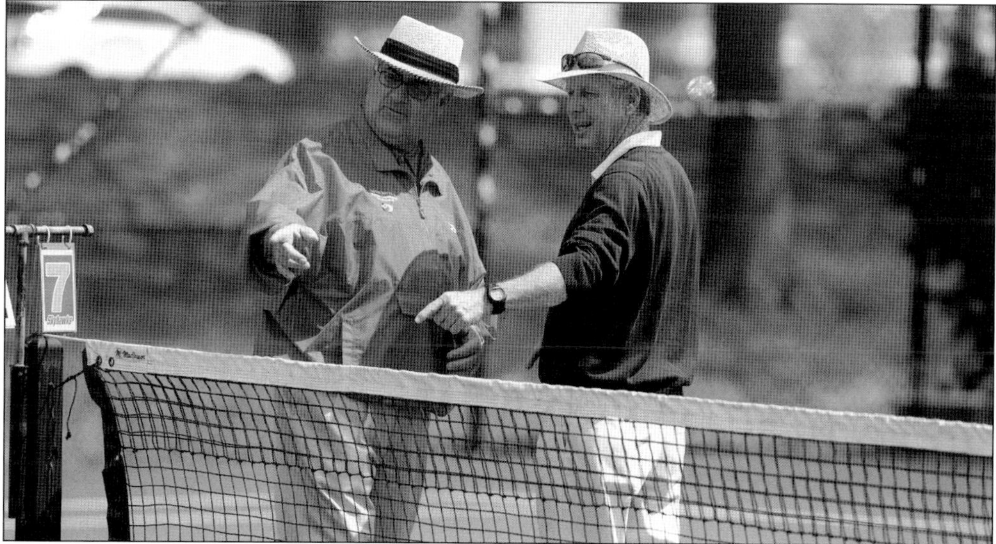

Dennis Taylor led UTM women's tennis from 1987 to 2019, earning 535 wins and a record seven Ohio Valley Conference (OVC) Coach of the Year awards. A UTM alum, he guided the Skyhawks to nine conference titles and their first NCAA Regional appearance in 2005. Taylor prioritized academics—his teams often posted GPAs above 3.75—and oversaw major facility upgrades. He coached 13 All-Americans and 74 all-conference players. Inducted into the UTM Athletics Hall of Fame in 2021, Taylor retired as one of NCAA Division I's winningest women's tennis coaches.

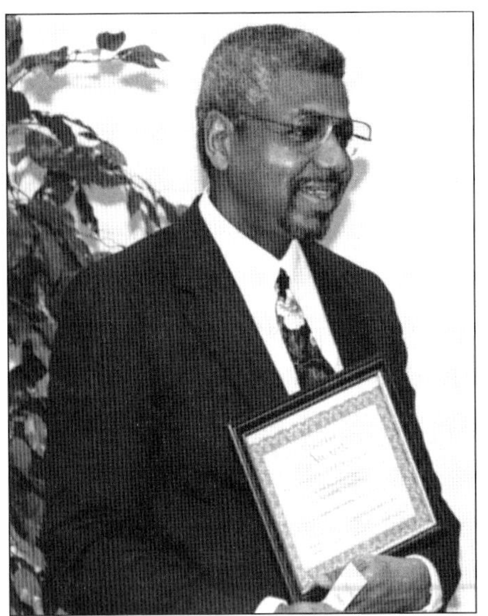

In 1988, Frank Black made history as the first African American to serve as UTM's vice chancellor for academic affairs. Before his appointment, he held academic leadership roles at several universities, including Jackson State University, the University of South Florida, and Murray State University. As vice chancellor, he acted as UTM's chief academic officer, overseeing faculty leadership, curriculum development, academic planning, and budget management. Black stepped down from the position in 1994 to join UTM's School of Education as a faculty member. He later returned to his former role on an interim basis in the year 2000.

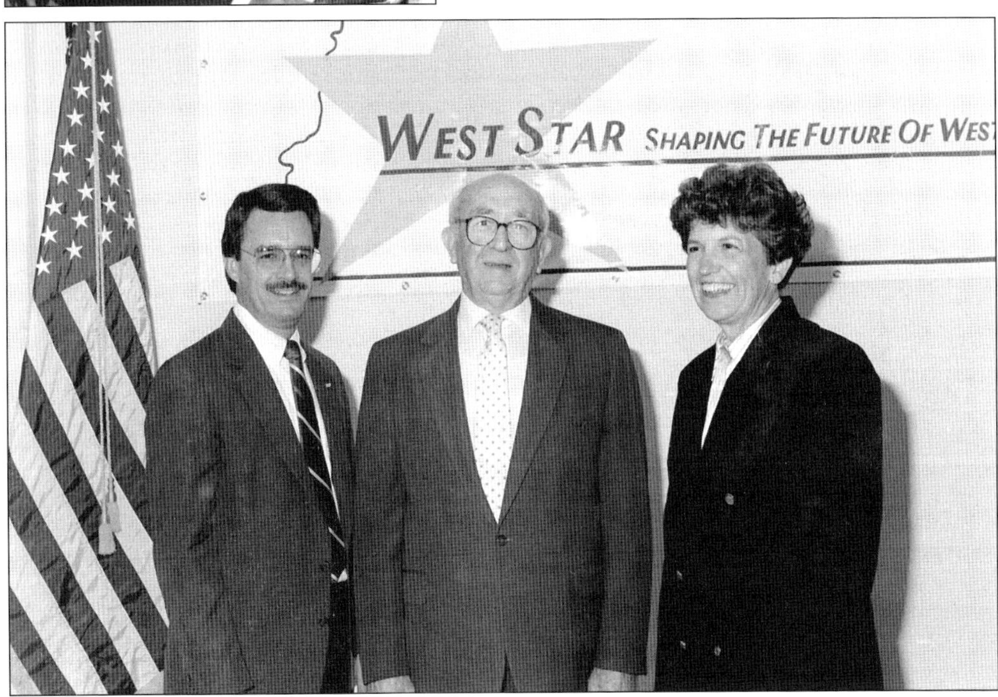

Founded in 1989 by Dr. Robert Smith, Dr. Nick Dunagan, and Dr. Charles Smith, the WestStar Leadership Program is Tennessee's oldest and largest regional leadership initiative, based at UTM. In 2024, the program celebrated 35 years of developing leaders across 21 counties in West Tennessee, with more than 900 graduates since its founding. WestStar's first executive director was Dr. Robert Smith, followed by Dr. Nick Dunagan, with longtime coordinator Virginia Grimes providing over three decades of steady leadership and support. Grimes was honored with a retirement reception in 2024, recognizing her 34 years of service and deep commitment to the program's success. Her professionalism, warmth, and dedication helped shape WestStar into a respected force for regional leadership and community development. Pictured from left to right on October 26, 1989, at a WestStar event are Dr. Robert Smith, Congressman Ed Jones, and Dr. Margaret Perry.

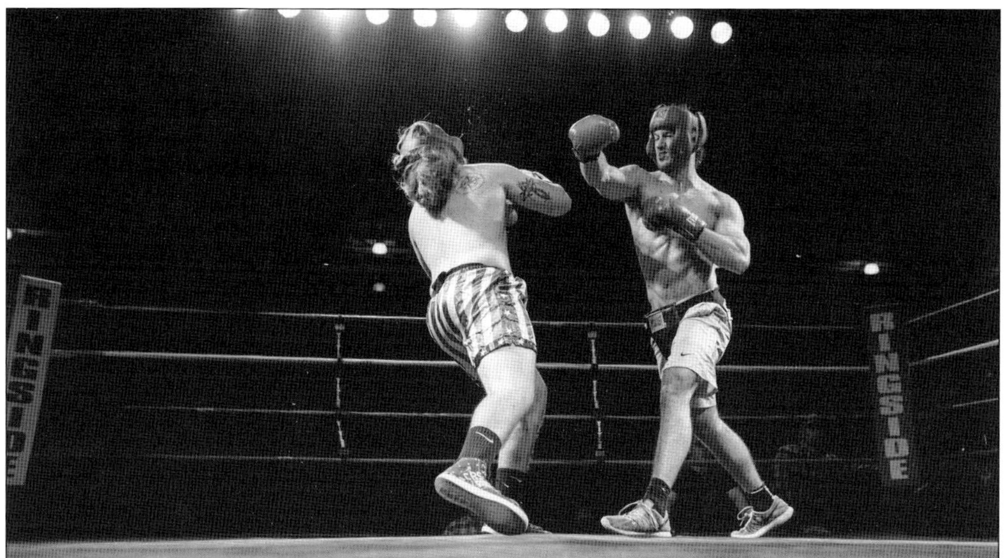

First held in spring 1990, Pike Fights is an annual boxing exhibition hosted by the Pi Kappa Alpha fraternity at UTM, featuring fraternity members from across West Tennessee who box to raise money for charity. Modeled after an event at Middle Tennessee State University, the first fight overcame last-minute hurdles and sparked a tradition. Though originally held on campus, recent events, such as the 2023 Craig Long Memorial Pike Fights in Dresden, Tennessee, continue to draw large crowds. Fighters compete in three one-minute rounds, judged by licensed officials. Safety is emphasized with weight classes, medical staff, and longtime referee Chris Edlin, who has officiated every bout. Renamed in 2007 to honor Craig Long, the event has raised over $200,000 for various charitable causes.

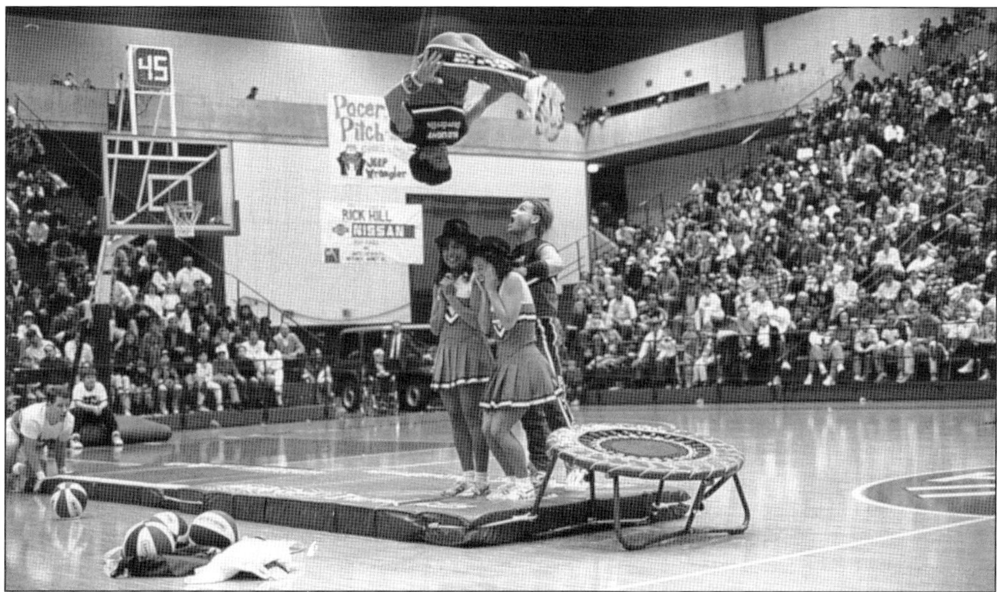

With quiet determination and a unified campus effort, UTM achieved NCAA Division I status and joined the Ohio Valley Conference in 1992. Led by chancellor Margaret N. Perry and guided by the slogan "All for One," the university reached key benchmarks, including a basketball attendance goal of 22,000, that had eluded previous efforts for more than two decades. The milestone solidified UTM's place among regional athletic peers and marked a new era in Skyhawk sports.

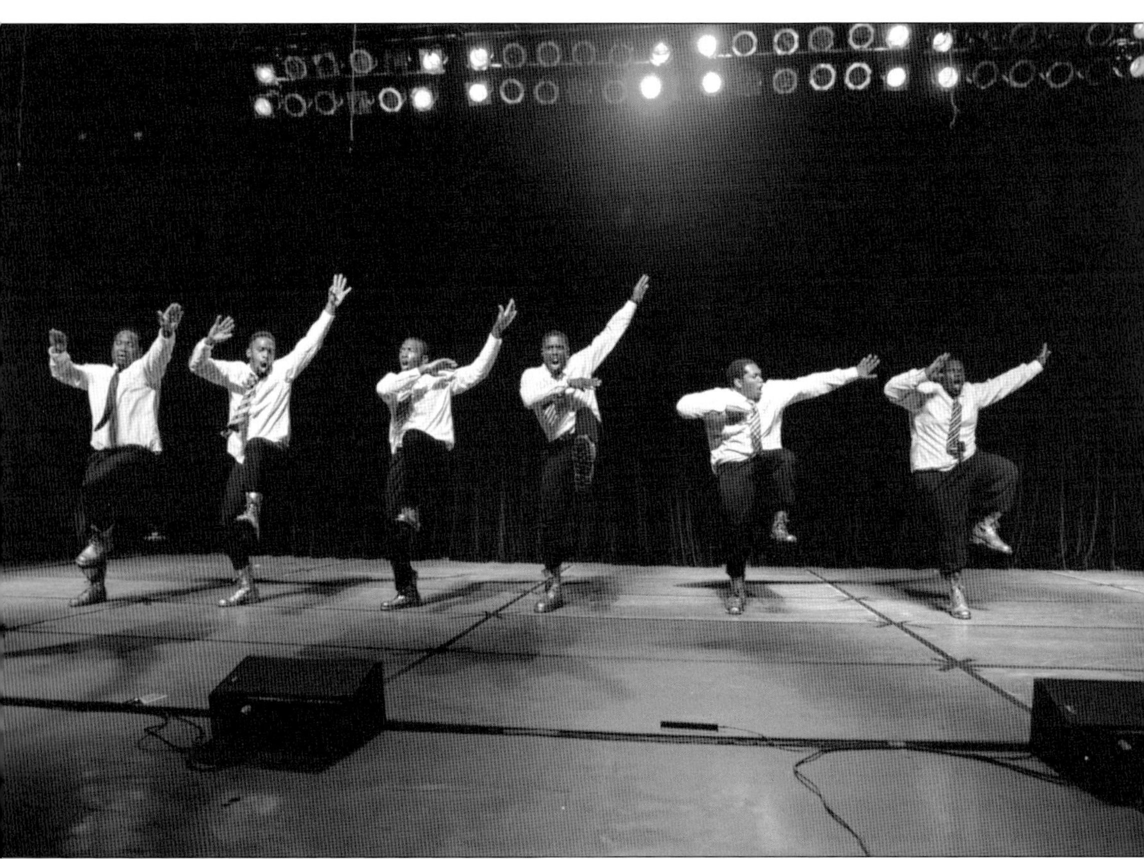

A signature event during Homecoming, UTM's Step Show showcases the artistry, tradition, and competitive spirit of NPHC fraternities and sororities. Rooted in African and African American cultural expression, stepping blends percussive footwork, body percussion, and synchronized choreography into electrifying performances. The 1994 Greek Show drew nearly 3,000 spectators to Pacer Arena and marked the first time a non-National Pan-Hellenic Council, Kappa Alpha Order, joined the competition. Beyond entertainment, the event supports philanthropic causes and celebrates unity, creativity, and cultural pride on campus. Pictured are members of Omega Psi Phi performing at Step Show in 2017.

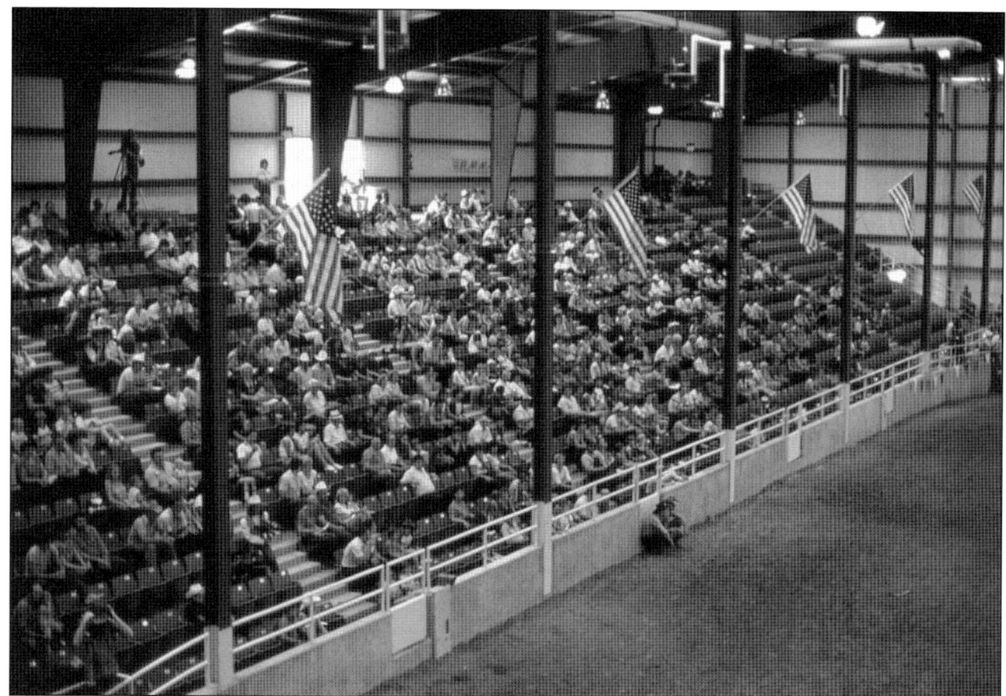

Completed in May 1984, the West Tennessee Agricultural Pavilion was designed to serve UTM and the region's farming community. The 82,000-square-foot facility featured a 24,000-square-foot arena with seating for 3,000, along with animal holding and grooming areas. A 150-stall barn was added in 1989. The pavilion quickly became a center for teaching, research, and public events. Leaders such as chancellor Charles Smith, UT vice president W.W. Armistead, and Speaker Ned Ray McWherter hailed it as a major step forward. McWherter called it "a dream come true" for its cultural and educational impact on West Tennessee.

In 1995, the facility and its surrounding structures were renamed the Ned McWherter Agricultural Complex, honoring the former governor's strong support for UTM and rural West Tennessee. The renaming also reflected McWherter's contributions to agricultural improvements, including new stalling facilities and plans for a swine and feed grain research center. At a dedication before the UTM Rodeo, chancellor Margaret Perry and UT president Joseph Johnson praised McWherter's impact, while McWherter credited the late Dr. Neils "Doc" Robinson as his inspiration. McWherter recalled Robinson saying the pavilion would be "like the performing arts center to New York City."

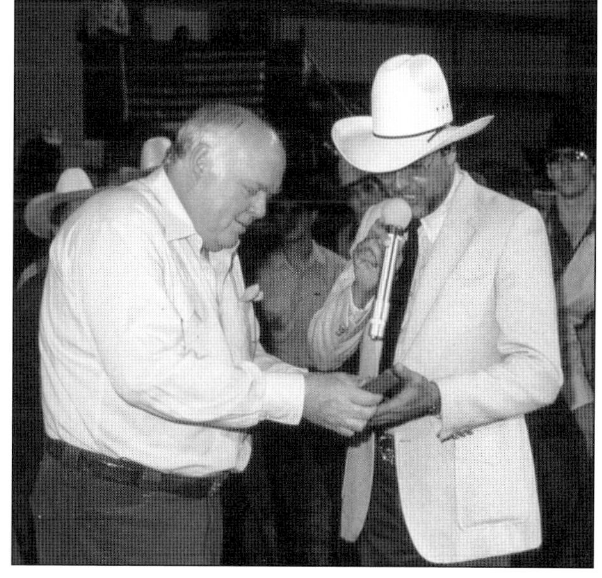

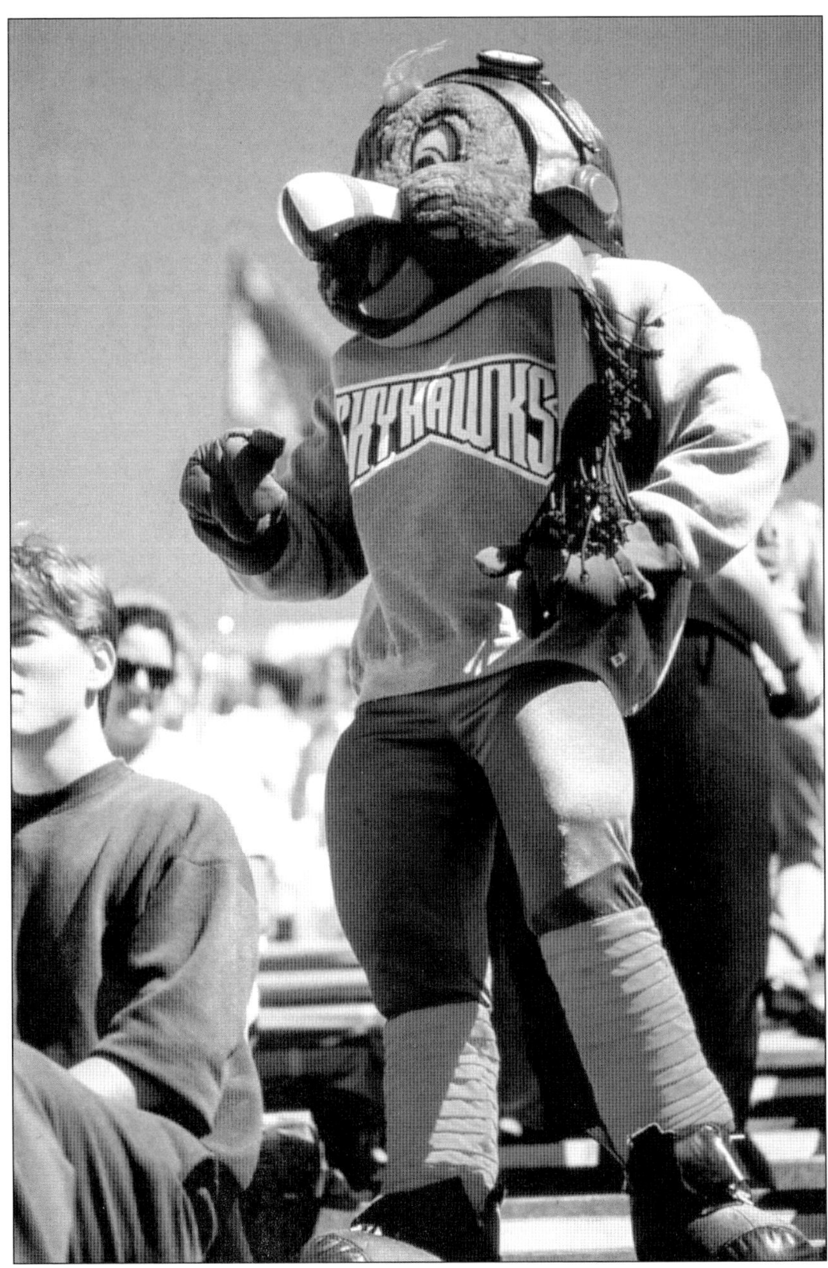

Captain is the official name of UTM's costumed Skyhawk mascot. The name was chosen for its gender neutrality and its alignment with the image of a mythical hawk that pilots an aircraft. UTM adopted the Skyhawks as its official mascot in 1995, selecting the name from several options to reflect key aspects of the university's history. The Skyhawk name connects to UTM's past in three distinct ways; firstly, the original institution on the site, Hall-Moody Institute, had athletic teams known as the "sky pilots"—a term once used to describe preachers, though students may also have been inspired by World War I flying aces. Secondly, during World War II, UTJC partnered with the Naval War Training Service to train pilots, with flight instruction taking place at an airport now occupied by Westview High School. Finally, the red-tailed hawk, a bird native to western Tennessee, provides a natural and regional tie to the Skyhawk identity.

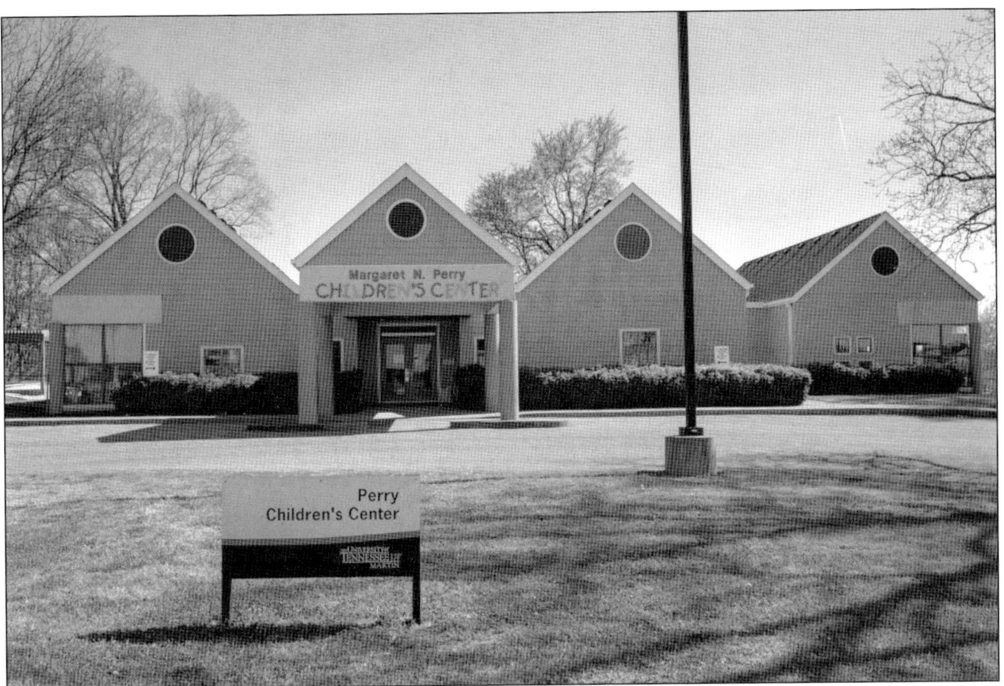

The increasing number of nontraditional students and student-parents led to a growing need for on-site childcare. In response, the Children's Center was built to fulfill that need. Completed in 1993, the 9,400-square-foot facility now serves as a day care center, preschool, and school for children with special needs. In 1998, it was named in honor of alumna and retiring chancellor Margaret N. Perry. In the photograph below, Joseph E. Johnson (center), UT System president, and his wife, Pat, review blueprints of the Children's Center with Chancellor Perry during a visit to the construction site.

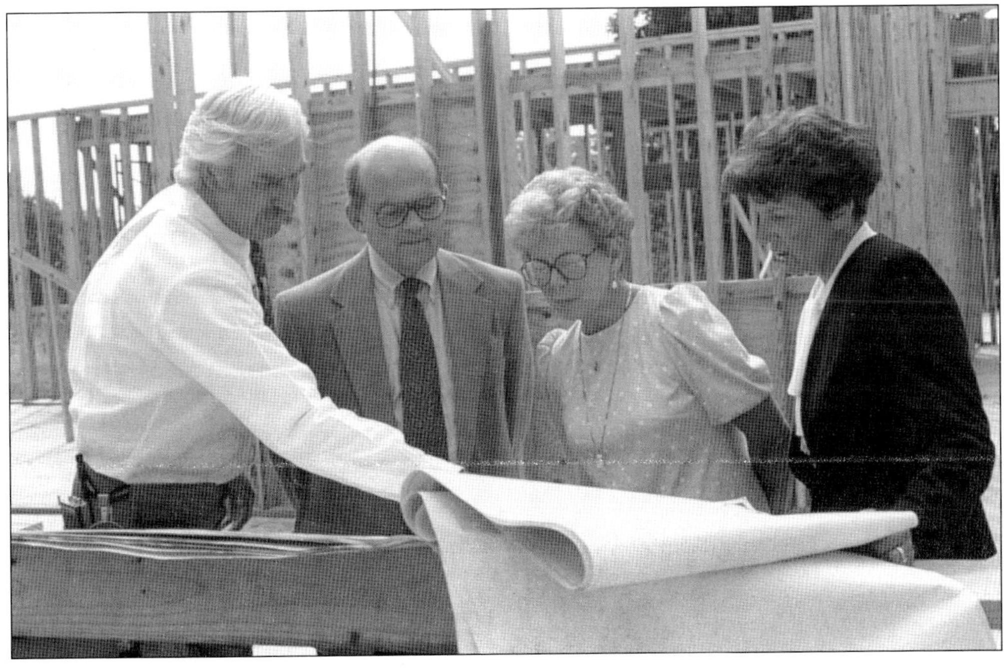

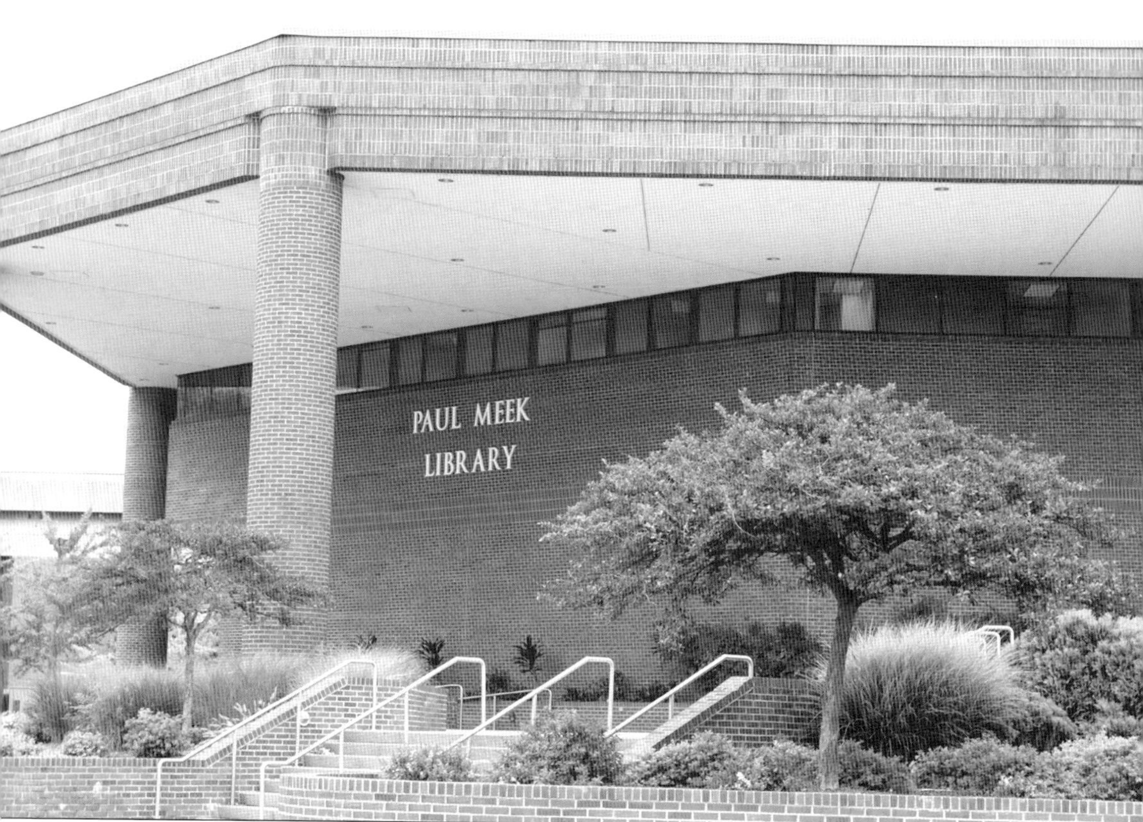

By the 1990s, the original Paul Meek Library had reached full capacity and was suffering from significant environmental issues that could not be remedied. Although the legislature declined to approve funding for a completely new facility, they did authorize a "retrofit" project. During the summer of 1993, the building was vacated, with collections and offices temporarily relocated to Clement Hall. The structure was then stripped down to just its concrete pad and support columns. Reconstruction was completed by the summer of 1995. The renovated library, now over 120,000 square feet—twice its original size—featured all the modern amenities required for a university research center, including a newly established special collections department.

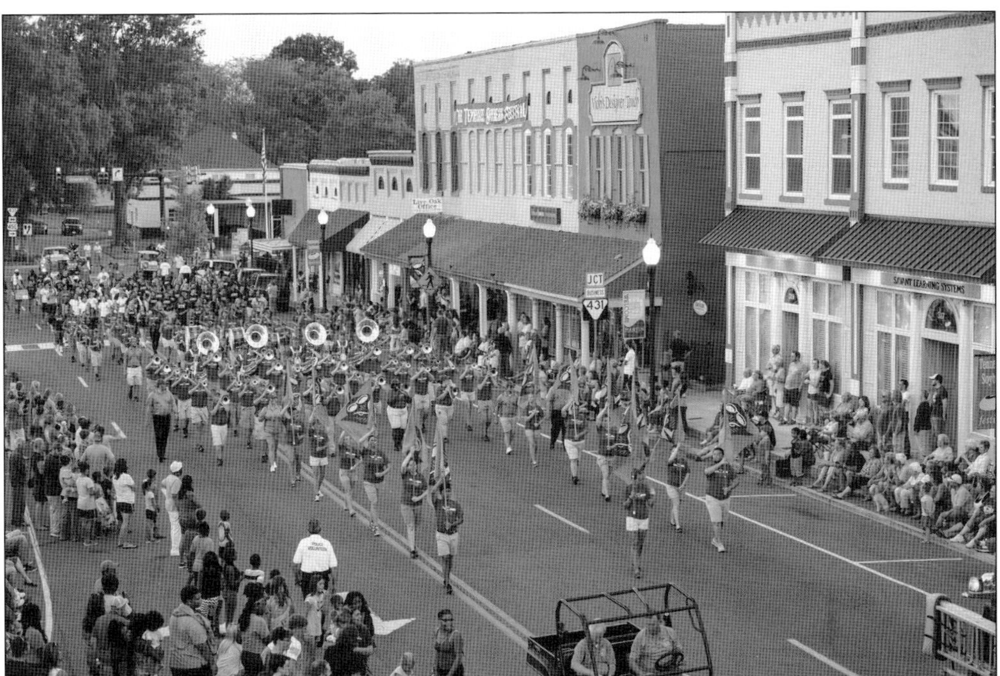

First held September 6–11, 1994, in Martin, the Tennessee Soybean Festival has grown into a beloved community tradition. Celebrating Weakley County's signature crop, the festival honors local soybean farmers while offering a wide variety of activities for all ages. Each year during the first week of September, UTM partners with the city to transform historic downtown Martin into a vibrant celebration filled with sideshows, carnival rides, live music, food and street vendors, art exhibits, a community barbecue cook-off, a parade, and more. The inaugural festival, held on the UTM campus, featured country music stars Tim McGraw and Suzy Bogguss during McGraw's Not a Moment Too Soon tour. Sponsored by the Soybean Producers of Tennessee, the City of Martin, and UTM, the first festival also introduced popular events such as the Prayer Breakfast, a community parade, youth field days, a wildlife expo, the Mayor's Luncheon, a downtown barbecue cook-off, and UTM Parents' Day.

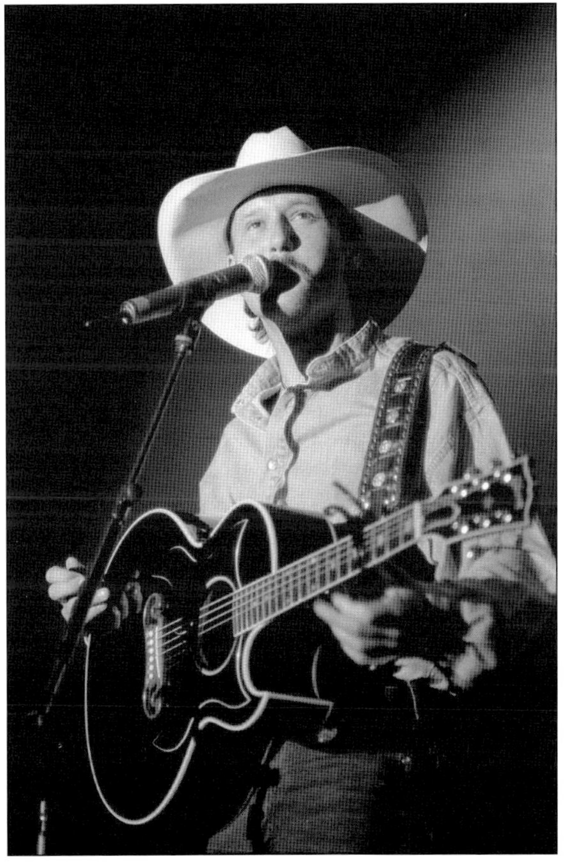

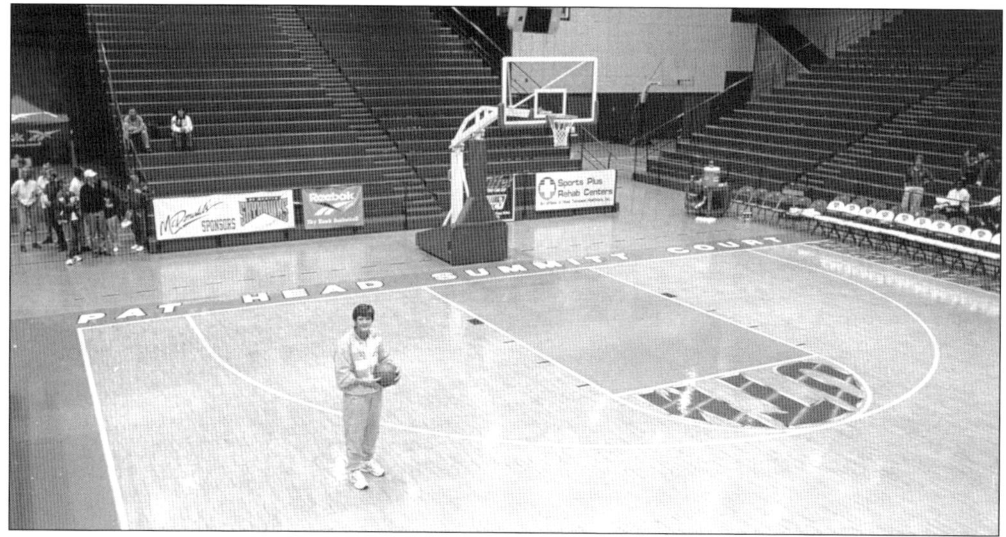

Pat Head Summitt returned to her alma mater on November 23, 1997, for a weekend of honors that included the naming of Pat Head Summitt Court inside the Skyhawk Arena at UTM. The legendary Lady Vols coach and former UTM star player led her Tennessee team to a 73-32 victory that day, christening the newly named court. The university also designated a campus street in her honor, joining her high school gym and UT Knoxville's Thompson-Boling Arena court—"the Summitt"—as lasting tributes. Summitt remains the only person with two active Division I basketball courts named after her.

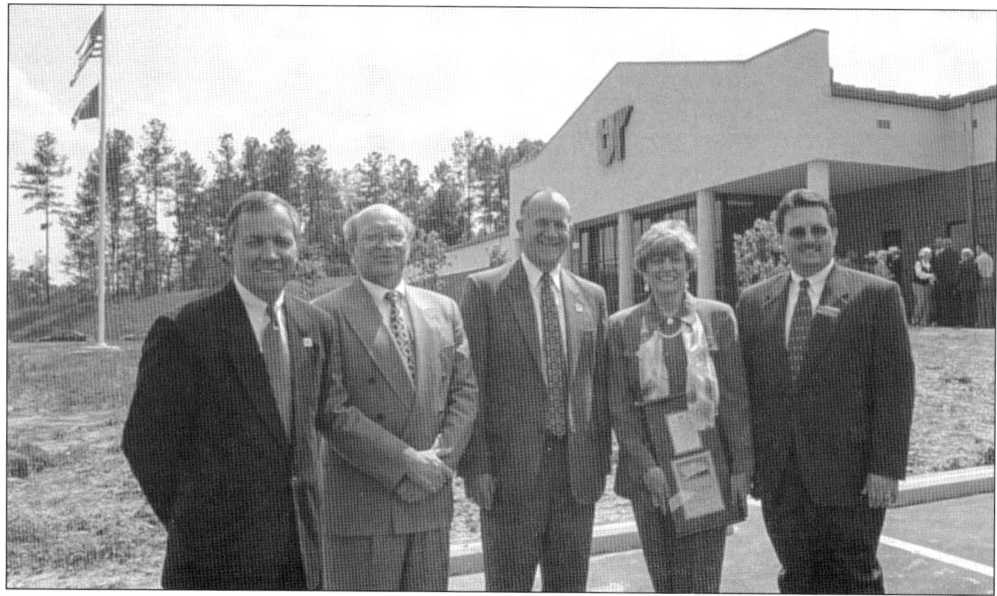

UTM has extended its reach across West and Middle Tennessee through a growing network of regional centers that bring higher education closer to home. The first center opened in 1998 in Selmer, thanks to a local partnership that included scholarship support and a commitment to workforce development. Since then, centers have been established in Parsons, Ripley, Jackson, Somerville, and most recently, Springfield. These centers offer more than 80 bachelor-level programs and select graduate programs, serving as vital hubs for rural and nontraditional students. "UTM is proud to partner with communities across the state to provide access to a highly acclaimed degree program and educational experience," said chancellor Yancy Freeman.

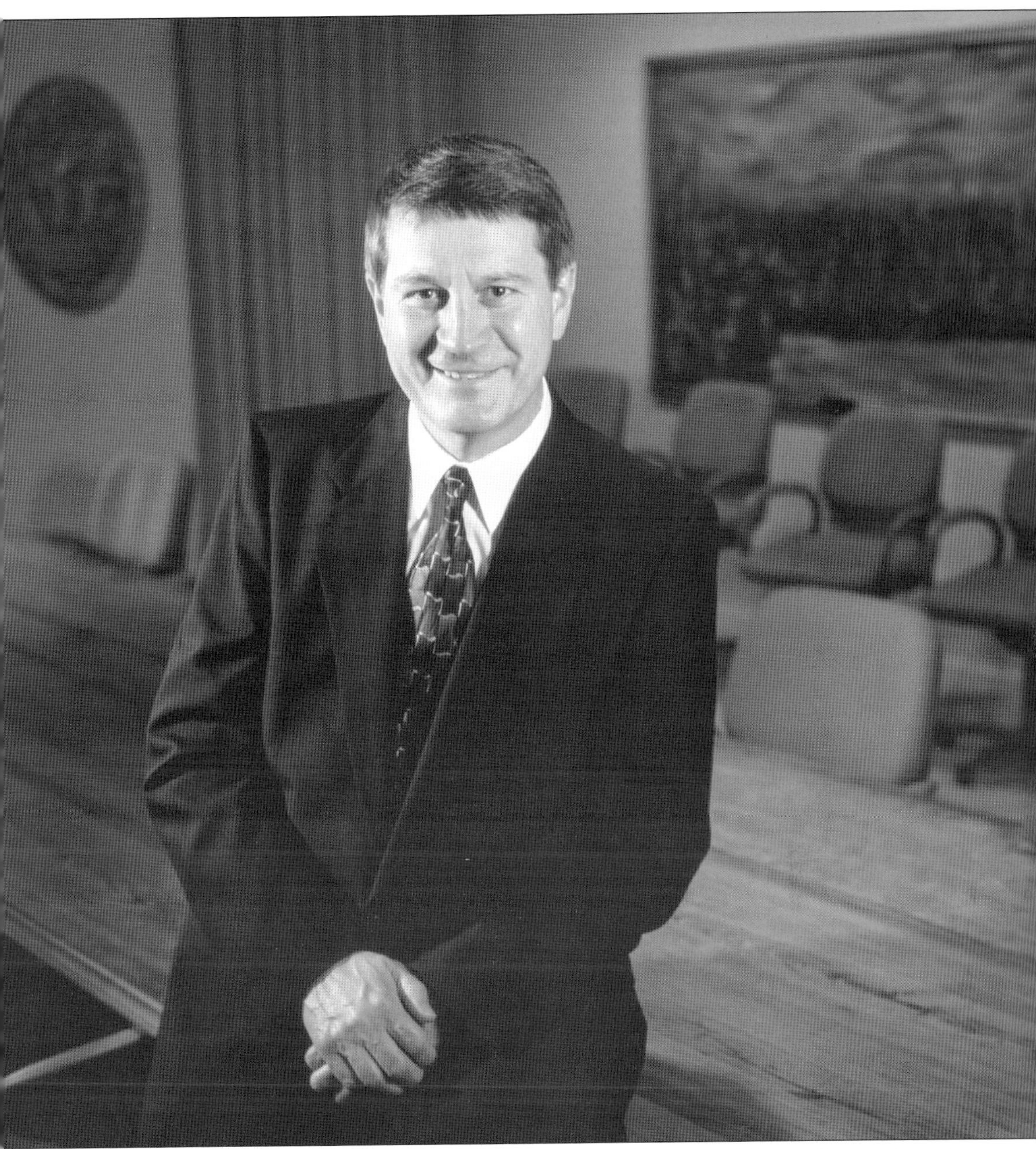

Dr. Phillip W. Conn became the seventh UTM chancellor in 1998, following Dr. Margaret Perry, and served until 2000. He began his career after completing graduate work at UT Knoxville, starting as a research specialist and later serving as executive director of the Kentucky Legislative Research Commission. By 1977, he had advanced to vice president of research and development, and he earned a doctorate in public administration from the University of Southern California in 1991. In 1994, Conn became president of Dickinson State University in North Dakota, a position he held for four years before accepting the chancellorship at UTM. Following his impactful tenure at UTM, he briefly served in the UT System before becoming president of Western Oregon University, where he worked until retiring in 2005.

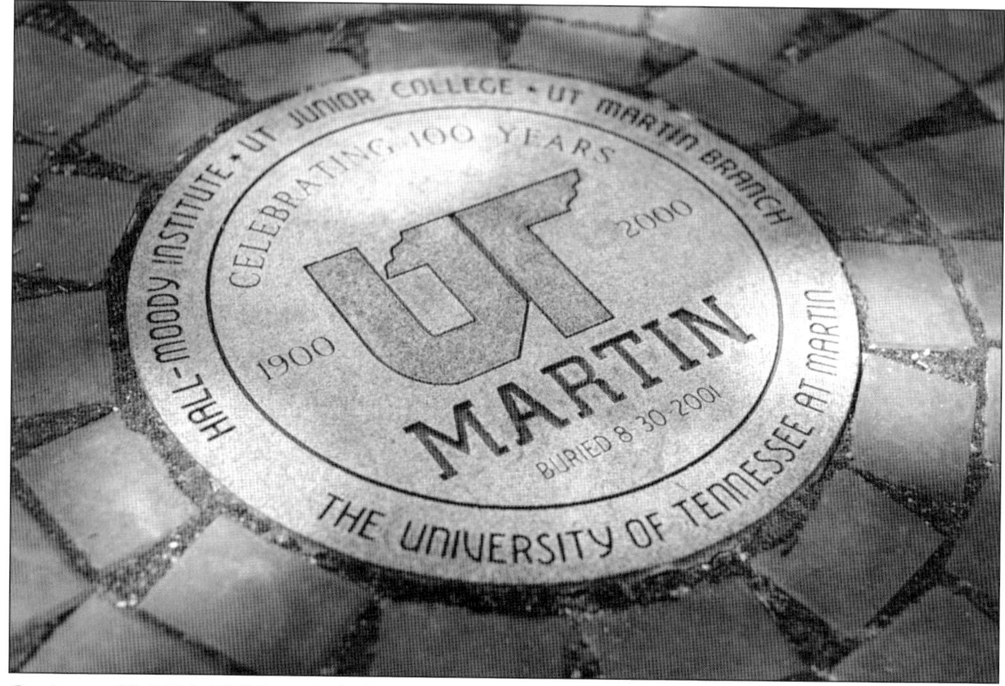

On August 30, 2001, UTM concluded its yearlong centennial celebration with a formal ceremony, burying a time capsule in Centennial Court, located in the campus quadrangle. The capsule is scheduled to be unearthed during the university's sesquicentennial celebration. Inside the capsule are items representing campus life at the time, including a UTM student's backpack filled with textbooks and class notes, a compact disc player with various CDs, a UTM yearbook, photographs of the community, a replica of the Hall-Moody Administration Building, and a scroll containing messages from students, faculty, and community members.

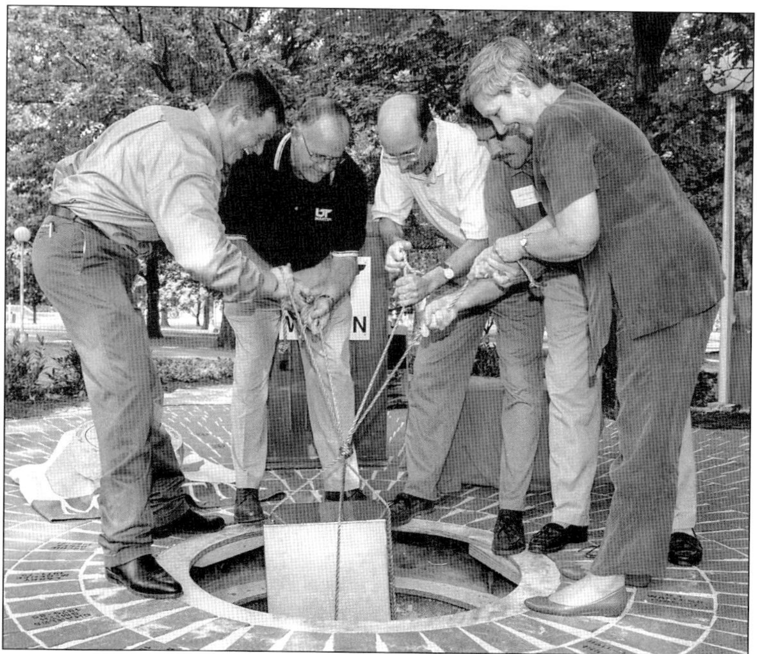

Lowering the time capsule are, from left to right, SGA president Clint Young, chancellor Nick Dunagan, archivist Richard Saunders, director of alumni affairs Jacky Gullett, and cochair of the centennial celebration and professor Dr. Kay Durden.

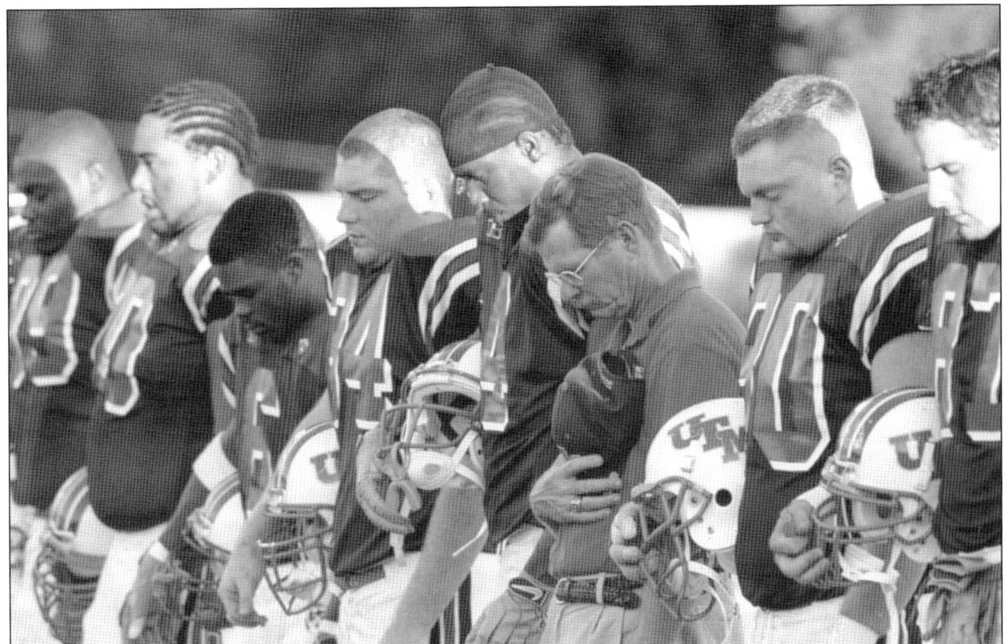

In September 2001, UTM faced a difficult choice following the terrorist attacks on September 11 in New York; Washington, DC; and Pennsylvania. The Skyhawks were scheduled to play Kentucky Wesleyan that Thursday night, September 13. While most collegiate and professional sports paused for a week, UTM's game was among the few played that week. According to former UTM athletic director Phil Dane, a conference call with Ohio Valley Conference athletic directors led to the decision. They agreed to follow Pres. George W. Bush's advice to continue daily life and prevent the terrorists from winning. Dane emphasized it was not a grand statement but simply because both teams were prepared. The Skyhawk team prayed before the game started, underscoring the solemn mood.

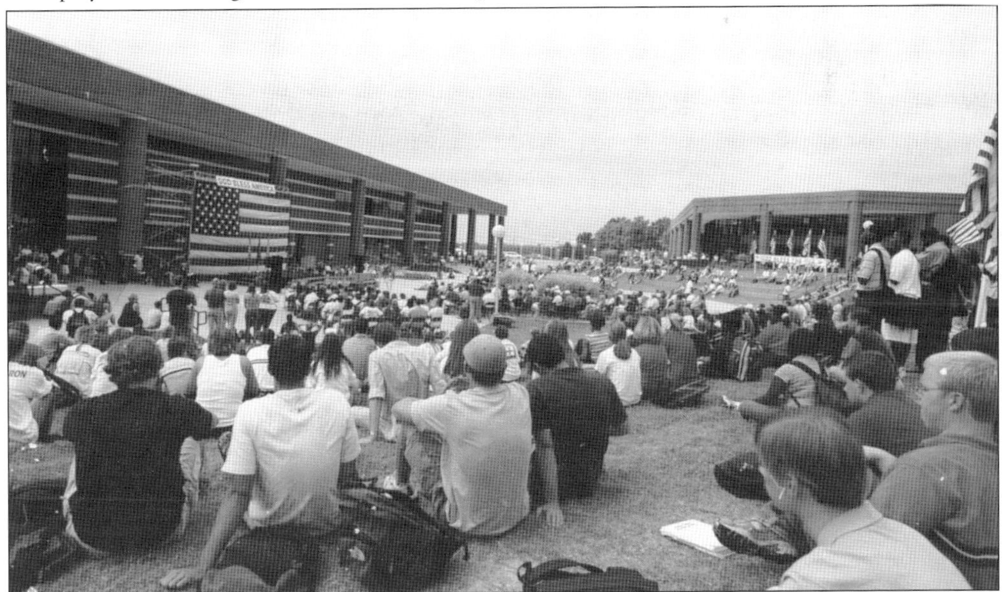

Students, faculty, and staff gather outside of the Dr. Edward J. and Carolyn P. Boling University Center (left) in 2002 to commemorate the one-year anniversary of the September 11 terrorist attacks of 2001.

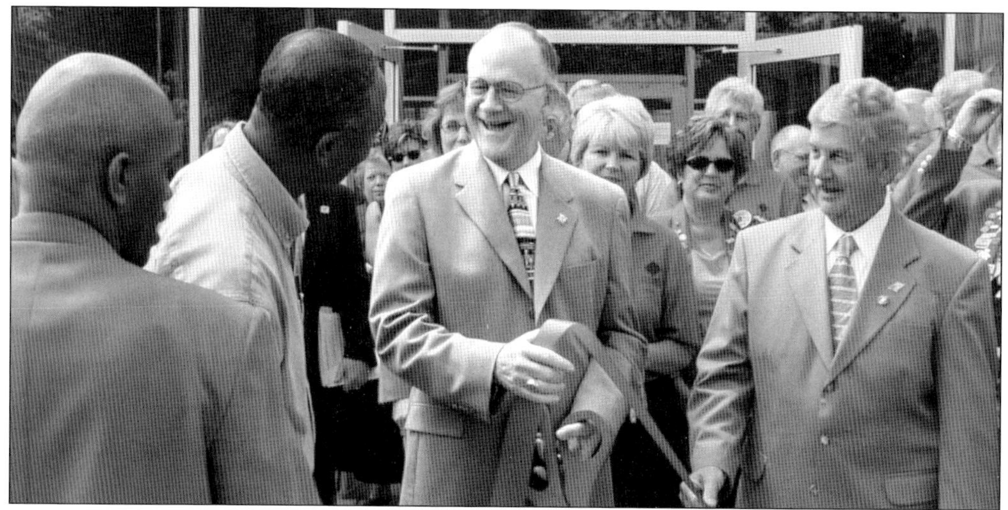

Dr. Nick Dunagan served as UTM's eighth chancellor from 2001 to 2007, capping a long and distinguished career that began in 1973. Over the decades, he held several key leadership roles and was instrumental in founding the WestStar Leadership Program, the state's oldest regional leadership initiative. A 1968 UTM graduate, Dunagan earned a law degree and a doctorate in higher education and served as a colonel in the Tennessee Army National Guard. He remains an active leader in the Martin community, especially in economic development and public service. He and his wife, Cathy, a fellow UTM alum, raised four children, all of whom share ties to the university.

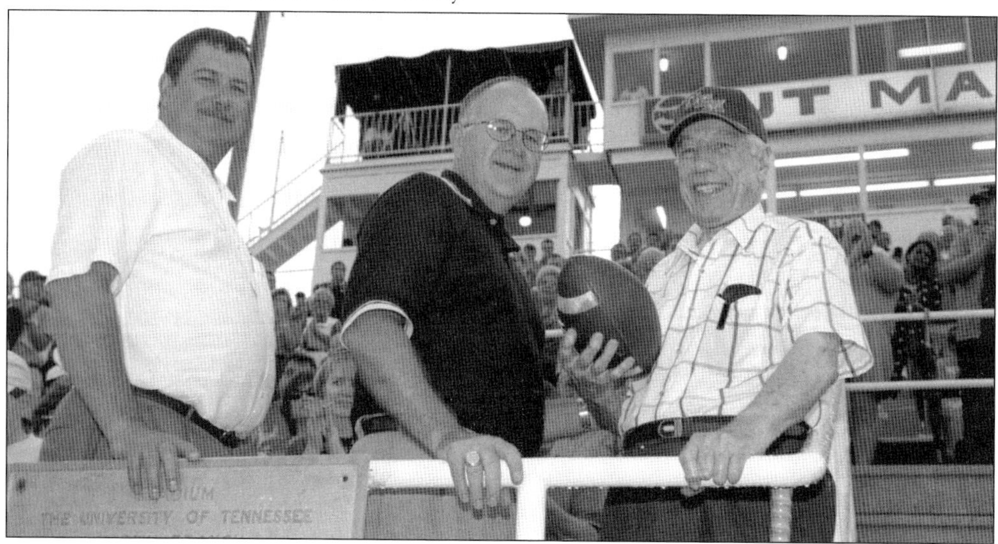

Hardy M. Graham Stadium has served as the home of UTM football for over 80 years, with a legacy that includes being one of the first lighted stadiums in West Tennessee. The playing surface, H.K. Grantham Field, was named in 1974 in honor of longtime coach and athletics director H.K. Grantham, and in 2001, the stadium itself was named for donor and supporter Hardy M. Graham. On September 17, 2016, university and community leaders gathered to dedicate a new four-story press box and academic facility on the west side of the stadium. The 20,000-square-foot addition includes a modern press level, club seating, an academic support space for the College of Agriculture and Applied Sciences, and a renovated visiting team area. Hardy M. Graham (right) is pictured with his son Newell Graham (left), a longtime donor and supporter of UTM academic and athletic programs, and UTM chancellor Nick Dunagan (center).

Photojournalist Ernest Columbus Withers Sr. speaks to a crowd in the Boling University Center's Watkins Auditorium during UTM's first-ever Civil Rights Conference titled "At the River I Stand–The Memphis Sanitation Strike. 1968." The conference was held February 28–March 1, 2001. February 2025 marked the Civil Rights Conference's 25th year of providing notable guest speakers, panels, and activities promoting civil rights and equality.

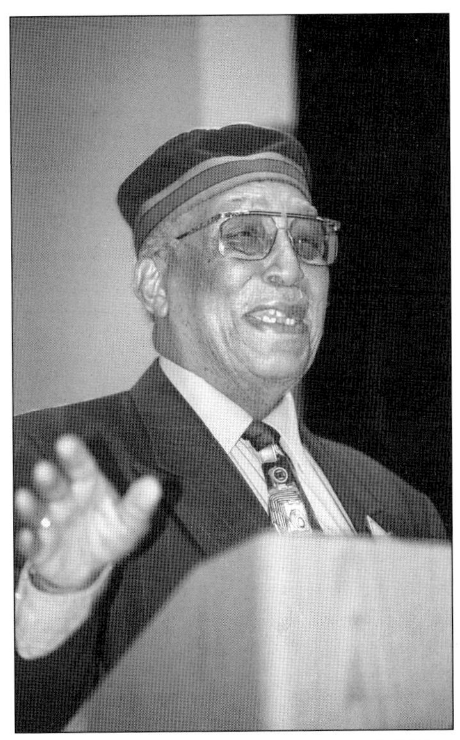

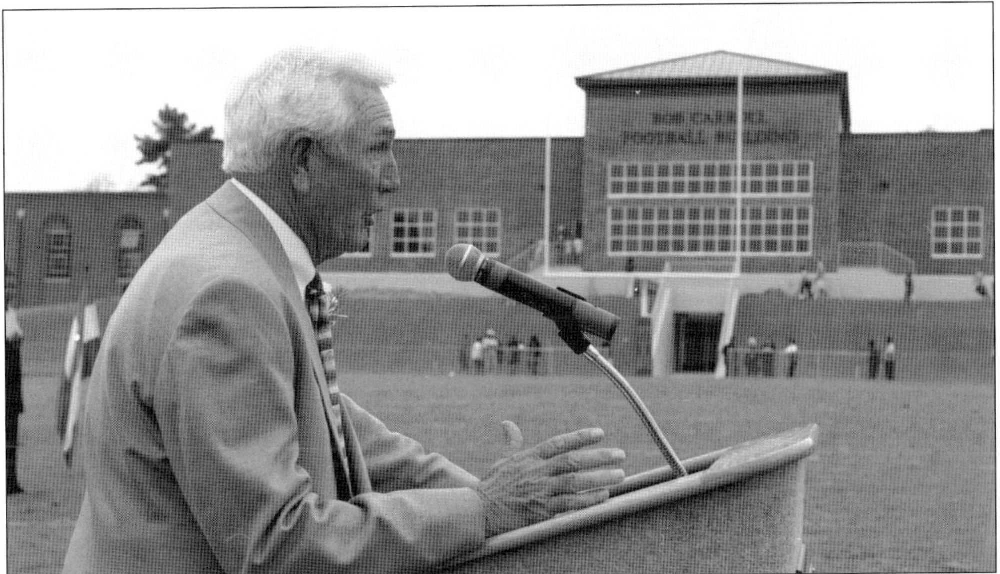

The Bob Carroll Football Building, dedicated on October 12, 2002, during UTM's homecoming game against Southeast Missouri, stands as the home of Skyhawk football. Located in the south end zone of Hardy M. Graham Stadium, the 17,000-square-foot facility includes offices, meeting rooms, a locker room, a training room, an equipment room, and a multipurpose room with a glass wall overlooking the field. Funded largely through private donations to the "Building for the Future" campaign—with major support from Kathleen Elam—the structure honors Bob Carroll's lasting impact on UTM football. "Anytime you think of UTM Football, you think of Bob Carroll," said the late Phil Dane, then director of athletics.

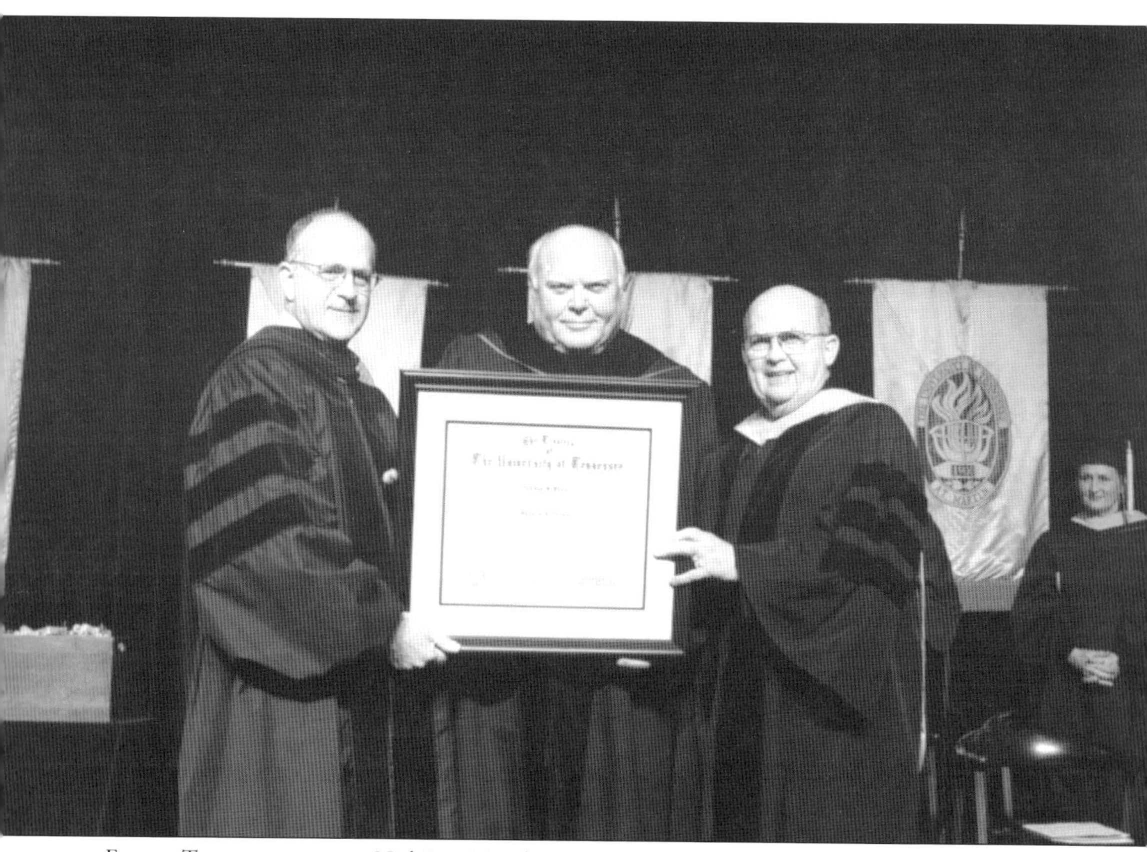

Former Tennessee governor Ned Ray McWherter received the first doctorate of leadership awarded by UTM during the university's fall commencement ceremony, Sunday, December 14, 2003, in the Kathleen and Tom Elam Center. The awarding of the honorary degree was approved June 19, 2003, during the UT Board of Trustees' annual meeting in Memphis at the Peabody Hotel. The degree is the first honorary degree of any kind awarded by UTM and is one of only six granted by the University of Tennessee. McWherter, a native of Weakley County, said the honor is something he will always cherish. "I thank the UT Board of Trustees for this wonderful honor, made even more special in that the degree comes from the university located in my home county," McWherter said before the June board meeting. "I frequently refer to UTM as 'my university,' and after today, that is especially true." Pictured are, from right to left, UTM chancellor Nick Dunagan, McWherter, and UT interim president Joe Johnson.

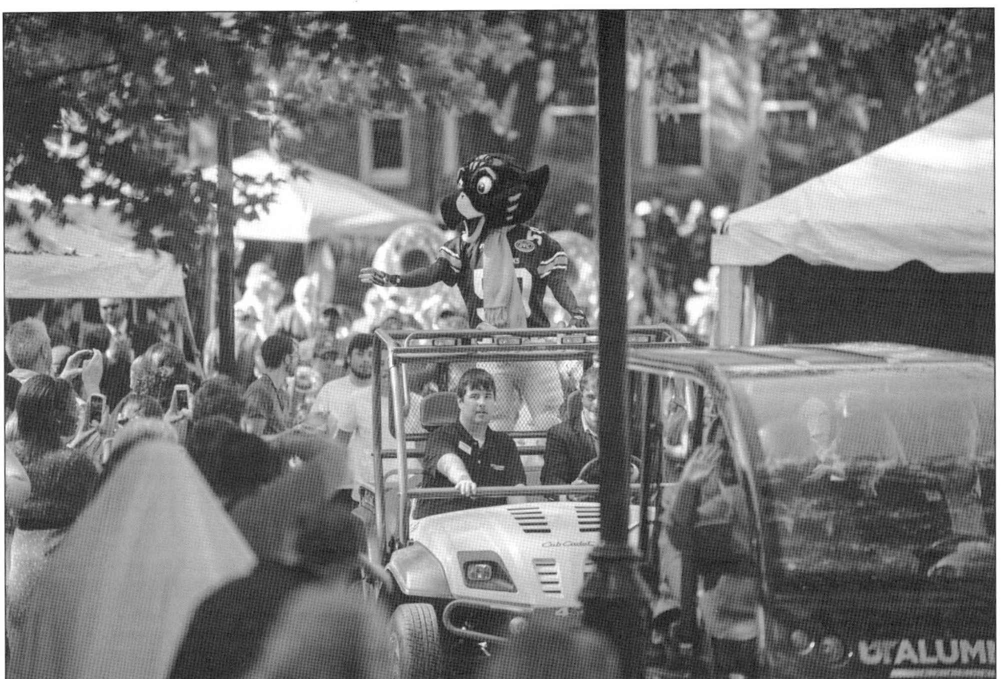

Quad City debuted in 2004 as a new centerpiece of UTM's homecoming, designed to bring alumni, students, and the campus community together in the heart of the quad. While the introduction of Quad City marked the end of the traditional homecoming parade—a beloved tradition dating back to UTJC's era—it offered a fresh, interactive experience with organization tents, live music, family activities, and opportunities for alumni to reconnect across generations. From rock climbing walls and petting zoos to pottery demos and themed reunions, Quad City quickly grew in scale and spirit. More than two decades later, it remains a highlight of homecoming weekend, celebrating the Skyhawk family with energy, tradition, and community pride.

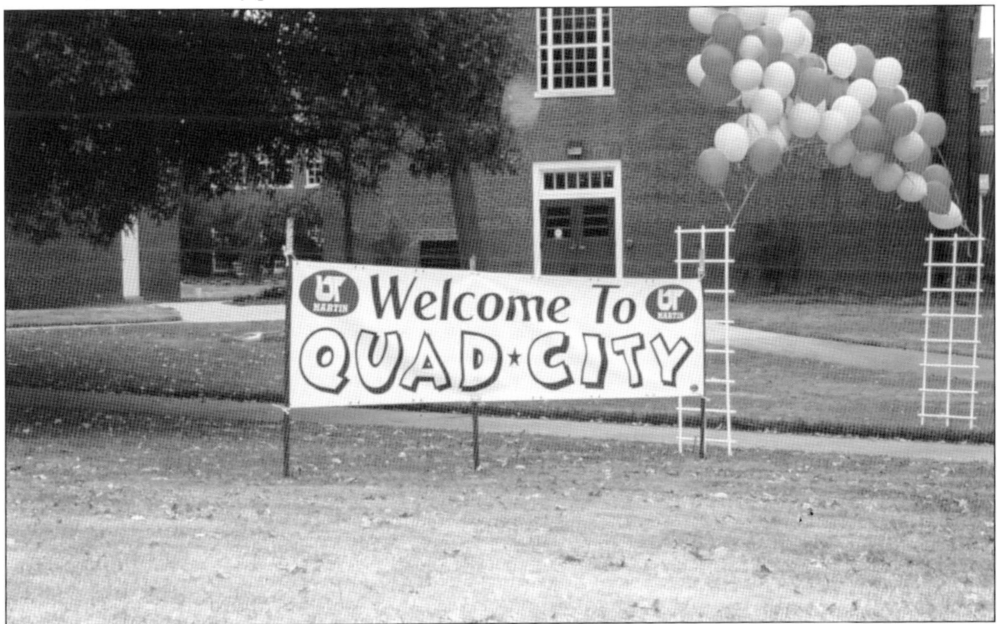

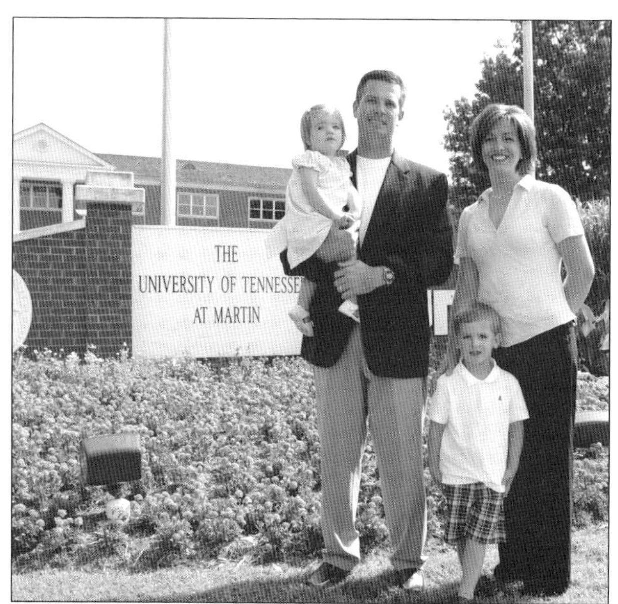

Jason Simpson, pictured with his wife, Julie, and children, Ty and Emma, on June 15, 2006 (the family would later welcome a second son, Graham), was named head coach of the UTM football program on January 17, 2006. A former UT Chattanooga assistant, Simpson quickly transformed the Skyhawks into one of the winningest programs of the Ohio Valley Conference (OVC). Now the longest-tenured head coach in the OVC, Simpson has compiled an impressive 115-87 overall record and an 87-48 mark in conference play over 18 seasons. His 115 career victories rank fourth all-time in OVC history, while his 87 league wins are the third most in conference history.

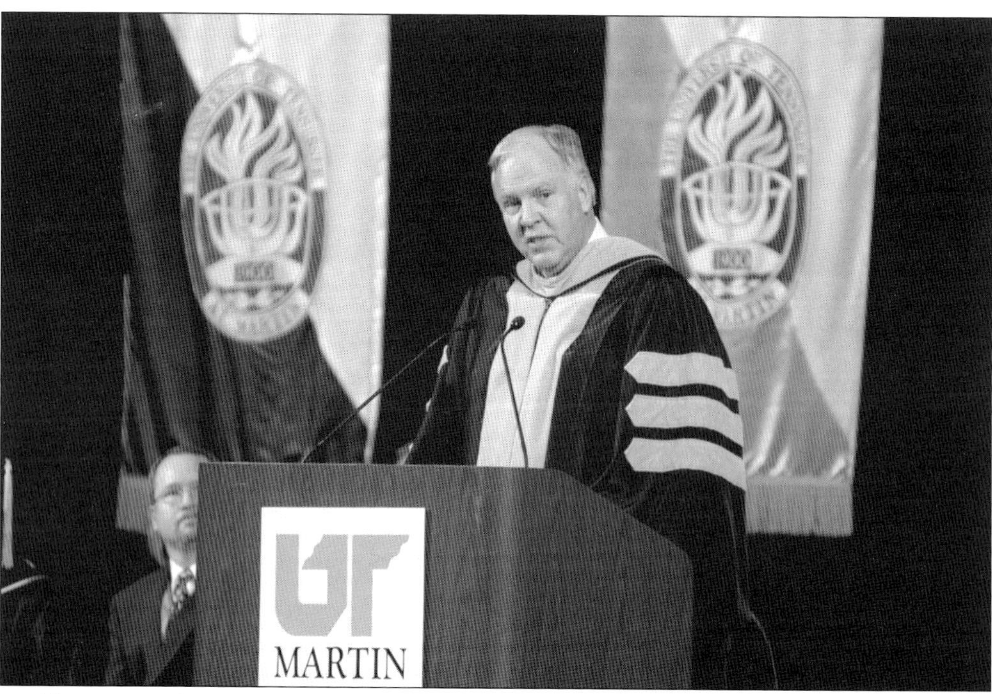

Dr. Thomas A. Rakes served as the ninth chancellor of UTM from 2007 to 2015, following his role as provost and vice chancellor for academic affairs. A seasoned leader in higher education, Rakes also held top academic and administrative positions at the University of Louisiana Monroe and began his career at the University of Memphis. Over his distinguished career, he authored 24 books and monographs, published more than 80 scholarly works, and managed more than $7.5 million in external grants. He served on numerous community and educational boards and consulted for over 40 colleges and corporate organizations nationwide. Rakes and his wife, Dr. Glenda Rakes, a professor of education at UTM, retired from the university in 2017.

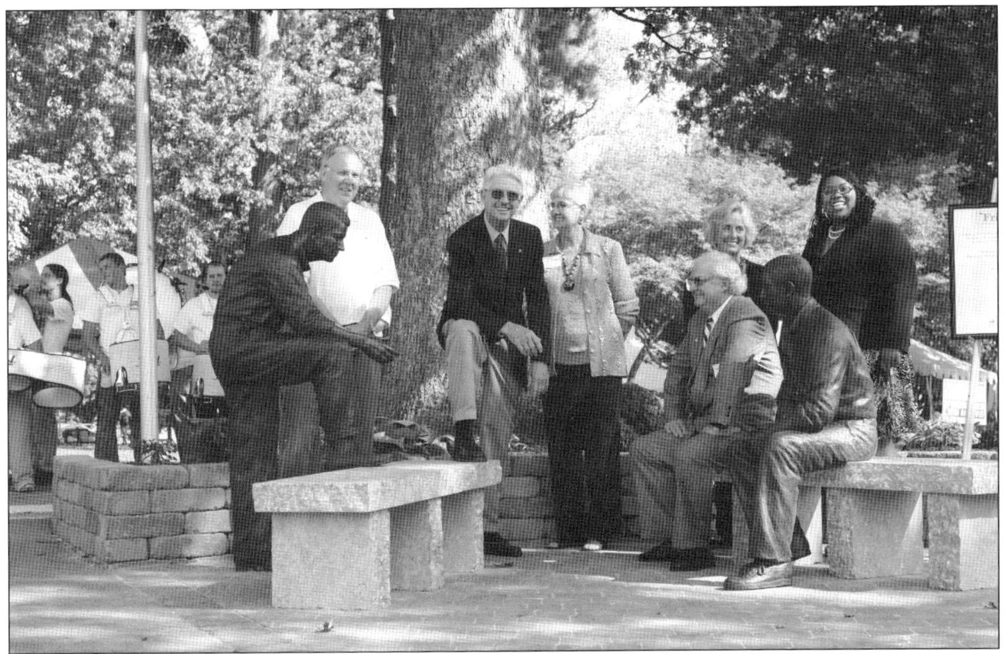

The first life-size bronze statues on the UTM campus were unveiled during homecoming 2007, made possible through a leadership gift from Dr. Paul Blaylock (class of 1968) and additional private contributions. The Friends statue area was inspired by a former chancellor's vision and championed by longtime vice chancellor for student affairs Dr. Phil Watkins, with support from former chancellor Dr. Nick Dunagan. The statues pay tribute to the meaningful mentoring relationships between students, faculty, and staff—bonds that often become lifelong friendships. A plaque nearby honors these connections: "A tribute to the faculty, staff and administrators who serve as mentors to students, past, present and future, at The University of Tennessee at Martin." The unveiling ceremony was attended by chancellor Tom Rakes; Dr. Watkins and his wife, Pat; Dr. Blaylock and his wife, Gaynelle Nolf; and SGA president Erin Chambers.

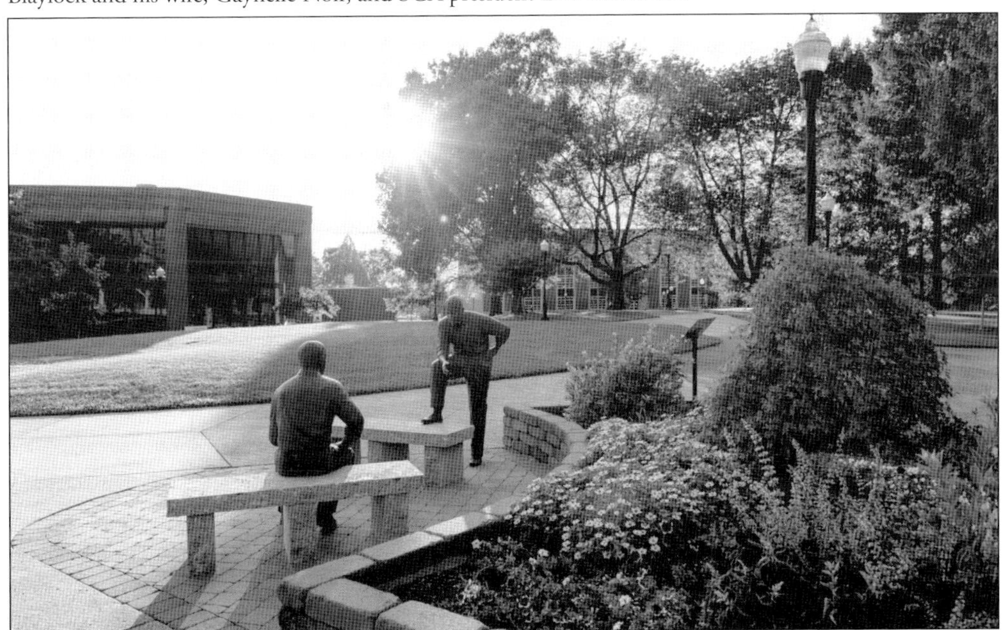

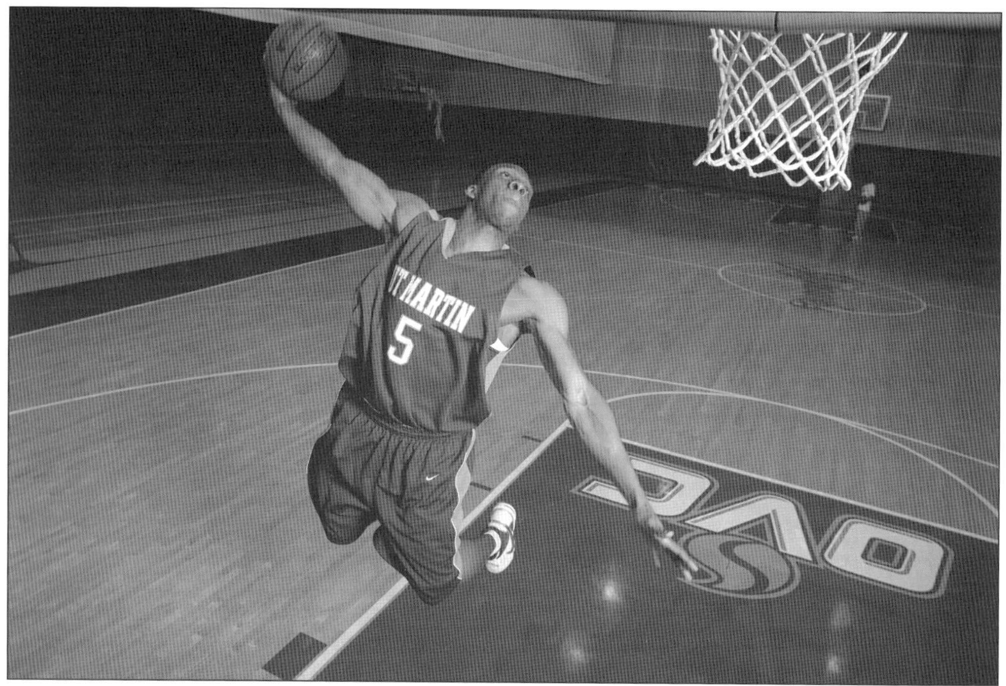

A two-time All-American and two-time OVC player and Male Athlete of the Year, Lester Hudson made history at UTM from 2007 to 2009, highlighted by the NCAA's first-ever quadruple-double and leading the Skyhawks to a school-record 22 wins, their first OVC title, and first Division I postseason berth. He set the OVC single-season scoring record with 880 points in 2008–2009, averaging 27.5 points per game, second only to Stephen Curry. Drafted by the Boston Celtics in 2009, Hudson played in the NBA before becoming a superstar in the Chinese Basketball Association, where he later became the league's all-time leading scorer and only two-time International MVP.

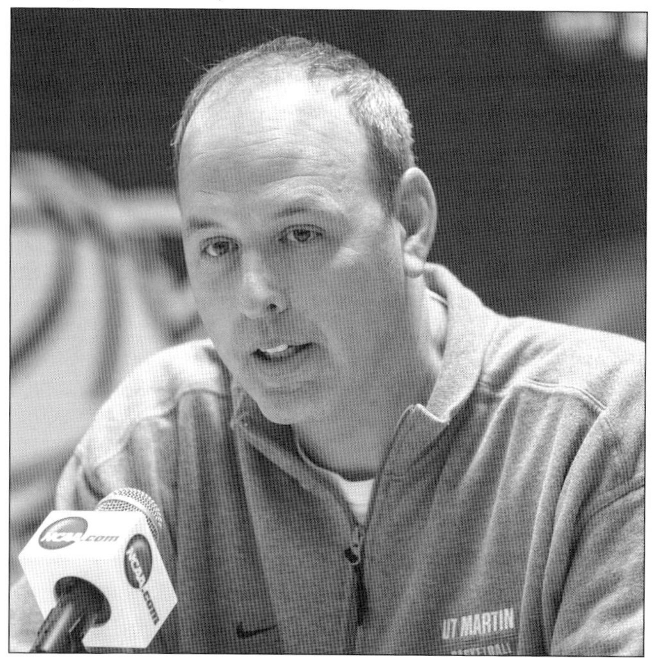

Kevin McMillan, the eighth head coach in UTM women's basketball history, has led the Skyhawks for more than 15 seasons. The program's all-time winningest coach, McMillan has recorded 281 career victories—the third-highest total in Ohio Valley Conference history—and has been honored with four OVC Coach of the Year awards. Under his leadership, the Skyhawks have captured 10 OVC championships, including six regular-season titles and four tournament crowns. UTM has made 10 postseason appearances during his tenure, highlighted by six consecutive trips and NCAA Tournament berths in 2011, 2012, 2013, 2014, and 2024.

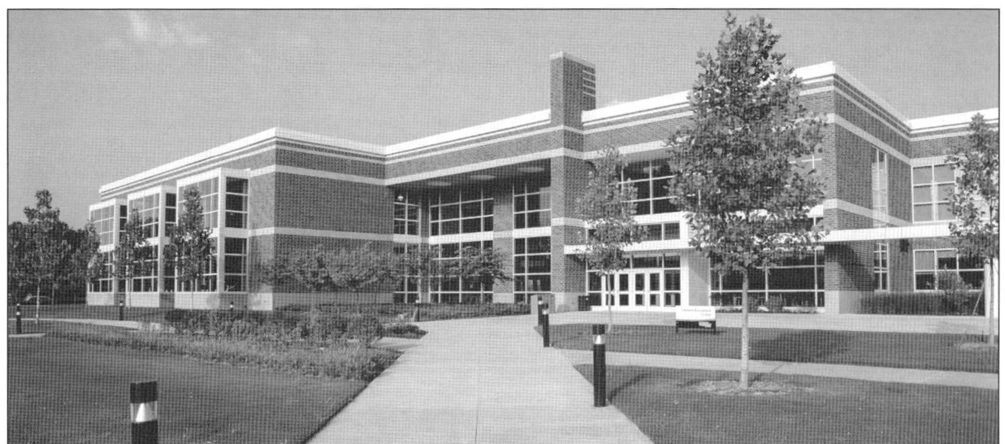

A ribbon-cutting ceremony on February 3, 2010, marked the grand opening of UTM's long-anticipated Student Recreation Center. At 96,000 square feet, the state-of-the-art facility features a four-court gym, weight and cardio areas, racquetball courts, group fitness rooms, a golf simulator, and an elevated track, all designed to promote wellness and student engagement. Chancellor Tom Rakes and UT interim president Jan Simek praised the vision and commitment of student leaders who helped bring the project to life. Simek emphasized the center's role in supporting the health and well-being of the entire campus community, while Rakes called it "a project better than we ever dreamed."

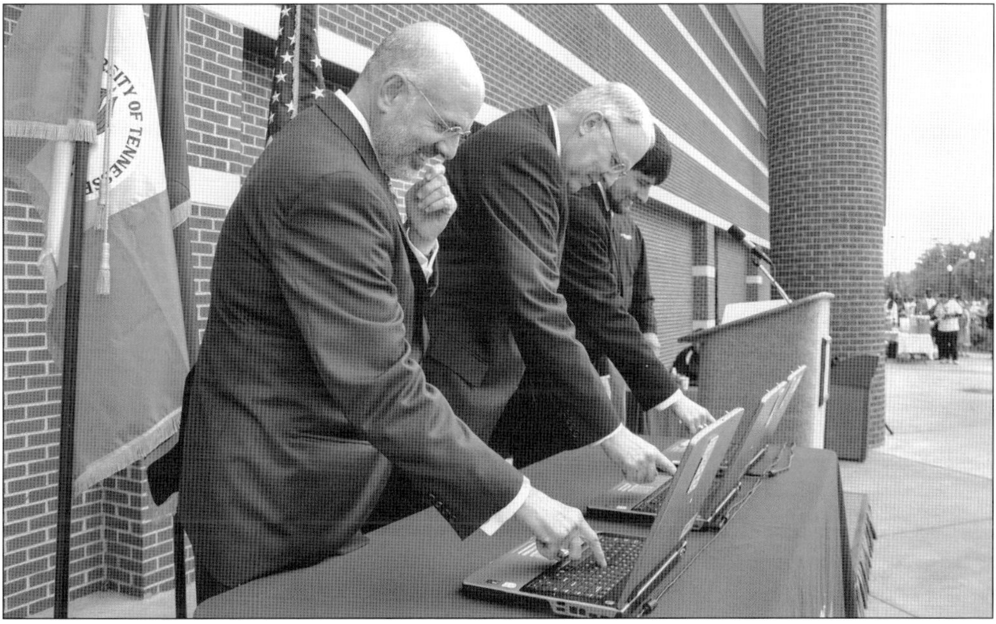

On April 17, 2012, UTM marked a bright new chapter in its history with the "Illumination Celebration," a ceremony to officially unveil its new campus lighting system. The event celebrated the installation of 665 energy-efficient, antique-style lampposts, replacing the 345 original "lollipop" fixtures that had illuminated campus for more than 40 years. Funded through a $3.2 million project, the new lights were 75 percent more efficient and provide increased visibility and safety, especially in previously unlit campus areas. The celebration symbolized both progress and preservation, blending modern technology with classic design. Pictured turning on the new lights for the first time at the "Illumination Celebration" are, from left to right, Dr. Joe DiPietro, UT System president; Tom Rakes, chancellor; and Alex Wilson, UT Martin Student Government Association president.

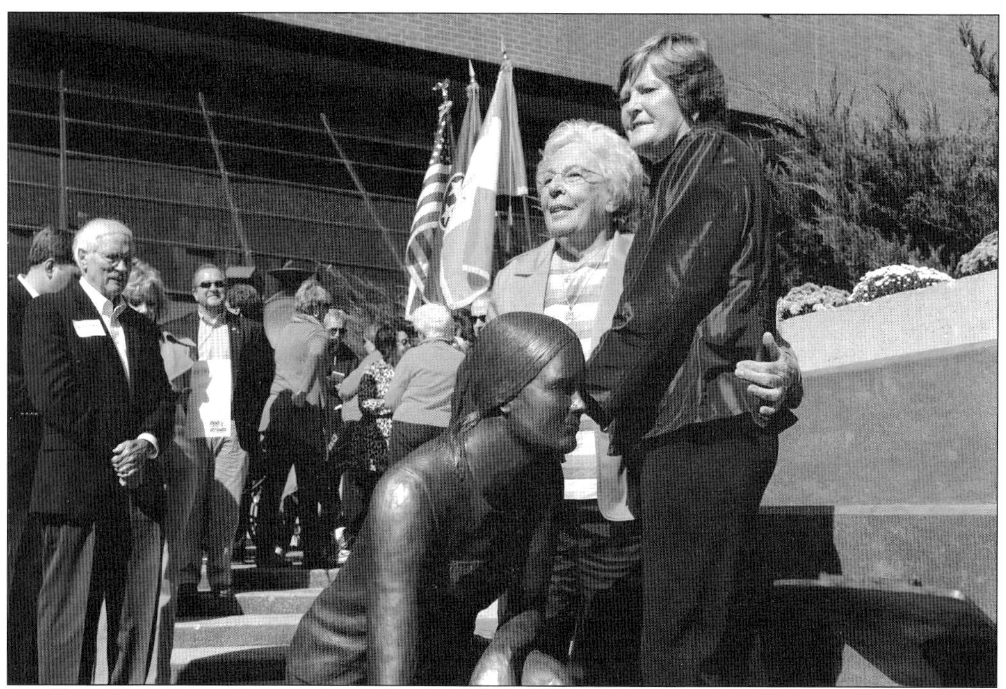

On October 6, 2012, a large homecoming crowd gathered outside the Elam Center to unveil "Coaches," a bronze statue honoring three pioneers in UTM women's athletics: Nadine Gearin, Bettye Giles, and Pat Head Summitt. The ceremony celebrated their lifelong dedication to expanding women's sports opportunities—Gearin as Summitt's college coach, Giles as longtime athletics director, and Summitt's iconic Lady Vols coaching career. Funded by private donations for Title IX's 40th anniversary, the statues inspire future generations. Summitt and Giles offered heartfelt speeches, with Giles warmly inviting visitors to "come and visit us" at the statues.

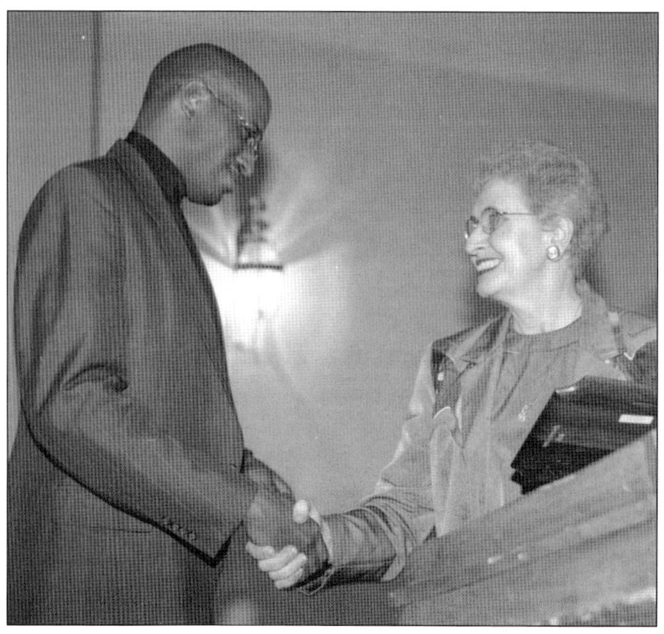

Van Jones, editor of the *Pacer*, made headlines by challenging the UTM community to face difficult truths. A 1990 graduate, he returned in 2014 as the keynote speaker at the communications awards banquet, receiving the Distinguished Alumni Award and joining an investigative journalism panel. Now a CNN contributor, best-selling author, and human rights advocate, Jones served as a special adviser to President Obama and championed the Green Jobs Act under President Bush. Former provost Jerald Ogg noted, "Van aimed to change the world—and he has." Jones credits UTM for laying the foundation of his success.

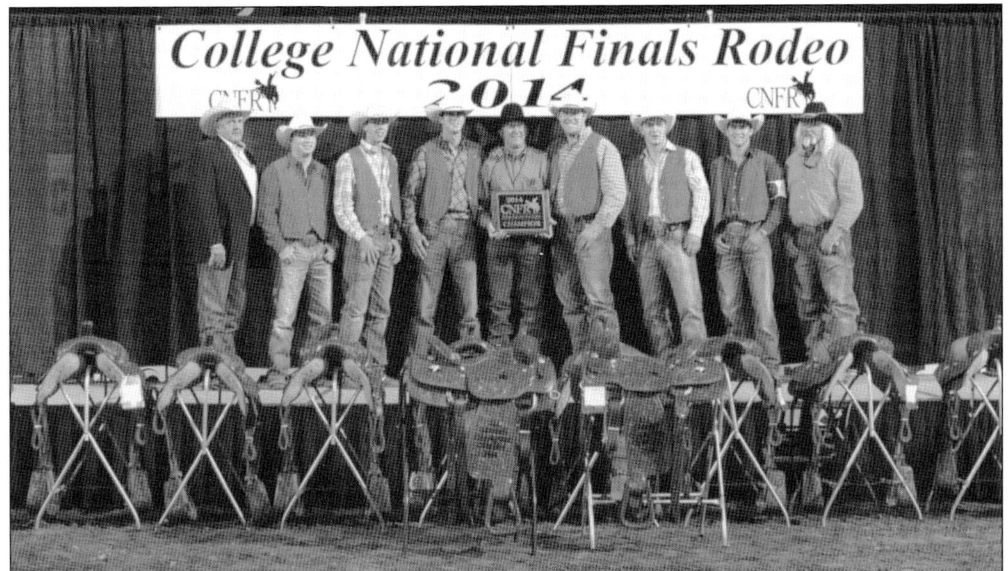

In June 2014, UTM's men's rodeo team made history by winning the university's first national championship at the College National Finals Rodeo in Casper, Wyoming. The Skyhawks scored 755 points to top a 56-team field, becoming the first collegiate rodeo team east of the Mississippi River to claim the title. Led by head coach John Luthi, the 2013 NIRA Coach of the Year, the roster included Will Lummus, Tyler Waltz, Clark Adcock, Tanner Phipps, John Alley, and Colt Kitaif. UTM honored the team in April 2023 with permanent signage on University Street commemorating their achievement.

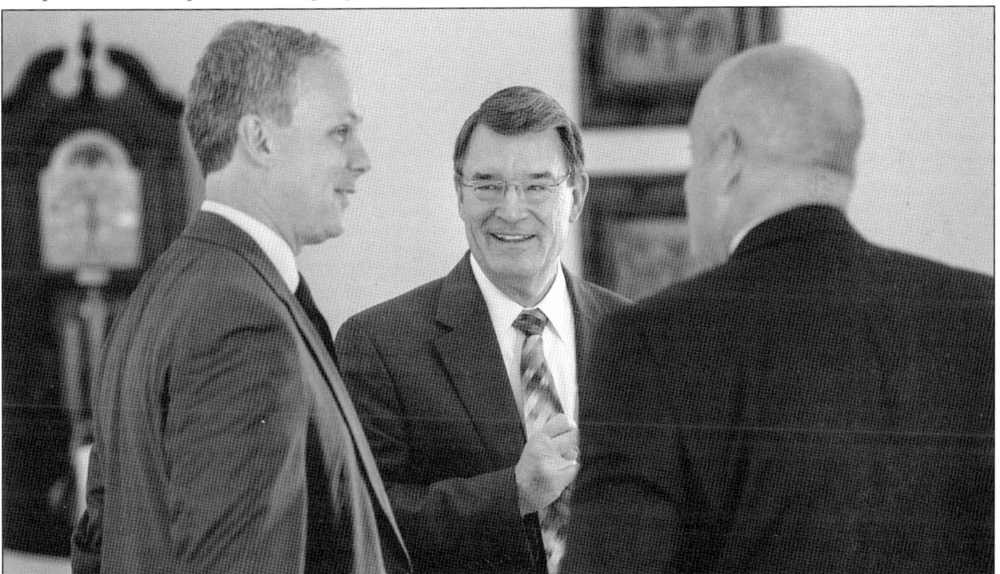

Dr. Robert M. Smith served as interim chancellor of UTM from 2015 to 2017, later becoming the university's 10th chancellor and earning the title of chancellor emeritus in March 2017. Under his leadership, UTM was removed from Southern Association of College and Schools Commission in Colleges probation, achieved record-breaking fundraising, and launched its first comprehensive marketing campaign. Smith also introduced new tuition models to support student success. His tenure included major campus expansion projects, such as the UTM Somerville Center and improvements at Graham Stadium. He also helped secure a historic $6.5 million gift to fund the Latimer-Smith Engineering and Science Building.

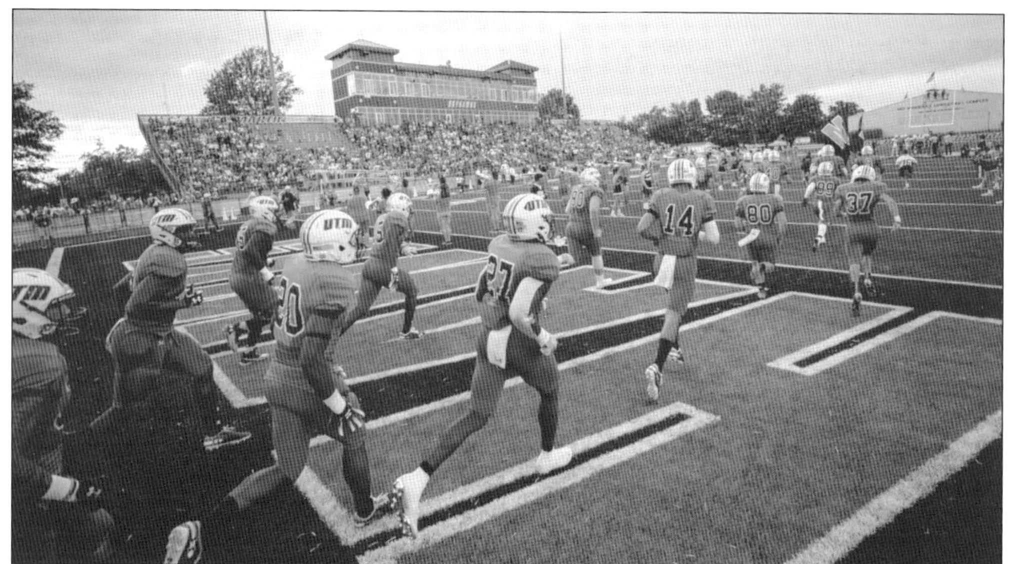

On September 17, 2016, university and community leaders gathered for a ribbon-cutting ceremony ahead of UTM's first home football game of the season to celebrate the opening of a new four-story, 20,000-square-foot academic and press box facility at Hardy M. Graham Stadium. The project provided modern classroom space and a state-of-the-art press area for athletics. Interim chancellor Dr. Robert Smith was joined by campus officials, donors, and student representatives in marking this milestone in Skyhawk athletics and academic facilities.

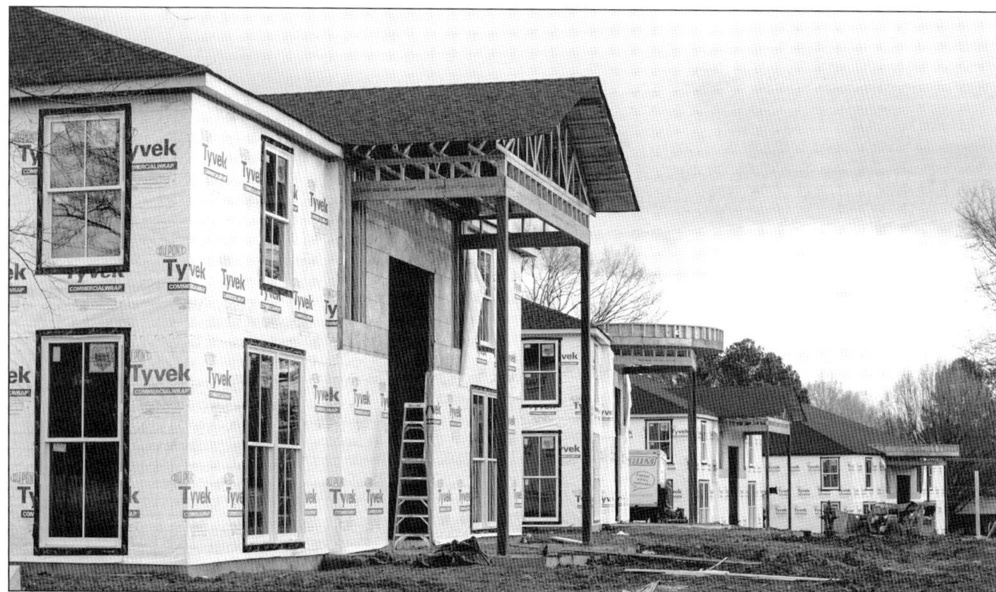

More than five decades after Panhellenic sororities arrived at UTM, four chapters—Alpha Delta Pi, Alpha Omicron Pi, Chi Omega, and Zeta Tau Alpha—celebrated the dedication of Sorority Village on April 28, 2017. The project began with a 2013 homecoming ground breaking attended by over 500 people. Each sorority contributed nearly $500,000 to build a 3,800-square-foot lodge near University Courts, replacing older Grove Apartment lodges. Alumni and campus leaders praised the project's significance. "It means that we have a home," said alumna Vicki Fry Whitworth. Chancellor Keith Carver called it "a tribute to the power of legacy."

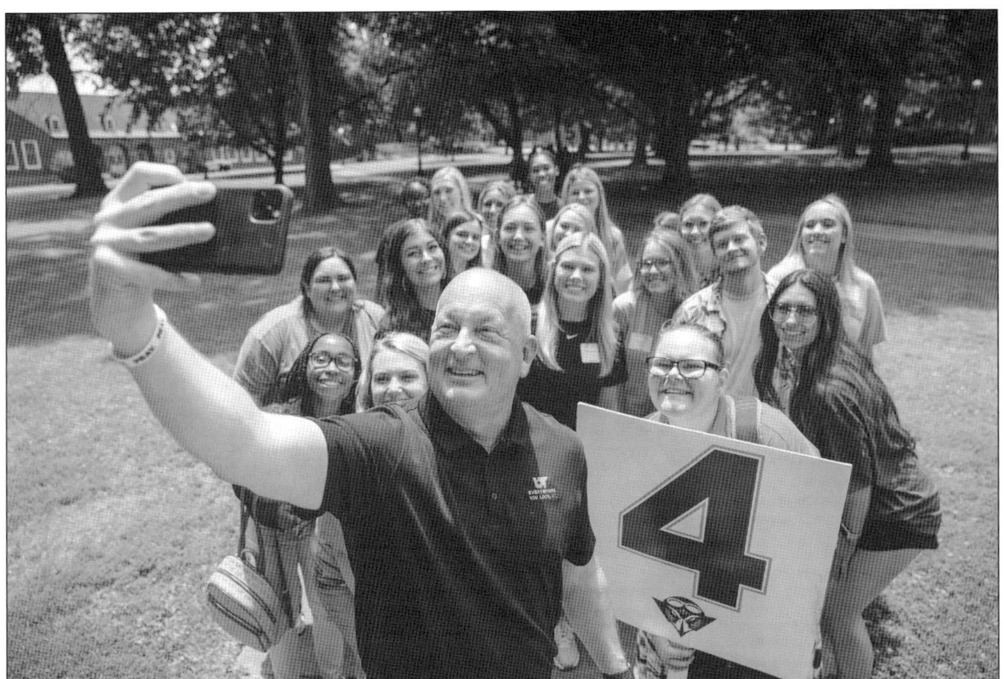

Dr. Keith Carver served as the 11th chancellor of the University of Tennessee at Martin from 2017 to 2023. During his tenure, UTM experienced renewed momentum, including the creation of a five-year strategic plan, a nearly nine percent increase in first-year freshman enrollment (from fall 2017 to fall 2018), and expanded academic offerings. Dual-enrollment partnerships were also formed with Jackson State and Southwest Tennessee community colleges. Carver was a dynamic and visible campus leader, known for his creative use of social media to connect with students and alumni through humorous and heartfelt videos. Under his leadership, UTM's athletics program grew to include 450 student-athletes, added beach volleyball as a women's sport, and completed facility enhancements, including a new playing surface at Hardy M. Graham Stadium. Prior to his time as chancellor, Carver held several leadership roles within the UT System, including executive assistant to the UT president and key development positions at UT campuses in Knoxville, Martin, and Memphis. In March 2023, he was appointed senior vice chancellor and senior vice president of the UT Institute of Agriculture. Dr. Carver and his wife, Hollianne, have three children and one grandson.

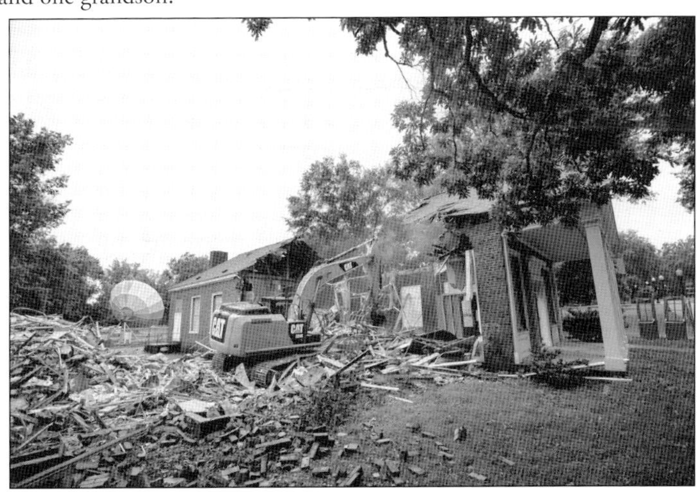

Demolition of the Communications Building began on June 6, 2019, to make way for the new Latimer-Smith Engineering and Science Building, the university's first new academic structure in 40 years.

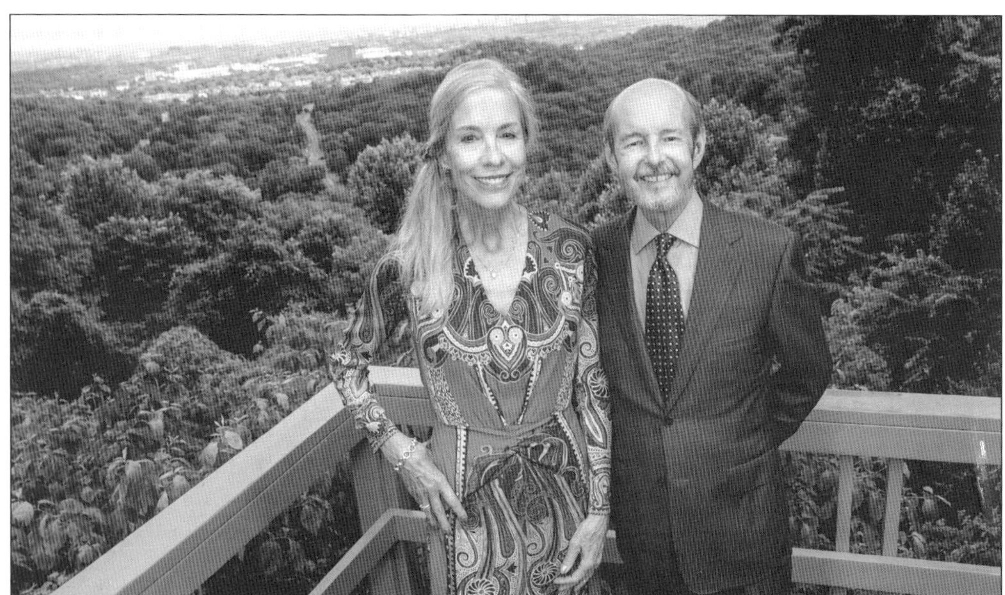

In June 2019, UTM alumnus Bill Nunnelly and his wife, Rosann, announced a transformative $22 million bequest to the university—the largest gift in UTM's history at the time. The Nunnelly Family Scholarship prioritizes students from Hickman County, Tennessee, where Bill was raised, and extends eligibility to six additional Middle Tennessee counties. In December 2022, Emmalee Mathews of Dickson became the first Nunnelly Scholar to graduate from UTM, exemplifying the life-changing impact of the Nunnellys' generosity. Bill Nunnelly passed away on February 11, 2022, but his legacy endures through the opportunities he created for first-generation college students across rural Tennessee.

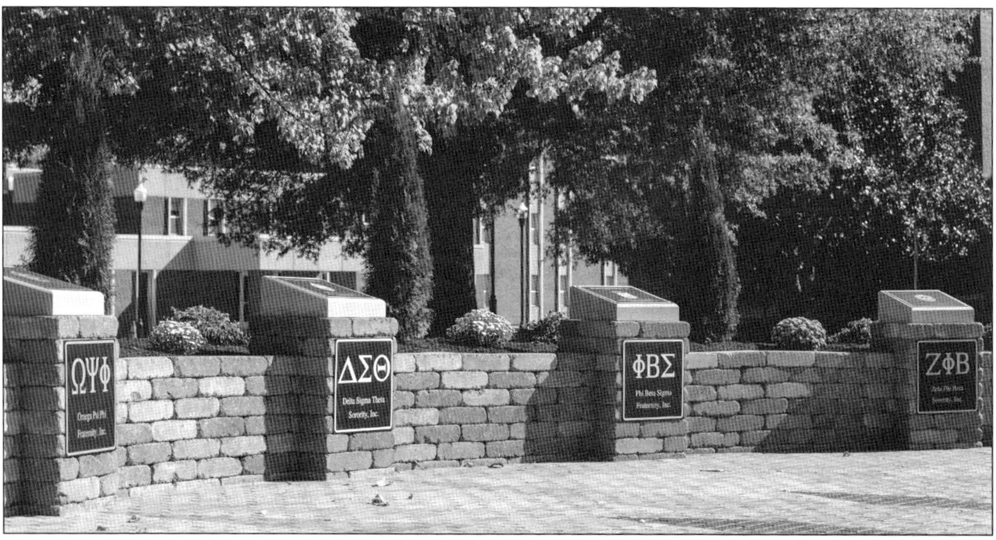

Since 1970, the Divine Nine—historically African American fraternities and sororities—have played a key role in student life at UTM by promoting leadership, service, academic success, and cultural unity. The first chapter, Delta Sigma Theta, was established in 1970, followed by eight others through 2010. These groups have enriched campus life and created a strong legacy of resilience and excellence. In 2019, UTM dedicated the National Pan-Hellenic Council Greek Garden at Unity Circle, honoring each chapter with a plaque. Unity Circle, originally dedicated in 2011, and the garden together celebrate the enduring impact of African American students at the university.

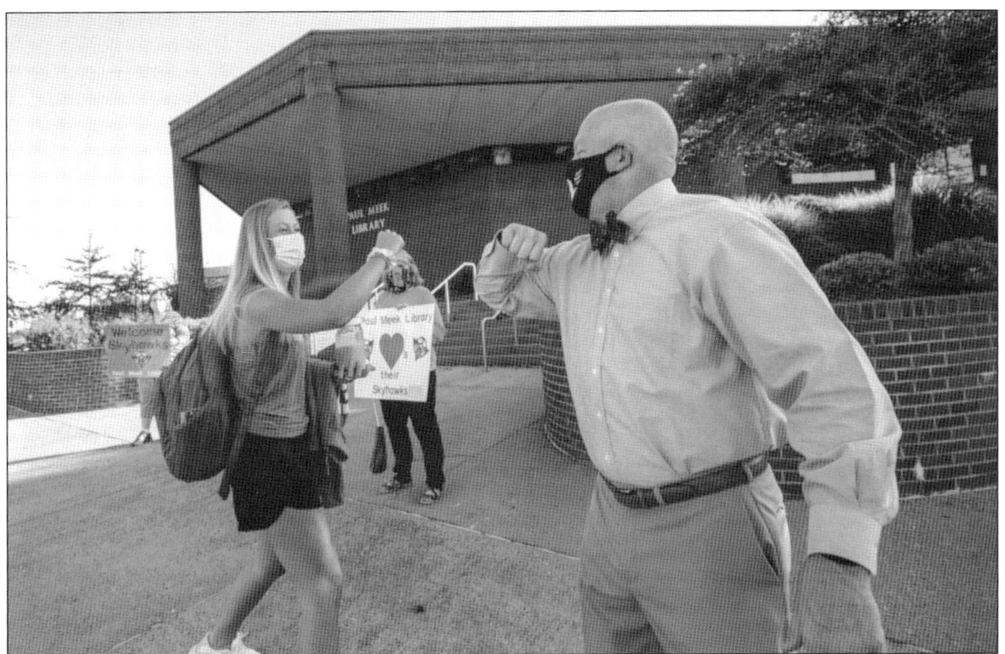

In March 2020, UTM shifted all classes online due to the COVID-19 pandemic, sent residential students home, and canceled large events. Virtual learning continued through summer as leaders planned for fall, weighing online, hybrid, and in-person options. A virtual commencement on May 2 honored over 700 graduates via Facebook and YouTube. In-person classes resumed gradually through 2022, guided by Centers for Disease Control and Prevention protocols. UTM used CARES Act funds for student support, including mobile hot spots. WUTM 90.3 FM kept broadcasting remotely. Despite challenges, students enrolled, graduated, and adapted, reflecting the university's resilience, innovation, and commitment to its campus community.

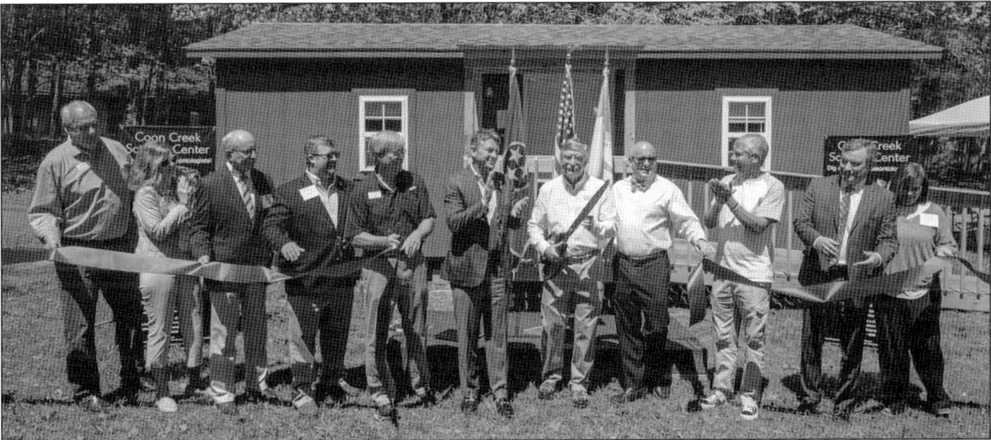

A ribbon-cutting on April 30, 2021, launched a new era for the UTM Coon Creek Science Center in McNairy County. Leased from the Pink Palace Museum, the 240-acre site preserves a 70-million-year-old marine seafloor containing nearly 700 fossil species. UT president Randy Boyd called it "arguably the largest classroom in the UT System," and chancellor Keith Carver praised its educational and research potential. Directed by Dr. Michael Gibson before his retirement, the center now offers field trips, teacher training, camps, and fossil digs. The site is managed by the UTM McNairy County Center/Selmer and serves all ages.

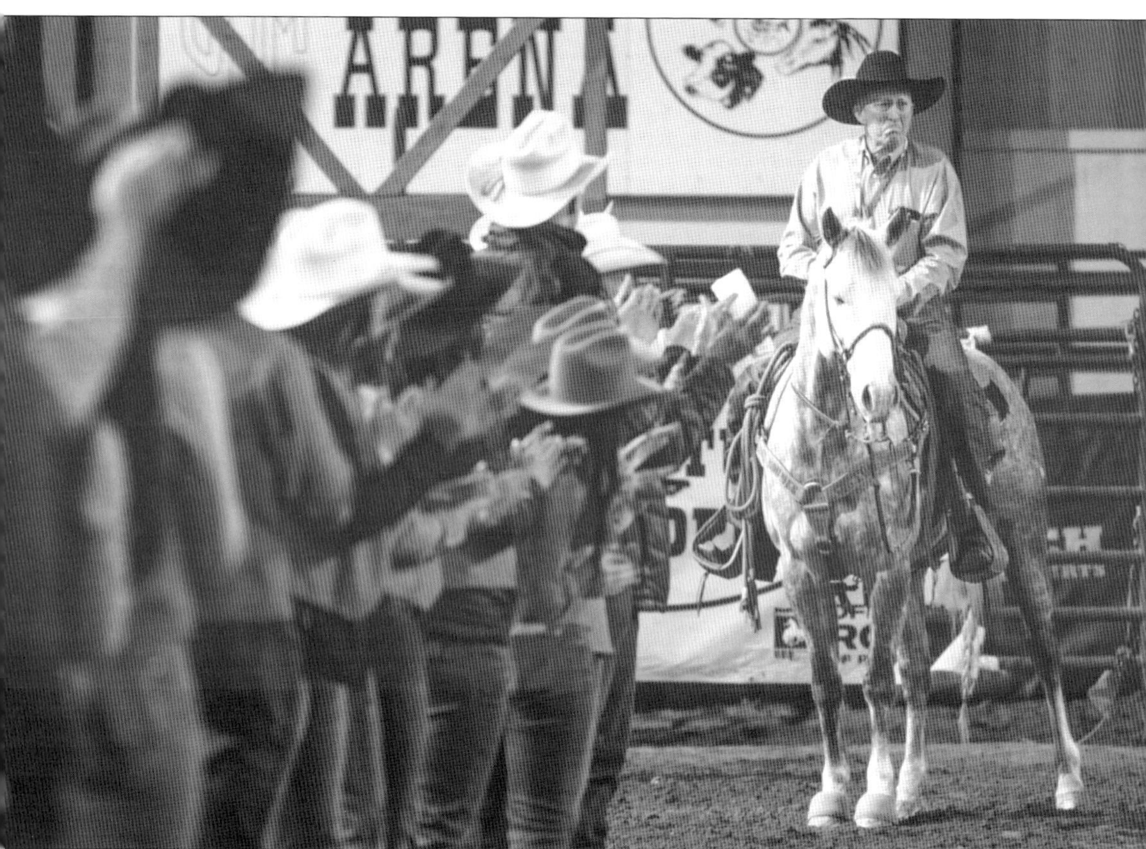

John Luthi retired in 2022 after 25 years as head coach of the UTM rodeo program, leaving behind a legacy as one of the most accomplished coaches in collegiate rodeo. Hired in 1997, Luthi led the Skyhawks to 19 Ozark Region championships—14 men's and five women's—and eight top-10 national finishes, including a historic national men's team championship in 2014, the first ever by a school east of the Mississippi River. He was named NIRA Coach of the Year in 2013 and coached standout athletes like Jeff Askey, the 2020 national bull riding champion. Luthi also helped make UTM's spring college rodeo one of the nation's best, with the event earning Rodeo of the Year honors 13 times in 14 years.

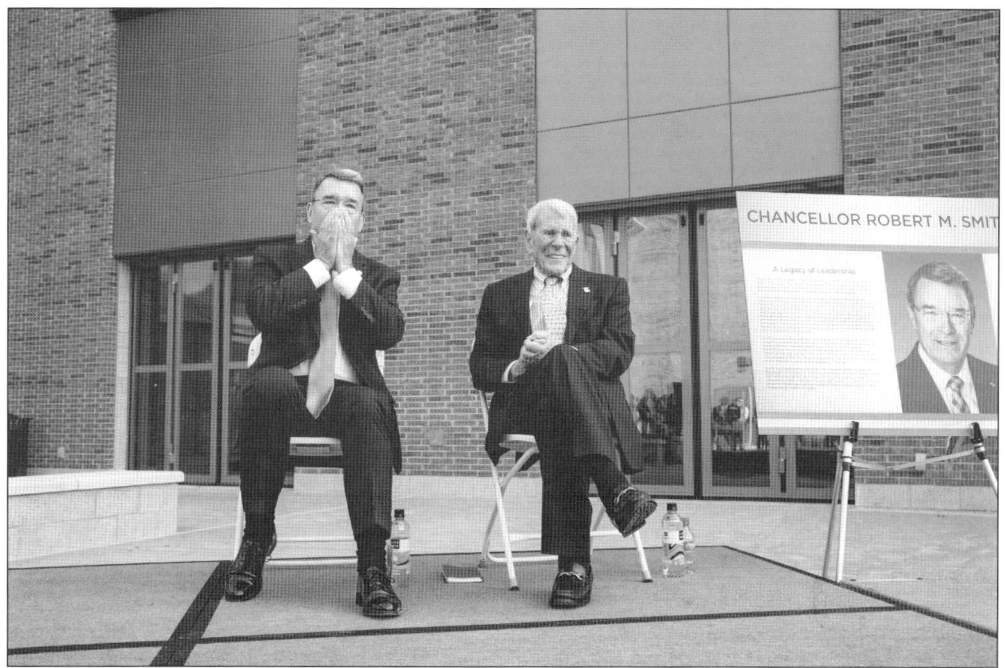

Chancellor emeritus Dr. Robert Smith (left) and Bill Latimer (right) react to the announcement of Smith's name being added to the new Latimer-Smith Engineering and Science Building during a dedication ceremony, Thursday, October 27, 2022. The new $65 million, 120,000-square-foot, three-story structure is situated along the quadrangle near the Business Administration Building. A $6.5 million gift from Union City's Bill and Carol Latimer provided the 10 percent match required by the state for construction of the state-of-the-art facility. Ground was officially broken on September 18, 2020, and the building opened for classes in the spring of 2023. The Latimer-Smith Building houses the departments of chemistry and physics, computer science, engineering, mathematics and statistics, and the preprofessional health sciences program. The building features classrooms, laboratories, offices, and a small observatory and was the university's first new academic building in 40 years.

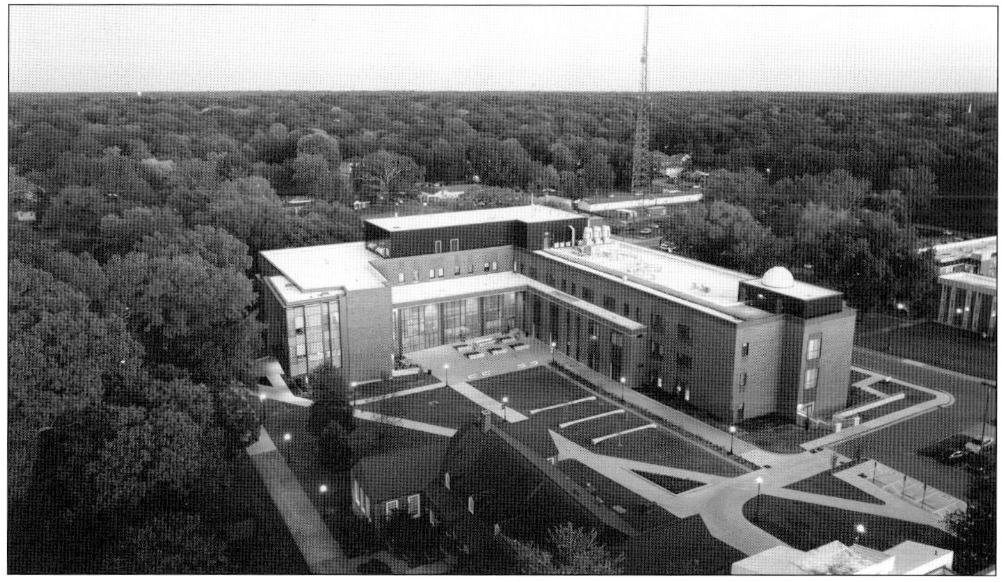

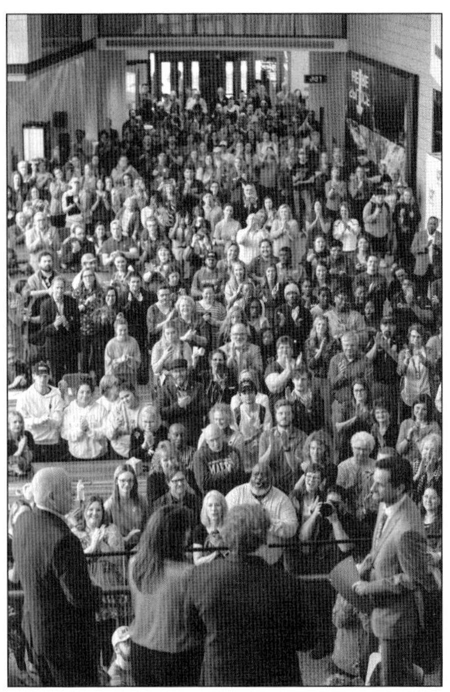

Hundreds of students, faculty, staff, and community members gathered to celebrate chancellor Keith Carver in the lobby of the Latimer-Smith Engineering and Science Building, February 22, 2023. During the celebration, Weakley County mayor Jake Bynum presented a proclamation to Carver and his wife, Hollianne Carver, in honor of his six years of service to UT Martin. Also pictured is Britton Carver, the Carvers' youngest child. Carver left UTM on March 1, 2023, to take a new role as senior vice chancellor/senior vice president of the University of Tennessee Institute of Agriculture.

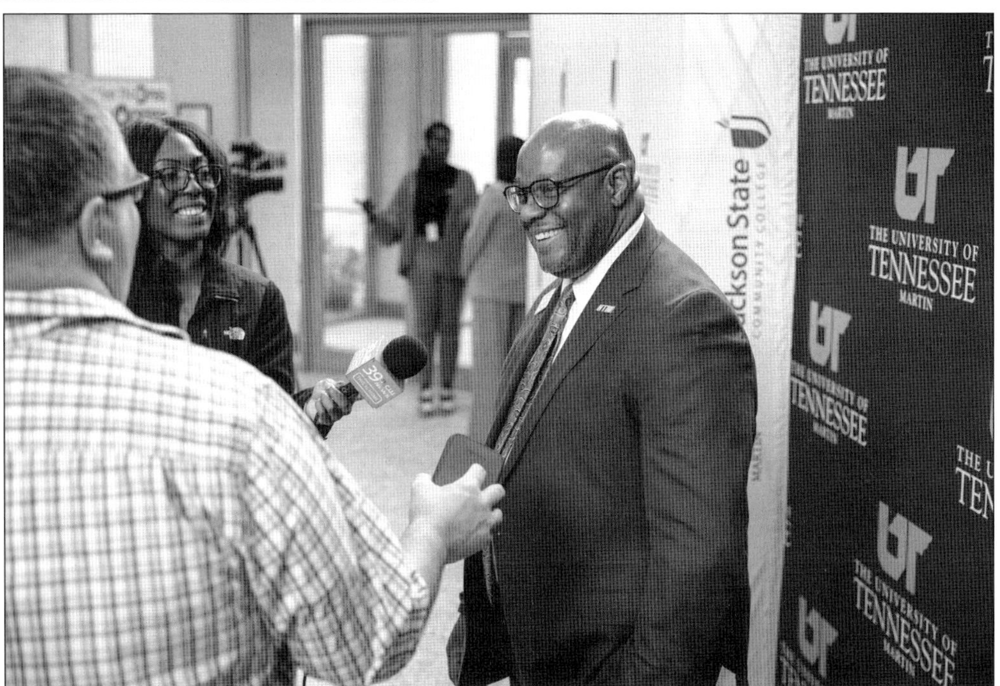

Dr. Yancy Freeman Sr. became the 12th chancellor of UTM on August 9, 2023, and the university's first Black chancellor. A Memphis native and first-generation college graduate, Freeman previously served as vice chancellor at UT Chattanooga. At UTM, he has overseen major growth, including a nearly 10 percent spring 2025 enrollment increase and a record 91.7 percent retention rate. He led the 2025–2030 strategic plan and launched the $18.5 million TEST Hub. In April 2025, $57.5 million was approved for a new business building. Freeman champions access and innovation across West Tennessee.

Dedicated in 2023, the Blaylock Inspiration Oracle stands near the Boling University Center as a lasting tribute to reflection, learning, and legacy at UTM. Designed as an open-air Greek Parthenon, the structure was made possible by a $2.4 million gift from Dr. Paul Blaylock, a 1968 alumnus, physician, and attorney. The Oracle features a circular layout, a central fountain, and inspirational plaques intended to offer wisdom and encouragement to all who visit. UTM chancellor Yancy Freeman described it as a space for contemplation, outdoor learning, and campus gathering. Ground was broken in 2021, and the Oracle now serves as a symbol of how a university experience can inspire a lifetime of purpose.

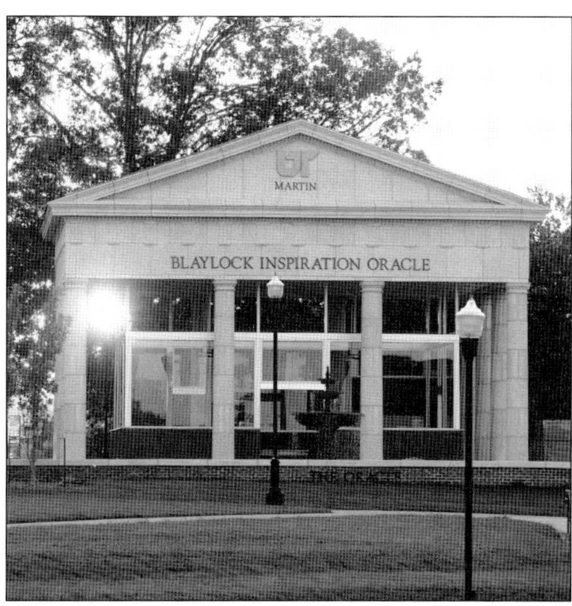

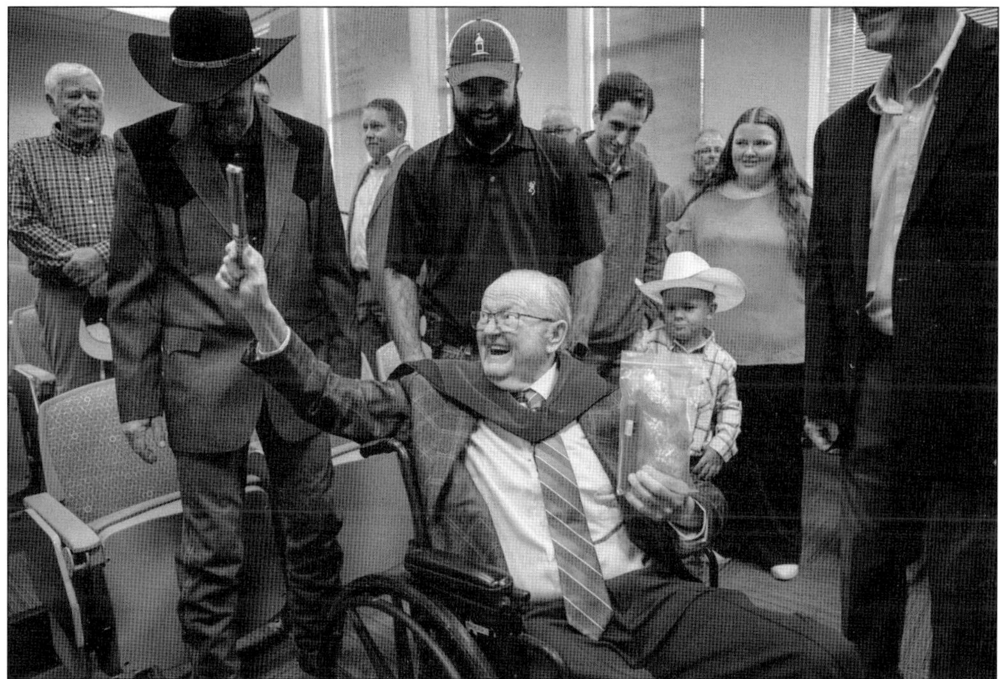

Dr. Rodney Thomsen, a 1975 UTM graduate and key figure behind the university's agricultural business program, was awarded an honorary doctorate on November 6, 2023, in Tosh Family Auditorium, where he once taught. Honored by colleagues, former chancellors, and students, Thomsen was praised for his 27 years of shaping lives and building one of UTM's most successful majors. He also led community events like Santa's Village and the UTM Rodeo. Chancellor Yancy Freeman, conferring his first honorary degree, recognized Thomsen's visionary leadership. Surrounded by loved ones, Thomsen shared cigars and said, "The best times of my life were at UTM."

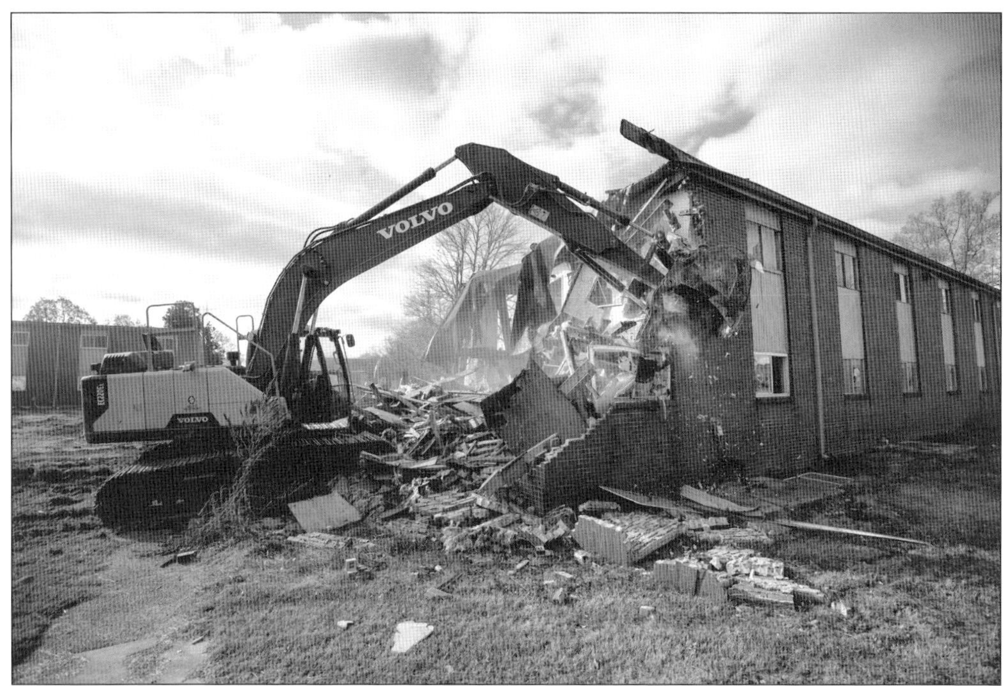

Constructed between 1964 and 1965 on land once donated by local businessman W.H. Lovelace, the Grove Apartments were built to house a growing population of students at UTM. Over the decades, the 10-building complex also provided housing for single male students, married students, and international students and served as a meeting space for campus sororities. Located between University, Moody, and Oxford Streets and Lovelace Avenue, the apartments were last occupied in May 2019. Demolition of the complex began on December 4, 2023, starting with asbestos abatement and progressing clockwise through the buildings. While future plans are still being determined, the cleared site is currently used as green space and a flexible gathering area for university events and activities.

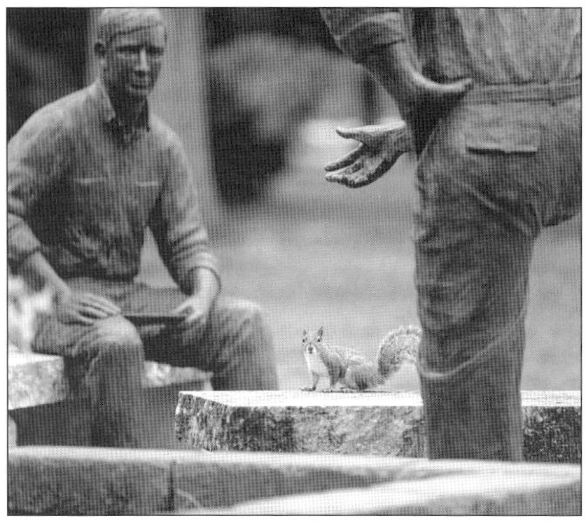

Squirrels are a familiar and charming sight across the UTM campus, often featured in university publications, social media posts, and even a popular student-run Instagram account, utmsquirrels. Their campus roots go back over a century. According to a May 1, 1947, issue of the *Volette*, "Martin had a little bushleague zoo" in 1922 that became too costly to maintain. "The strain of feeding the beasts grew to be too much of a burden on the municipal treasury, so they expressed the big monsters to the Memphis zoo and turned the possums and coons and squirrels and things loose." The squirrels thrived and are here to this very day.

Five

Chancellors 1927–Present

The University of Tennessee at Martin has been led by a series of distinguished chancellors who have each contributed to the institution's growth and development. The role of the chancellor is pivotal, serving as the chief executive officer of the campus and reporting directly to the UT System president. The chancellor's responsibilities encompass promoting academic excellence, providing visionary leadership, strategic planning, budget management, fostering diversity, and engaging with the wider community.

UTM's leadership history began with C. Porter Claxton (1927–1934), followed by Paul Meek, who served in various capacities from 1934 to 1967 and became the first to hold the title of chancellor when the institution gained equal status within the UT System in 1967. Subsequent chancellors include Archie R. Dykes (1967–1971), Larry T. McGehee (1971–1979), Charles E. Smith (1980–1985), Margaret N. Perry (1986–1997), Phillip W. Conn (1998–2000), Nick Dunagan (2001–2007), Thomas A. Rakes (2007–2015), Robert M. Smith (2015–2016), Keith S. Carver Jr. (2017–2023), interim chancellor Philip A. Cavalier (March–August 2023), and currently, Yancy E. Freeman, who assumed the role on August 9, 2023.

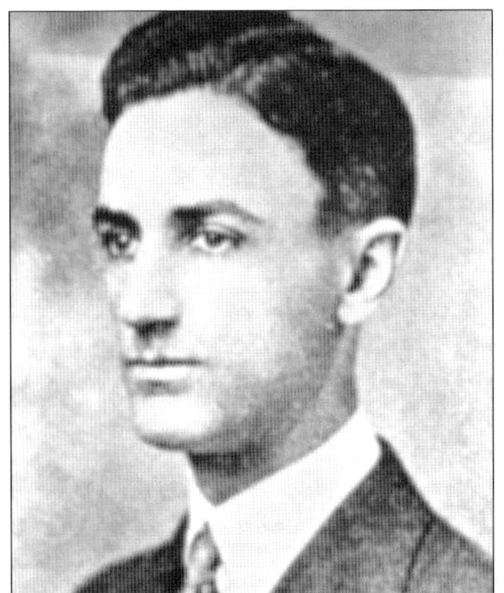

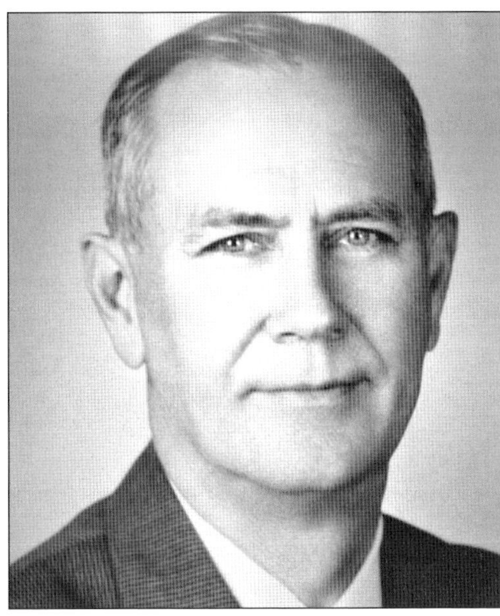

C. Porter Claxton (left) was born on April 23, 1898, in Greensboro, North Carolina, to Philander Priestly Claxton, a noted Tennessee educator, and Anne Elizabeth Porter. Claxton served as executive officer of UTJC from 1927 to 1934 and died on August 20, 1963. Paul Meek (right) was born on February 9, 1897, in Martin, Tennessee, to Felix McCrager Meek and Charlotte Temperance Atkinson. From 1934 to 1967, he held key leadership roles at UTM—including executive officer, dean, UT vice president, and chancellor. He died on November 2, 1972.

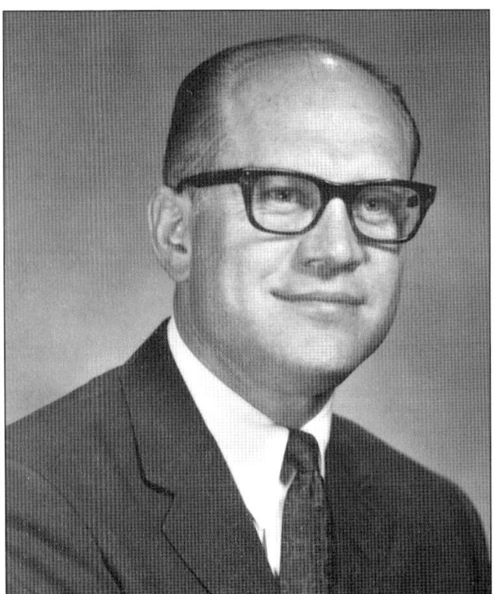

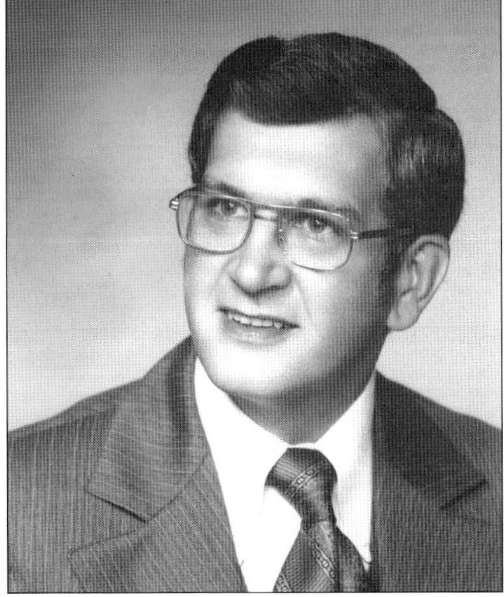

Archie R. Dykes (left) was born on January 20, 1931, in Rogersville, Tennessee, to Claude Reed Dykes and Rose Quillen. He served as the third chancellor of UTM from 1967 to 1971, following Dr. Paul Meek's retirement. Larry Thomas McGehee (right) was born on May 18, 1936, in Paris, Tennessee, to George Eugene McGehee and Margaret Elizabeth Thomas. McGehee succeeded Dykes and served as chancellor of UTM from 1971 to 1979. McGehee died on October 25, 2008, at his home in Spartanburg at the age of 72.

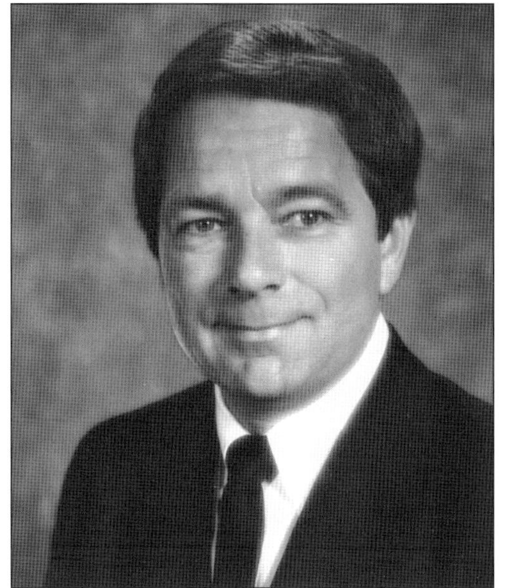

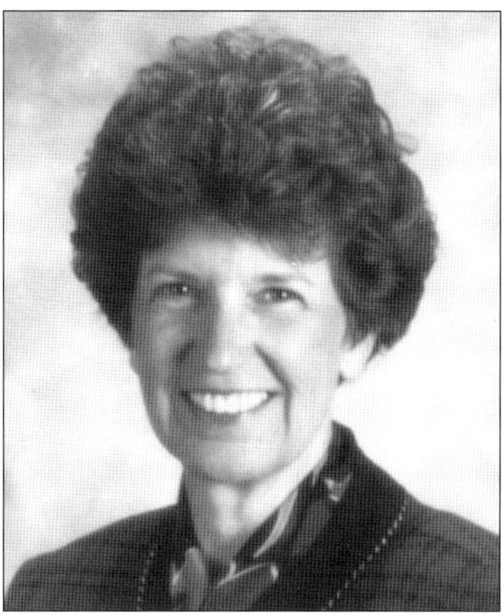

Charles E. Smith (left), a native of White County, Tennessee, was the son of Cecil Edward Smith and Christine S. Newsome. He served as the fifth chancellor of UTM from 1980 to 1985, leaving the role to become vice president of the University of Tennessee System. Margaret N. Perry (right), born April 23, 1940, in Waynesboro, Tennessee, became UTM's sixth chancellor in 1986, serving until 1997. She was the first UTM alumna to hold the position and the first woman to serve as chancellor or president of any public university in Tennessee.

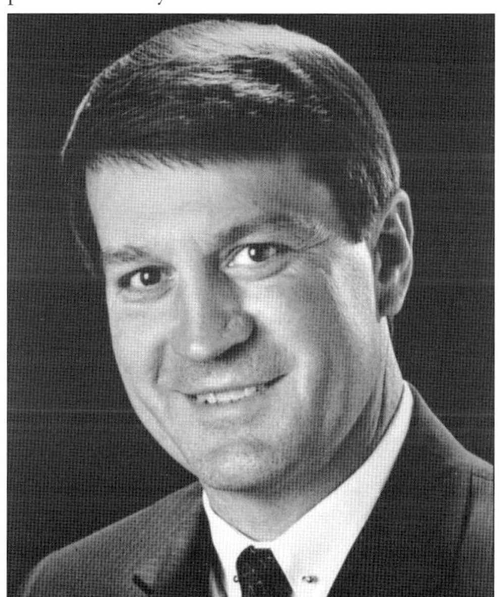

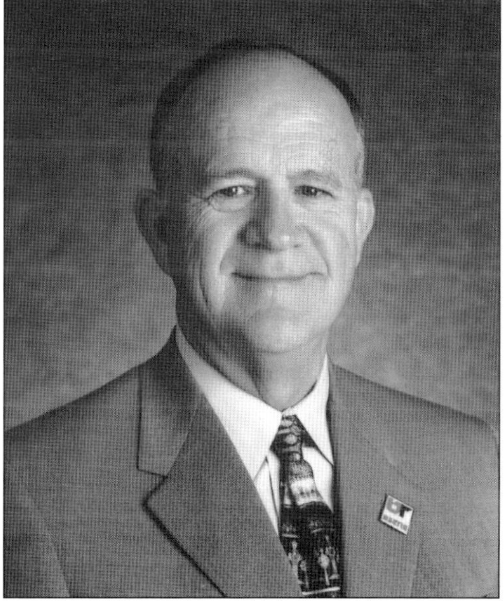

Phillip W. Conn (left), born on January 4, 1942, in Decatur, Alabama, later relocated to Cleveland, Tennessee. He served as the seventh chancellor of UTM from 1998 to 2000. Nick Dunagan (right), a Caruthersville, Missouri native and 1968 UTM graduate, was the university's eighth chancellor from 2001 to 2007. He also held the role of interim chancellor three times (1985–1986, 1997–1998, and 2000–2001) and served as executive director of the WestStar Leadership Program, the oldest and largest regional leadership initiative in the state.

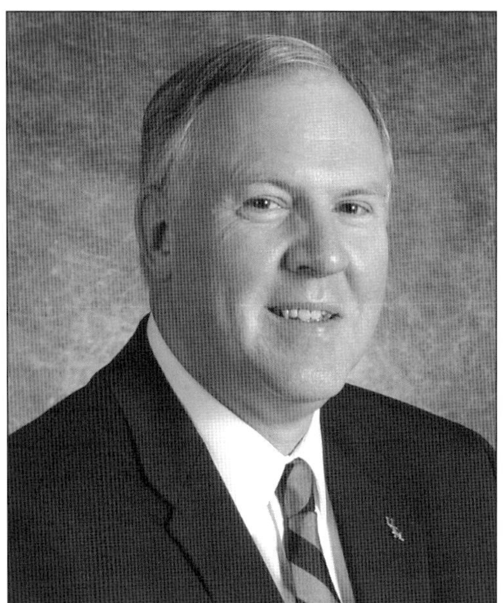
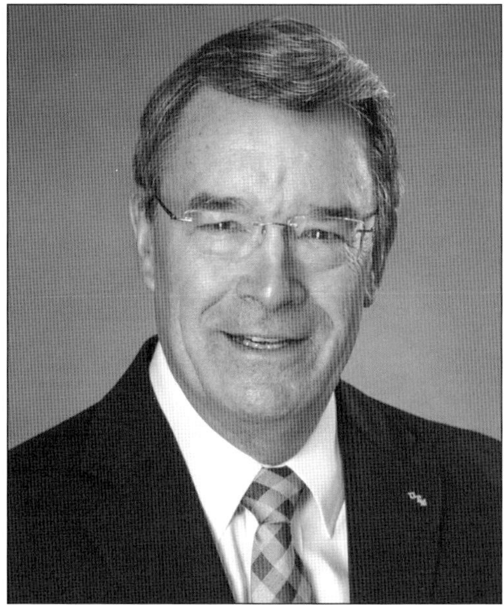

Thomas A. Rakes (left) served as UTM's ninth chancellor from 2007 to 2015, after joining the university in 2002 as vice chancellor for academic affairs and professor of educational studies. He was named provost in 2005, and later in 2015, he returned to teaching. Robert M. Smith (right), who served as interim chancellor from 2015 to 2017, was named UTM's 10th chancellor in 2017 and later honored as chancellor emeritus. From 1987 to 1999, Smith was dean of UTM's School of Arts and Sciences, where he cofounded the WestStar Leadership Program and served as its executive director for a decade.

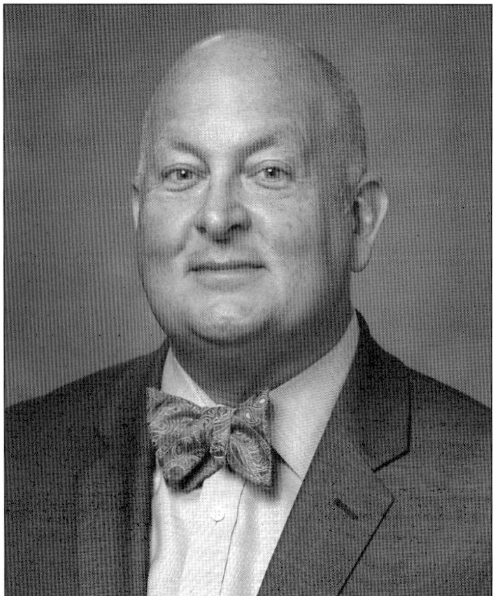
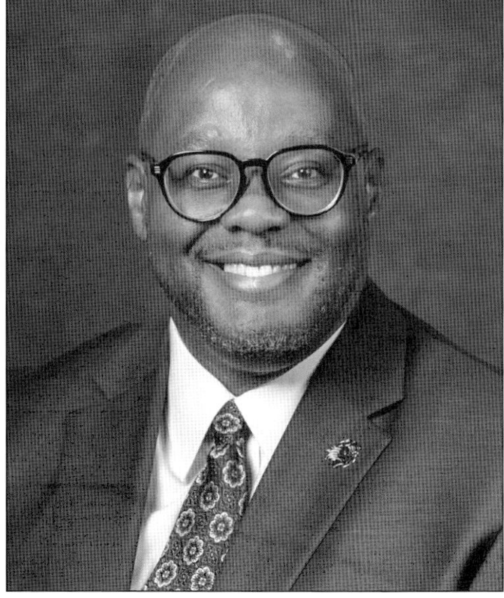

Keith Carver Jr. (left), a native of Frog Jump, Tennessee, began serving as the 11th chancellor of UTM on January 3, 2017, and led the university until 2023. He stepped down to assume on the role of senior vice chancellor and senior vice president at the UT Institute of Agriculture. Yancy Freeman Sr. (right), who grew up in Memphis, Tennessee, became UTM's 12th chancellor on August 9, 2023, making history as the university's first Black chancellor. Before his appointment, he was vice chancellor for enrollment management and student affairs at UT Chattanooga.

Bibliography

Carroll, Robert L. *The University of Tennessee at Martin: The First One Hundred Years.* Franklin, TN: Hillsboro Press, 2000.

Graves, Neil. A Picture *History of Hall-Moody: UTM's Parent Institution.* Martin, TN: The University of Tennessee National Alumni Association/the University of Tennessee at Martin, 1975.

Hall-Moody Junior College, the *Last Leaf 1900–1927*

Hall-Moody Normal School, *The Call: Portraying the Joys and Sorrows of our School Life for the Year 1920–1921*, Vol. 1.

The University of Tennessee Junior College, the *Checkerboard* /Yearbook, 1928.

The University of Tennessee at Martin, the *Addenda.*

———. Alliene and Jimmie S. Corbitt Special Collections and Archives, University Archives.

———, *Campus Scene.*

———, the *Pacer.*

———, the *Spirit*/university yearbook, 1930–2010.

———, the *Volette.*

www.utm.edu

Consistent with our mission to preserve history on a local level, this book was printed in South Carolina on American-made paper and manufactured entirely in the United States. Products carrying the accredited Forest Stewardship Council (FSC) label are printed on 100 percent FSC-certified paper.

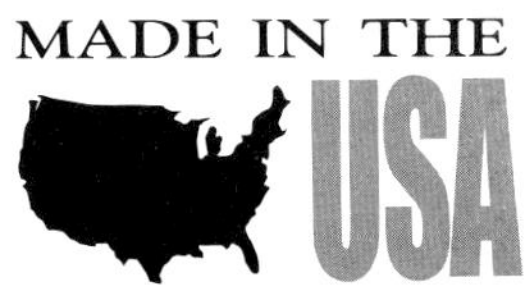